WH

Asian American Women on Skin Color and Colorism

Edited by

NIKKI KHANNA

NEW YORK UNIVERSITY PRESS

New York

NEW YORK UNIVERSITY PRESS
New York
www.nyupress.org
© 2020 by New York University

References to Internet websites (URLs) were accurate at the time of writing. Neither the author nor New York University Press is responsible for URLs that may have expired or changed since the manuscript was prepared.

Library of Congress Cataloging-in-Publication Data
Names: Khanna, Nikki, 1974–   author.
Title: Whiter : Asian American women on skin color and colorism / Nikki Khanna.
Description: New York : New York University Press, [2020] | Includes bibliographical references and index.
Identifiers: LCCN 2019012043| ISBN 9781479881086 (cloth : alk. paper) | ISBN 9781479800292 (pbk. : alk. paper)
Subjects: LCSH: Asian-American women—Social conditions. | Colorism—United States. | Race relations—United States. | Racism—United States.
Classification: LCC E184.A75 K495 2020 | DDC 305.800973—dc23
LC record available at https://lccn.loc.gov/2019012043

New York University Press books are printed on acid-free paper, and their binding materials are chosen for strength and durability. We strive to use environmentally responsible suppliers and materials to the greatest extent possible in publishing our books.

Manufactured in the United States of America

10 9 8 7 6 5 4 3 2 1

Also available as an ebook

For my daughter, Olivia Savitri

maganda • beautiful

I gathered
my role models
from television shows
some spoke my language
but had skin
lighter
than mine.

"that's what you're
supposed to look like,"
Society whispered
in my ear
"here's how you get there,"
"look over here,"
"see, this is ideal"

white
with a dash of
exotic
and a surfer boy
on my arm
waves of blonde.
that is what
I want.

—*Cheyanne Ramón*, FILIPINA AMERICAN

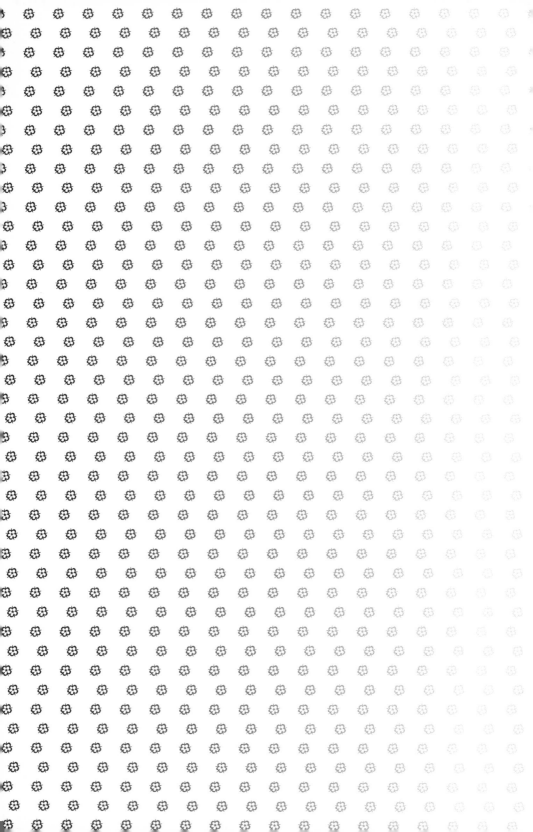

CONTENTS

Introduction

Nikki Khanna

"Whiteness will make you win," she tells me.

She smiles brightly before my screen, and I watch as she tries to sell me a skin-whitening pill in a fifty-second Thai commercial.[1] I can only see the Asian actress from the shoulders up, though from her face I can easily see that she is strikingly attractive, with ebony hair and porcelain skin. I glance down at my own skin, quickly comparing our skin tones. Without the pill, she warns, the whiteness she has invested in will vanish, and as if to illustrate her point, her skin slowly fades to black and her on-screen expression turns despondent and depressed with each darkening frame. The product name, Snowz, aptly chosen to evoke whiteness, reminds me of the flakes that fall from winter skies—white, pure, nearly translucent. The skin of the second model in the commercial, perhaps like snow, is bright and white as she beams with a cheery smile before my computer screen; apparently she has invested in the dietary supplement of glutathione that will prevent her, as the ad claims, from becoming a "faded star." Her light skin and wide grin are in direct contrast to the gloomy, black-skinned model next to her. I am simultaneously captivated and disgusted by the ad, the juxtaposition of light and dark and smiles and frowns, the unapologetic and explicit racism. I am immediately taken back to my childhood.

Far from Thailand, or anywhere in Asia for that matter, I grew up in suburban Atlanta in the 1980s. As a child, I often spent weekends with my parents and younger brother at the local Indian grocer, standing among displays of colorful Indian sweets, brass statues of Hindu gods and goddesses, and imported tubes of whitening creams and bars of whitening soap stacked ever so neatly on store shelves.

Like the two Thai actresses in the Snowz commercial, Indian models, all light-skinned and nearly white, smiled to me from every package and tube, promising "total fairness" and "complete whitening." As a child waiting in busy check-out lines, impatient and often bored to tears, I would occasionally occupy my time by checking my skin color next to the seven shades of the "expert fairness meter" printed on the side of a Fair & Lovely package. Strategically holding my arm next to the box, I felt satisfied when I found my shade; it most closely matched the second-lightest skin swatch. I smiled.

Growing up in the Indian American community, and as a mixed-race-part-white child at that, I already understood the value of having light skin.

≈

The 2016 online Snowz advertisement was heavily criticized both within and outside of Thailand for its blatantly racist message and was promptly pulled by its parent company, though skin-whitening products like Snowz and Fair & Lovely remain popular throughout Asia and around the world, and are only the tip of the iceberg. Skin whitening (also called skin lightening or skin bleaching) is a multi-billion-dollar global industry that promises consumers "translucent," "bright," "fair," and "white" skin through moisturizers, foundations, night creams, anti-aging serums, sunscreens, lip balms, face washes, soap bars, facials, foot creams, deodorants, and even feminine washes, pills, laser treatments, and whitening injections. Light-skinned, near-white models peddling products with names like Snowz, Fair & Lovely, Bright, White Perfect, White-Light, Lightenex, Whitenicious, Fairever, White Beauty, CyberWhite, Refined White, DiorSnow, Snow UV, and Blanc Expert conjure images of whiteness and its explicit link to beauty, flawlessness, and femininity. The product tag lines, too, reinforce the message that white is beautiful and read like musty artifacts from a bygone era: "From Ebony to Ivory" (Glutamax), "Whatever Keeps My Skin the Purest White" (Bird's Nest), "Reveal Your True Inner Fairness" (L'Oreal White Perfect), "Turn Down the Dark, Turn Up the Bright" (Elizabeth Arden), and "Dark Out, White In. Increase Your Face Value" (Pond's White Beauty Facewash).

Figure I.1. Advertisement by Pond's White Beauty with the tagline, "Dark Out, White In. Increase Your Face Value." Marketed in Asia, it promises consumers that they can "get fairer skin right from the first wash."

Throughout Asia, Africa, Latin America, and the Middle East, advertisements for skin-whitening products are aimed at consumers, most notably women, who are routinely told that their dark skin is unattractive and a social liability.[2] The advertising is everywhere: splashed across roadside billboards, in the pages of glossy fashion magazines, and on television commercials seemingly aired on repetitive loops between regularly scheduled programming. Across South Asia, a common theme for skin-whitening commercials goes something like this: A dark woman is unhappy with her life—she is often portrayed with a saddened look as depressed, dejected, and discouraged. She cannot get hired, get promoted, or find a mate. She uses said cream and, voila! She lands the coveted job, the elusive promotion, and/or the handsome and successful husband.[3] These "Cinderella" or "ugly-duckling-to-swan" advertisements[4] are provocative, highly controversial, and (let's be honest) unabashedly racist, yet they are exceedingly effective because of widely shared cultural beliefs that dark skin is a stigma and a physical handicap in marriage and job markets. The ads mirror the message of many societies: *Light skin is superior to dark.* For women, the message is even more sobering: *Those with light skin are beautiful and will marry and be successful; if you have dark skin, too bad for you.*

In a study of 312 cultures, fifty-one were found to use skin color as a marker of beauty, and in all but four, light skin was favored.[5] Hence in much of the world, skin shade is significant and light skin an enviable asset. According to sociologist Margaret Hunter, most Americans have a general understanding of discrimination between racial groups and its insidious effect on people of color, but she notes that "hidden within the process of racial discrimination, is the often overlooked issue of colorism."[6] "Colorism," a term first coined by novelist Alice Walker in 1983,[7] refers to the practice of discrimination whereby light skin is privileged over dark—both between and within racial and ethnic communities. The bulk of the literature on colorism typically focuses on intragroup bias—that which occurs *within* racial and ethnic groups. African Americans, for example, have a long history of discriminating against each other on the basis of skin tone; those with lighter skin are relatively more privileged within the African American community, while those with darker hues are typically discriminated against by their lighter-skinned counterparts. However, colorism also occurs *between* racial groups (e.g., whites who privilege light-skinned African Americans over African Americans with darker skin) and even *between* ethnic groups (e.g., Asian ethnic groups discriminating against each other, such as lighter-skinned Japanese discriminating against darker-skinned Cambodians). Scholar Darrick Hamilton and his colleagues conceptualize colorism "as a byproduct of racism,"[8] and Margaret Hunter argues that "colorism would likely not exist without racism, because colorism rests on the privileging of whiteness in terms of phenotype, aesthetics, and culture."[9] Perhaps "racism" and "colorism" can be conceptualized as cousins or as parent and child—distinctly different, but nonetheless closely related.

Colorism affects racial and ethnic groups worldwide, and its harmful effects are well documented in the United States, particularly for African Americans. Research shows that light-skinned African Americans tend to have better health, greater job prospects, higher-status occupations, higher earnings, greater wealth, and more years of schooling than those with darker skin;[10] light skin is also linked to perceived intelligence and trustworthiness.[11] Dark-skinned African Americans face within-group bias from other African Americans, but also bias from other racial groups, including whites, who tend to favor those with light skin. This practice dates back to slavery, when white slave owners privileged those with light skin over those with dark tones; they gave them the more desirable indoor jobs (while darker-skinned slaves labored in the fields), opportunities for education and skilled labor (privileges unavailable to most slaves), and for some, even their freedom.[12] In fact, during the slave era, free blacks in America were often lighter in color than those who were enslaved.[13]

Long after slavery ended, the preference for light skin continued—even *among* African Americans. During the Jim Crow era, light-skinned blacks often used exclusionary practices to discriminate against those with darker skin, and they segregated themselves physically and socially by creating their own elite social clubs, fraternities, sororities, neighborhoods, churches, preparatory schools, colleges, business organizations, and even vacation resorts.[14] Qualifying "tests," such as the paper bag test, were used to control membership, and only those lighter than the dye of a paper bag would be granted entry.[15] The pressure for light skin was also evident in the homemade and store-bought skin whiteners used by African Americans during the Jim Crow era to access light-skin privilege[16]—including widely marketed brands such as Nadinola, which guaranteed black women a "clear, bright, Nadinola-light complexion," and Dr. Fred Palmer's Skin Whitener, which promised that they could be "lighter, clearer and more beautiful than [they] ever dreamed." Though skin-lightening products aimed at black women are less visible (albeit not absent) in American markets today, the bias for light skin persists: when Barack Obama ran for his first term as president, Senator Harry Reid, then the Democratic majority leader, predicted that Obama could become the nation's first black president because he had "no Negro dialect" and was "light-skinned."[17] He apologized for the politically incorrect gaffe, though perhaps he hit on an uncomfortable truth: Americans, white and otherwise, react more favorably to light skin as compared to dark even today.[18]

A closer look at colorism among African Americans further reveals that for black women, in particular, light skin is associated with physical attractiveness[19] and success in the marriage market.[20] Scholar Mark E. Hill argues that light skin is more valuable to black women than to black men, drawing attention to what he calls "gendered colorism."[21] Beauty, often defined in the American context as possessing light skin, is a form of social capital or "currency" for women,[22] and Margaret Hunter notes that "study after study has shown that light-skinned African American women marry spouses with higher levels of education, higher incomes, or higher levels of occupational prestige, than their darker-skinned counterparts."[23]

This "gendered colorism" is also evident in American media. Most black actresses, especially those cast in lead roles, are light in complexion. Hollywood actress Zendaya, who is multiracial and light skinned, observes that because of her skin color, she represents Hollywood's "acceptable version of a black girl."[24] Consider, too, Halle Berry, Thandie Newton, and Paula Patton—all three are light-skinned "black"[25] actresses with some degree of white ancestry, though black male actors tend to show comparatively more range in skin tone (think Sydney Poitier, Wesley Snipes, Denzel Washington, and Idris Elba, for whom dark skin is perceived as more acceptable and often presented as masculine).[26] Catherine Knight Steele, a professor at Colorado State University, even finds colorism in American children's cartoons. In her analysis of the animated Disney series *The Proud Family*, which features a black family (a rarity in children's media), the central female character, Penny, and her mother are illustrated with light skin and Eurocentric features; this is in direct opposition to the father, who is darker by comparison. Moreover, the lighter-skinned characters are depicted as intelligent, while those with darker skin are portrayed as "clownish" and "less intelligent," reinforcing colorist beliefs about African Americans.[27]

Gendered colorism is further seen in the music industry as light-skinned black women take center stage. In a 2018 interview with *Ebony* magazine, Mathew Knowles, father to American pop star Beyoncé, asks, "When it comes to Black females, who are the people who get their music played on pop radio? Mariah Carey, Rihanna, the female rapper Nicki Minaj, my kids [Beyoncé and Solange Knowles], and what do they have in common?"[28] The answer: light skin and Eurocentric features. His daughter, Beyoncé, is known for her light skin and long, blonde, straight hair. While black male performers typically show a range in skin tones (some examples include Tupac, Snoop Dogg, Jay-Z, Usher, Kanye West, and Drake), black female vocalists are overwhelmingly light-skinned. Perhaps then it is not surprising that some of these women, such as Beyoncé and Nicki Minaj, have been accused of lightening their skin; there is value in doing so.

The bias for light skin is even found in mainstream media outlets accused of photoshopping black and brown women to appeal to the white masses (for examples, see the unnaturally lightened hue of actress Gabby Sidibe on the cover of *Elle* in October 2010; recording artist Beyoncé in a print ad for L'Oreal in 2012; and actress Kerry Washington on the cover of *Instyle Magazine* in March 2015). Moreover, colorism within the African American community is well documented in research and in documentaries such as *Dark Girls* (2011) and *Light Girls* (2015), which give voice to African American women and the discrimination they face within the African American community—particularly from other black women. The coin of colorism, however, is two-sided; it involves dark-skinned women who feel negatively stereotyped and rejected by light-skinned women for being too dark, and light-skinned women who feel rebuffed by their darker-skinned counterparts for not being "black enough."[29] Negative stereotypes, valuations of beauty, and perceptions of black authenticity are intimately inter-twined with skin color in the African American community.

In addition to the extensive literature on African Americans and colorism, there is a burgeoning body of work on Latinx[30] populations in both Latin America and the United States.[31] Light skin in these communities is similarly privileged, and skin tone affects one's life chances and opportunities. Latinx populations show wide range in skin color, and studies suggest that, as with African Americans, light skin is linked to better mental and physical health, more years of schooling, higher occupational status, and higher income. Light-skinned Latinos in the United States also tend to live in more affluent neighborhoods with high property values, are more likely to marry "higher-status" spouses (those with higher levels of education, income, and occupational prestige), and are considered more attractive than those with darker tones.[32] Perhaps this explains ex–baseball slugger Sammy Sosa, a native of the Dominican Republic, who over the course of several years went through a very public shift in skin shade— from deep brown to nearly white. When asked about the transformation, Sosa reportedly remarked, "It's a bleaching cream that I apply before going to bed and whitens my skin some,"[33] suggesting that darker-skinned Latinxs face many of the same pressures as African Americans.[34]

Moreover, although colorism occurs within Latinx communities, skin-color bias also stems from other groups, including whites. A 2015 study by sociologist Lance Hannon, for example, finds that whites are much more likely to view light-skinned Latinxs as smart as compared to those with darker skin—a phenomenon he labels "white colorism."[35] This is problematic given the power of whites in American society, and Hannon writes that in the school context, for example, if whites equate lighter skin with intelligence, it may impact the level of expectations white teachers have for Latinx students. This light-skin-equals-intelligence bias likely also influences hiring, promotions, pay, and even access to political power. Raquel Reichard, a Latina feminist and scholar, observes that "from state and local officials to Congress to the current 2016 presidential candidates, most Latino politicians . . . are light-skinned or straight-up white-passing. Just take a look at the Latino politicos getting the most media attention right now, Republican contenders Ted Cruz and Marco Rubio."[36] Arguably, their light skin makes them palatable to American voters.

Colorism and Asians

Though research on colorism in the United States has grown in recent decades, especially as it pertains to African American and Latinx populations, less attention has been given to Asian Americans, for whom colorism is equally pervasive and deeply entrenched. Colorism exists in just about every part of Asia and affects Asian diasporas, including most Asian American communities—most notably affecting those descended from South and Southeast Asia (e.g., India, Pakistan, Cambodia, Singapore, Thailand, Philippines, Vietnam, Indonesia), as well as those from Japan, China, South Korea, and other parts of Eastern Asia. The preference for light skin is deeply rooted both in Asian ethnic cultures and in European colonization, which makes Asians rather distinct from other racial groups, and throughout Asia, light skin typically functions as a marker for wealth and class, caste, and proximity to whiteness.

Because colorism among Asian populations is understudied and, until recent years, nearly absent in public discourse, this is often surprising to many non-Asians—even to some scholars well versed in colorism. In her 2013 article, professor of law Trina Jones, an African American woman, writes about her own surprise when first learning about colorism in Asia, and when reflecting on her first visit to Asia, she writes that she began to notice a "fascinating phenomenon—the ubiquitous presence of skin-lightening or skin-'brightening' products . . . in grocery stores and at cosmetic counters in department stores [in Asia]." Describing her own unfamiliarity with colorism in Asia and the skin-whitening practices there, she adds, "As an African-American academic who had written about skin color differences among African Americans, I was familiar with the conventional use and sale of skin-lightening products by and to the African-American community. But these new products were directed at a different market. I did not give much thought to the significance of skin color differences among Asians and Asian Americans. I erroneously and naively assumed that skin color was a nonissue within these groups. My 2001 visit to Japan, Vietnam, Thailand, and Hong Kong began to open my eyes."[37] Jones is not alone. While colorism is pervasive across Asia, this fact is unknown to many non-Asians.

Nonetheless, most of Asia has a preoccupation (and perhaps an obsession) with light skin. Japan, for instance, has "long idolized ivory-like skin," as sociologist Evelyn Nakano Glenn notes—skin that is "'like a boiled egg'—soft, white, and smooth on the surface."[38] Historically, Japanese women shielded themselves from the sun and covered their skin with thick, white pancake makeup because white skin has long been linked to social perceptions of beauty, sophistication, and high social class. The adulation of white skin is reflected in an ancient Japanese proverb that translates to "a fair/white complexion hides faults," which suggests that as long as a Japanese woman possesses light skin, she can be forgiven for any shortcomings.[39] The connection between light skin and whiteness is common in the Western world, though writer and blogger Seimi Yamashita asserts that the preference for light skin in Japan is not associated with Europeans nor with a desire to be Caucasian, and has existed in Japan since the Heian Era (from about 794 AD to 1192 AD), when rich, noble women remained indoors, protecting their light skin.[40] In fact, according to Eric Li and colleagues, white skin is tied to Japanese racial identity and Japanese notions of beauty, which, they argue, are seen as "quite different from and even superior to Western whiteness."[41]

While deeply rooted in Japanese history, the preference for light skin continues today. "*Bihaku*," a Japanese term coined in the early 1900s with the emergence of whitening products, translates to "beautifully white."[42] The pressure to be *bihaku* can be seen in modern Japan in the wide range of skin whiteners on the market, on roadside billboards that exclusively showcase light-skinned Japanese women, and even on online dating and matching sites where the younger generations use apps to edit their profile photos to make their faces look brighter and whiter.[43] Moreover, as in ancient times, light skin continues to be a sign of high social class, while darker skin is perceived as unattractive and associated with lower-class people who work outside in the sun. Even in

Figure I.2. Skin-whitening products line a supermarket shelf in Kuala Lumpur, Malaysia. Whitening products are popular throughout Asia, and frequently sold in Asian food markets across the United States. Source: Shutterstock.

modern-day Japanese American beauty pageants, the preference for light skin is evident in the "no tanning" rules for contestants because dark skin is, in Japanese society and Japanese American society, linked to the peasant class or those who work in the fields.[44] According to sociologist Rebecca King-O'Riain, some contestants even rub lemons on their faces to try to lighten their skin.[45]

The association of wealth and light skin, according to scholars Joanne Rondilla and Paul Spickard, can be found in other parts of Asia as well, such as Cambodia, the Philippines, and Taiwan. One Cambodian respondent in their 2007 study described the connection, saying, "[People] want to look whiter because it's associated with wealth and status," and another respondent, Taiwanese, similarly claimed that "light skin is the standard of beauty in Taiwan. . . . Wealthy people tend to be light skinned, while darker people are associated more with low socioeconomic status."[46] In Taiwan, more than half of all women pay "big money" to lighten their skin,[47] some paying as much as three hundred to five hundred US dollars per session with dermatologists who promise white skin—these appointments may include prescribed pills, skin-whitening injections, and in-office treatments with chemical concoctions for the face and body. Rondilla and Spickard argue that customers are not necessarily seeking whiteness (in other words, to be Caucasian), but rather they often want to look like "rich Asians."[48]

In China, skin whiteners account for one-third of all facial skin-care products,[49] and as in Japan, skin color is a signifier of both social class and beauty. A popular Chinese adage passed through the generations is, "One white covers up three ugliness,"[50] suggesting that white skin compensates for physical unattractiveness. In a 2018 study of women and culture-based meanings of skin color, one respondent, Chinese, observed that "if you are white, you are beautiful no matter how you look. . . . Whiter skin color automatically upgrades you."[51] Thus, white skin is not merely an indicator of physical beauty, but is perhaps its most significant measure.

Chinese women traditionally whitened their skin by swallowing crushed pearls or by applying white chalk or rice powder to their skin,[52] though contemporary women can purchase whitening products that are routinely advertised by light-skinned, multiracial, Asian-white models; go to whitening salons that hype laser-operated machines promising to lighten one's "entire body . . . in just one hour";[53] or simply whiten their online faces. A Chinese company whose app makes its users appear thinner and whiter in their "selfies" was valued at nearly five billion dollars in 2016, though critics charge that the app imposes "an ideal of pale skin" on consumers, especially women.[54] The fixation on white skin is also apparent on some Chinese beaches where female bathers don full body suits and "face-kinies"— brightly colored rubber face masks with holes for the eyes, nose, and mouth, which are designed to protect their skin from the sun in a culture that has a "terror of tanning."[55] Face-kinies, popular in China, can also be purchased for day-to-day use to shield one's face from the sun's rays. Even beauty pageants in China glamorize pale skin, and, according to Gary Xu and

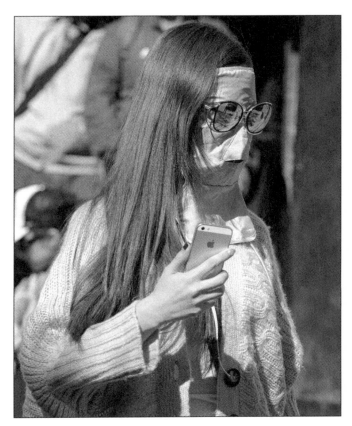

Figure I.3. A Chinese woman wears a face mask or "face-kini" in Lhasa, Tibet. Face-kinies are primarily produced in China and are designed to protect one's face from the sun's UV rays.
Source: Shutterstock.

Susan Feiner, they reinforce "the standardization of beauty features based on Anglo-European norms"[56] and an "imitation of whiteness."[57]

Some argue, however, that as in Japan, whitening in China is not about mimicking Eurocentric ideals. Ye Tiantian, blogging in 2015 about her own experiences with colorism, says that for her, it is not about imitating white people: "It is true that I cannot represent all of the consumers in the skin whitening market, but I am pretty sure that I and most of the people I know buying these products are not trying to make ourselves look like white people. We don't want to be white," but adds, "I cannot tell you for sure that it has nothing to do with white privilege."[58] At least, she posits, that is not the whole story behind the skin-whitening market in China. Chinese women have been lightening their skin for centuries, and the practice dates back to the Qin Dynasty (221–206 BC), when having a white complexion was seen as noble and aristocratic.[59] Even today, people lighten their skin because they do not want to be perceived as poor. Light skin implies social status, and scholar Evelyn Yeung further argues that even the consumption of whitening products "can be a display of wealth. . . . [b]ecause cosmetics are considered luxury items," signifying to others one's disposable income in China's growing consumerist culture.[60] Rae Chen, who describes herself in an op-ed as a "light-skinned Chinese woman," similarly views colorism in China as more of a "status symbol than a racial one," though she admits that, regardless of the motivation, the message remains that light skin is superior to dark.[61]

Other Asian societies prize light skin not simply because of its link to social class but because of their colonial roots and history of European conquest, when Caucasian standards of beauty became embedded in the psyches of the colonized. In 1952, French psychiatrist Frantz Fanon, in his book *Black Skin, White Masks*, argued that colonization has had a deep impact on the human psyche, and Pal Ahluwalia further explains that "the effects of colonialism permeated the black body and created a desire to wear a white mask, to mimic the white person in order to survive the absurdity of the colonial world."[62] Performative whiteness was arguably a survival technique for the oppressed and a tool for the upwardly mobile to access status, and in postcolonial Asia, perhaps aspirations for whiteness have lingered.

This colonial legacy can be seen in the ways in which whitening products are routinely advertised to the masses. In the Philippines, the mass consumption of skin-whitening products is, according to Joanne Rondilla, a reflection of its colonial history (the Philippines was colonized by Spain and then the United States for over four hundred years) and the controlling images of the media, such as television, film, magazines, and the Internet, which, even today,

Figure I.4. Print advertisement for Lancôme's Blanc Expert, featuring actress Emma Watson. Light-skinned Asian women, multiracial Asian-white women, and even Caucasian women are used in the advertising of skin whiteners across Asia.

idealize light skin and Western standards of beauty.[63] Companies advertise how their product will "whiten" skin and promise that their product will make one's skin "pure," "fair," "white," or "translucent," literally calling upon European standards of beauty. Other key terms in whitening advertisements—"flawless," "radiance," "purify," "brightness," "clarity," "luminous"— according to Rondilla, "*imply* a Eurocentric beauty standard that is imposed on Asian and Asian American women" (emphasis added).[64] This beauty standard is further reflected in the use of light-skinned Asian models (often multiracial with white ancestry) and even European models who are the face of whitening products in print and commercial advertisements across Asia. From 2011 to 2013, for example, Caucasian actress Emma Watson, of *Harry Potter* film fame, was the face of Lancôme's advertisement campaign for their Blanc Expert skin-whitening serum, which was advertised in Asian markets.[65] She received widespread criticism for her role in advertising the product, though Caucasian women have long been employed to market skin whiteners to Asian women across Asia.

Vestiges of European colonization are also evident in the Philippines in marrying practices wherein darker-skinned Filipinxs are encouraged to marry lighter. Joanne Rondilla and Paul Spickard describe this practice of "marrying up" as a way to access social status and power, but also whiteness itself.[66] One interviewee explained, "My father suggested I have children with my White ex-boyfriend so he could have mestizo [multiracial] grandchildren. I think years of this colonial way of thinking and all the American propaganda has made it so that my father (and most other Filipinos) think that everything 'American'—White American—is superior."[67] The preference for whiteness is even seen among those of Filipinx descent living in America. Professor of psychology Kevin Nadal describes situations where he witnessed multiracial black-Filipinx Americans being teased or called "*egots*" (a derogatory term for black people), while multiracial white-Filipinx Americans were praised for their light skin and white heritage. According to Nadal, many Filipinx Americans are proud of their identity, though they still carry a "colonial mentality" in which all things Western and white are seen as superior to anything Filipinx.[68]

In India, too, centuries of European colonization have left an indelible mark. In Bollywood (India's multi-billion-dollar film industry), the light, near-white actors and actresses who grace the silver screen are not reflective of the brown masses. The blue and green eyes and light skin of Bollywood's elite reveal a society that is obsessed with lightness, though historians are divided over why. For some, the obsession is rooted in India's caste system, a rigid form of social stratification rooted in Hinduism that dates back centuries.[69] Jyotsna Vaid, professor of psychology and women and gender studies at the University of Texas at Austin, explains that the Sanskrit term for "caste" also means "color,"[70] and historians have long speculated whether colorism is deeply embedded in Indian culture and Hindu religion. Indeed, dark skin in India is frequently associated with the lowest castes and connotes dirt and evil.[71]

Assistant professor of law Neha Mishra argues, however, that while the two lowest castes, the Shrudras and the Dalits, are indeed the darkest-skinned people in India, linking skin color and caste is a gross oversimplification.[72] There are varied degrees of skin tone in most castes, and skin color is more location-specific than caste-related; those in the northern regions of India tend to have lighter skin than those in the south. Moreover, Jyotsna Vaid contends that there is "nothing in the ancient Vedic texts or religious scripture to suggest a favoring of lighter over darker skin,"[73] and Lori Tharps similarly challenges the notion that colorism has ancient roots in India when she observes that "there are Hindu gods and goddesses with dark skin who have long been considered both beautiful and benevolent, crushing the theory that in India dark skin has always been associated with negative characteristics or inherent evil."[74]

For many historians, Indian obsession with light skin is un-equivocally linked to, or at the very least exacerbated by, centuries of British colonization—when Europeans held power, status, and esteem over their darker subjects. British colonizers made "invidi-ous comparisons" between light-skinned and dark-skinned Indians, asserting that the former were more attractive and intelligent than the latter,[75] and they empowered lighter-skinned (and sometimes part-white) Indians during their rule, further elevating lightness and whiteness in colonial India.[76] According to Tharps, the British granted them prestigious positions in government, industry, and education, while those with dark skin were left with menial jobs, often in roles subservient to their British masters. Accordingly, Tharps writes that "whether or not a belief system that favored light skin over dark was already in place before colonization, the British took a giant step in institutionalizing colorism."[77]

Though British rule ended in 1947, the preference for all things European arguably remained, including European physical traits such as light skin, and this preference is clearly evident in modern India. "Fair" and "lovely" are terms that are nearly synonymous and are forever linked in India's most popular whitening cream by the same name. Skin whitening is big business in India, and its ubiq-uity is seen in the glut of whitening products on the market, from face creams and soaps to deodorants that whiten dark underarms and feminine washes and creams that lighten brown nipples and vaginas.[78] The national obsession with light skin is further reflected in the multitude of advertising billboards that use European models to advertise Indian products to Indians in India,[79] the creation of Facebook apps that allow users to lighten their skin color in profile pictures (such as one marketed by Vaseline in 2010),[80] and even in the practice among some Indian couples of seeking Caucasian egg donors so that they can have light-skinned, blue-eyed babies through in-vitro fertilization (IVF).[81] Seeking light-skinned donors seems to be a trend according to some IVF specialists in India, and one father who conceived a daughter via IVF with a Caucasian donor egg reveals at least one reason why: "There is no denying that it is easier to get fair girls married."[82]

In South Asian cultures where arranged marriages are common (such as India, but also Pakistan, Bangladesh, and Sri Lanka), parents often seek light-skinned partners for their children. Hence, as with African American women (described earlier), light skin, especially for South Asian women as compared to men, is an asset and is just as valuable as, or perhaps even more valuable than, one's educational background and social class. In fact, a survey of nearly twelve thousand Indians by the online Indian matrimonial site Shaadi.com reveals that in three north Indian states, light skin is the most important criterion when choosing a mate.[83] Further, in an analysis of marital advertisements that appeared in India's *Sunday Times* on a single day in 2013, skin tone for prospective brides was mentioned 40 percent of the time, though it was never mentioned in ads for prospective grooms, illustrating the gender asymmetry in colorism in Asia. Moreover, of the ads for females that described skin color, none included terms that indicated dark skin, but rather they used terms such as "fair" and "rosy."[84]

Just as in South Asia, skin color is valuable social capital in South Asian American marriage markets. Growing up, my parents subscribed to the *India Abroad*, a popular newspaper that serves the Indian American community. Out of curiosity, I often sat at the kitchen table scrutinizing the matrimonial section, where Indian parents placed ads similar to those in India for their sons and daughters in hopes of finding them suitable mates. To make their adult children sound attractive, parents advertised their children's prestigious educations, high-status jobs, good family values, caste, and, quite often (especially if they were advertising for their daughter), their "fair," "light," or "wheatish" skin color. In the marriage market among South Asians, fair skin, or skin that is the color of wheat, is an indicator of beauty and represents tangible "symbolic capital" for women in marriage negotiations.[85] Some recent examples of matrimonial ads:

NI parents seek alliance for daughter 1979/5"4' slim/very fair accomplished hotel professional in Florida, can relocate. Send bio/ photo. (*India Abroad*; ad placed on May 4, 2018)

Hindu Punjabi parents seek suitable match for beautiful, fair, slim, and homely, 5'6"/1980 US born and raised MD daughter. Email Biodata/Pictures. (*India Abroad*; ad placed on May 21, 2018)

Aristocratic reputed Hindu Business Family, settled US, over 30 years; seeking educated, well-placed, business professional for their very fair and very beautiful, US citizen daughter 31, Graduate. Email: bio/photo. (*India Abroad*; ad placed on June 8, 2018)

Men's ads do not typically advertise their skin color, yet they don't hesitate to ask for light-skinned brides.[86] For example,

Seeking fair attractive girls 32–35; for USA born handsome groom Height 5'10". Operating a multi-million dollar investment/manage-ment business. From well-established family. Email/photo/biodata. (*India Abroad*; ad placed on May 25, 2018)

Social activist Fatima Lodhi, who was raised in Pakistan, describes the pressures to whiten her skin because of those who told her, "No one will marry you."[87] As in other parts of South Asia, Pakistani women face intense social pressure to have light skin—what author Maria Sartaj calls a "hideous complexion complex" suffered by the entire nation, but suffered most of all by women. She observes that dark Pakistani women, like herself, are mocked and devalued, and argues that dark skin is treated like a "disease" in Pakistan.[88] Clearly, Pakistan is not alone.

Furthermore, the literature on colorism typically focuses on skin color, though colorism can also be extended to include other traits that approximate European notions of physical beauty. Blue eyes in Asia are prized, and this was made quite obvious to me growing up. My north Indian great-grandmother had blue eyes, as do many of my second and third cousins, many of whom live in India, and this has become a source of family pride, probably because of their uniqueness amid millions of dark eyes (let's face it, blue eyes stand out there), but conceivably also because of their connection to whiteness. Some of our family conversations: "Perhaps one of our ancestors is European?"; "Maybe a great-great uncle was from Germany or Eastern Europe?" In my family, there was great interest in and even excitement at the thought, and certainly Eurocentric features, such as light eyes, are adored. I was not immune. I, too, wanted the light blue eyes that were so coveted in my community and in my family. If my great-grandmother had them, and my white mother had them, why couldn't I?

Eye shape and nose shape also matter, and their importance in many communities is arguably tied to colorism. Eyelid tapes and glues, which claim to create an extra fold in the eyelid, are heavily marketed across East Asia.[89] Even a plastic set of "eyelid trainers" can be purchased that are designed to create a double eyelid presumably for those Asian consumers with creaseless monolids. I found a pair online for under twenty-five US dollars on Amazon that advertises, "Just like to wear glasses, take 5 minutes one day, one month can get beautiful double eyelid!"[90]

Surgical alternatives are more invasive, permanent, expensive, and perhaps more controversial. Nonetheless, cosmetic surgery is booming in parts of Asia. South Korea, for example, currently has the highest rate of plastic surgeries (per capita per year), outpacing both the United States and Brazil.[91] Two of the most popular procedures in Asia include nose jobs (rhinoplasty) to narrow the nose and make it project more (usually with silicone implants or

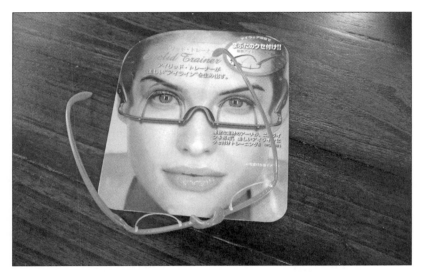

Figure I.5. Packaging for eyelid trainers. Though marketed to East Asian consumers, the model for the product is a European woman with double-lidded, blue eyes. Source: Nikki Khanna.

cartilage grafted from the ear, rib, or septum) and eyelid surgery (double blepharoplasty) to give Asians an extra fold in the eyelid—something present in nearly all Caucasians, but only naturally found in about 15 percent of East Asians.[92]

While these surgical procedures may invoke images of "white-worship," many women argue that these surgeries are not about looking Western at all.[93] *New York Magazine*'s Maureen O'Connor, who is Chinese and white, argues that these phenotypic modifications are not about "hiding one's race or mimicking another" but about attaining particular aesthetics popular in Asian cultures. According to Dr. Robert Flowers, a white surgeon and a pioneer in blepharoplasties, Asian patients do not want to be white—they simply want to be "beautiful Asians."[94] In fact, O'Connor contends that those who believe eyelid surgery is about erasing one's race are usually white themselves, and she asks, "[Is] that a symptom of in-group narcissism—white people assuming everyone wants to look like them?"[95] Similarly, writer and journalist Euny Hong, in a 2013 op-ed in the *Wall Street Journal*,[96] writes about her own eyelid surgery and argues that "Asians, for the most part, get the surgery for themselves and for each other—not to approximate a Caucasian appearance." In fact, she notes that after her eyelid procedure, none of her non-Asian friends (including her white friends) even noticed—and she did not seem particularly concerned when they didn't. For Hong, the surgery was not about or for them.

Likewise, many cosmetic surgeons (like Dr. Robert Flowers above) argue that these surgeries are about attaining Asian standards of beauty, not mimicking white women. Joanne Rondilla and Paul Spickard, however, challenge this interpretation by pointing out that these so-called Asian beauty standards "just happen to coincide with the way they perceive White women to look."[97] Is it merely a coincidence that what Asian women deem beautiful happens to mirror Caucasian standards of beauty—such as double-lidded eyes? Rondilla and Spickard argue that "in fact, it has everything to do with such beauty standards,"[98] and they claim that the cosmetic-surgery industry profits from the idea that Asian women must correct their ethnic features. They further point out that the popularity of cosmetic surgery in Asia happened, in part, because of colonialism. Local populations, particularly women, were influenced by Western notions of beauty introduced by their Western colonizers, and it was during this time that they first began seeking plastic surgery in large numbers.

Whether these tapes, glues, gadgets, and surgeries are about attaining whiteness is highly debatable, though undoubtedly Western standards anchor beauty culture in parts of Asia—and most certainly in the United States. In 2013, Chinese American talk show host Julie Chen revealed the pressure she felt to surgically alter her features—not from her Chinese American community but from white Americans. She underwent eyelid surgery in her twenties to look less Chinese after a (white) news director told her that she would be more appealing to American audiences without her "Asian eyes," and a prospective (white) talent agent warned, "I cannot represent you unless you get plastic surgery to make your eyes look bigger."[99] Pressure to fit into white-dominated American society may only compound the issue of colorism for Asian Americans.

The Voices of Asian American Women

In this book, Asian American women, with their own stories and in their own words, describe their experiences with skin-color privilege and discrimination both within their respective ethnic communities and within American society. Few books examining skin color focus exclusively on Asian populations and, unlike previous books on colorism, mine focuses exclusively on women because the research suggests that while Asian/Asian American men and women both feel the effects of skin-color discrimination, it is women who bear its brunt—especially because of the link between skin color and perceptions of beauty and femininity.[100] A conversation with my father just before my wedding illustrates this. In the weeks leading up to my winter nuptials, I decided (for the first time, I might add!) to tan at a local tanning bed—yes, yes, I know, cancer-wise, not a particularly wise decision. But, I did it. After the first tanning session, when I returned home quite pleased with and proud of my burgeoning brown color, my father asked, rather exasperatedly in fact, "Why are you tanning?!" Well, it was December, and whatever deep color I had gained in the summer had now faded to my natural yellowish-pale tone. I matter-of-factly replied that I did not want my skin to match my white wedding dress as I sauntered down the aisle—to which my father then asked, rather perplexed, "Indian woman are always trying to get lighter, why are you trying to be darker?" Undoubtedly, colorism is more salient for women as compared to men, and I cannot picture our conversation happening between a father and son. My younger brother did not tan before his wedding, though I cannot imagine anyone commenting on it if he had.

I focus on Asian American (as opposed to Asian) women because those of Asian ancestry living in the United States conceivably face compounded pressure for light skin (and other European physical traits) because of (1) the cultural importance given to these traits in their respective Asian ethnic communities, and (2) the added pressure towards whiteness in a white-dominated society. Perhaps Asian American women feel less constrained by colorism as compared to Asian women given that they are geographically and, in many cases, generationally removed from their ancestral countries of origin and Asian cultural pressures. In fact, Joanne Rondilla and Paul Spickard find that first-generation Asian immigrants "have more (or at least more overt) colorism issues" than Asian Americans born in the United States.[101] Undoubtedly the pressure for light skin and Eurocentric traits is more covert for Asian Americans, but I argue that the pressure is strong in the United States as well. According to law professor Trina Jones, the color hierarchy in the United States (as in Asia) privileges light skin, and in the American context, "lightness is associated with intelligence, honesty, industry, and beauty, while darkness is associated with laziness, immorality, criminality, and ignorance."[102] Moreover, Asian American women, like all women in the United States, are routinely bombarded by images of white models and actors on American television, Internet sites, magazines, and billboards. A quick online search of "beautiful women," for instance, reveals mostly white faces, and *Vogue* covers through the years typically feature white women.[103] Celebrities who grace *People* magazine's "Most Beautiful People" covers are almost always white—rarely are they women of color,[104] and never have they been Asian American in its near-thirty-year history. In American society, Eurocentric traits are the gold standard of beauty.[105]

Like the women included in this book, I have grown up in two worlds: one, Indian American, where light skin is clearly valued over dark, and Eurocentric traits are favored (my younger brother has light blue eyes and, believe me, I have never heard the end of it); and two, American culture, where I grew up surrounded by white faces in school, in my community, and in the films and television shows that I watched (and still watch). Even I, mixed-race with an Indian father and a white mother, with light skin, dark brown eyes, and brown hair, who is often read as white, went through a phase when I wanted the traits of the white women in my fashion and teen magazines, such as light eyes and light hair. Perhaps pressures for lightness and whiteness would have been more pronounced for me had I been raised in India surrounded

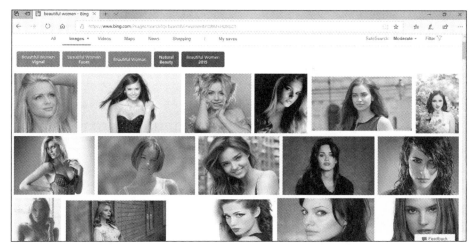

Figure I.6. An online search of "beautiful women" on the popular search engine Bing reveals mostly Caucasian-appearing women. Source: Nikki Khanna.

by endless advertisements for whitening creams peddled by near-white Bollywood starlets. However, I know that I and many others experience comparable pressure right here in America, even if the message is more veiled than the overtly racist and colorist ads across Asia that shamelessly promise consumers that their whitening product will address all of their "whitening needs" (Estee Lauder's CyberWhite) or reveal their "true inner fairness" (L'Oreal's WhitePerfect). This blatant messaging is rare in America, though the lesson is nonetheless the same. Just as girls and women in India and other parts of Asia are taught the value of light skin, I learned that whiteness is the epitome of status and beauty in American society.

An important caveat: Growing up, I loved when I was tanned. I thank my South Asian ancestry for my ability to quickly achieve a deep golden hue in summers, something that was enviable to many of my white friends. Tanned skin is considered attractive in American culture, and this is something that clearly differentiates the United States from most of Asia;[106] however, tanning cannot be likened to skin whitening. Scholar Sriya Shrestha describes what she sees as a false equivalency between tanning and skin-whitening practices, noting that this "false parity" ignores the power dynamics that make light skin desirable for people of color.[107] Light, white skin is powerful and is associated with increased opportunities and privilege; tanned skin, though a beauty norm in the West, does not hold the same power. Social advocate Sabina Verghese further describes tanning as a "social luxury" for white women.[108] While her own dark skin tone has been used by others to gauge her worth, beauty, and intelligence, white women "maintain a sense of privilege" and do not endure "backlash that comes with having dark skin tone." I, too, can tan to achieve an aesthetic popular in the United States—like other light-skinned women, I am praised for my temporarily browned summer skin and, at the same time, remain relatively insulated from cultural judgments and negative stereotypes about my darkened tone.

Moreover, white women may tan at the beach or apply darkening lotions for a "healthy glow," but whether any of them would trade their white skin for good is another matter altogether. Comedian Chris Rock, African American, said it best in his 1999 standup routine: "There ain't a white man in this room that would change places with me. None of you. None of you would change places with me, and I'm rich!"[109] Perhaps this is because light skin along with racial whiteness in the United States is associated with intelligence, wealth, national belonging, and citizenship, and impacts access to opportunities. Despite the tanning culture, Sriya Shrestha argues that "white people want to be white."[110] Just as in Asia, light skin is esteemed in the United States, and Asian American women must simultaneously manage the Eurocentric pressures both in their Asian ethnic communities and in American society at large.

Scholar Eugena Kaw describes an additional pressure felt by many Asian American women that goes beyond merely trying to conform to Eurocentric norms for the sake of beauty: Asian American women may also alter their looks (their skin, hair, eyes, and noses) because they feel they must "conceal the more obvious forms of their ethnicity in order not to stand out and be targeted for racial stereotypes."[111] According to race scholar Mia Tuan,

Asian Americans are often seen as "forever foreigners," even if their families have been in the United States for generations.[112] Their foreign-sounding names, language, accent, facial features, and/or skin color mark them as "other." Writer Rae Chen, herself light-skinned, describes her experiences growing up in Canada and observes that her darker-skinned Chinese friends and family experience comparatively more micro-aggressions and racial profiling, which has made schooling and job hunting difficult for them.[113] Hence, some Asian Americans may lighten their skin, slim their nose, or modify their eyelids to "shake off [their] perceived otherness" (as did talk show host Julie Chen, described earlier) as a strategy to blend in and evade bias.[114] In Julie Chen's case, surgically altering her eyelids conceivably opened job opportunities in American broadcasting that may have otherwise been closed to her. In fact, she admits that her career "did take off" once she had the surgery.[115]

My own experiences growing up in the United States have been largely shaped by my gender, my race, and, most importantly, my skin color. I am a mixed-race woman and light-skinned. I look back at myself standing in the Indian market as a kid, checking my skin tone next to the seven shades of the "expert fairness meter" printed on the Fair & Lovely package, while smiling to myself. I am embarrassed at that memory, and at both my understanding and misunderstanding of colorism. Like most people, I had no word for it then. I knew light skin was favored, but I did not recognize as a child what that really meant—what it meant for me, and what it meant for my darker-skinned family members (such as my father, grandparents, aunts, uncles, and cousins) and for other Americans of color with dark skin. Only as an adult do I understand colorism for what it is—a repressive, sexist, and racist practice that disadvantages much of the world's population. The intent of this book is to give voice to Asian American women—of all shades and hues. Skin-color discrimination directed towards and found among Asian Americans is understudied and, to some extent, missing from current discussions of colorism. My hope is that this collection of essays will, first and foremost, be a collective platform for women to share their own stories in their own words, and, second, draw attention to both the varied and common experiences of Asian American women in the twenty-first century to inform what we know and understand about colorism among these communities.

Plan of the Book

The book is divided into six distinct sections, and each section reflects a theme related to colorism. In the first section, "Colorism Defined," the authors introduce the concept of colorism as it pertains to their lived experiences as Asian American women. Through their stories, they explain how they learned about the significance of their skin shade and its association with class, wealth, intelligence, beauty, and femininity. Through their stories, they also explain how the meanings connected to skin color are deeply embedded in both American and Asian cultures, and they reveal the chief source of these messages—mass media and family, often mothers and grandmothers. One college student describes pressure from her Indian mother to "maintain" her light skin and the conflict it has caused between them; her story mirrors mother-daughter struggles shared by many women throughout the book. Moreover, the authors describe the pressure to conform to beauty norms, especially as females, and how they came to understand the shared and sometimes conflicting definitions of beauty in America, Asia, and Asian America. According to one writer, her dark skin is seen as "deviant" in Japan and among Asian Americans, though she contends that it is viewed indifferently, and sometimes even positively, in America.

In Part II, "Privilege," authors examine their own privilege, or lack thereof, as it pertains to the color of their skin. The contributors range widely in skin color, and for some women, their skin color is an asset, though for others, it is a social liability. The literature suggests that possessing light skin is valuable, though the authors in this section reveal that privilege is shaped not only by the particular tone of their skin but by the context in which they are viewed. Because colorism is global, their skin color takes on different meanings depending upon location—for example, what may be privileged in Asia, may not be in the United States.

The privilege that they experience is also dependent upon the ethnicity and race of the audience before them. Colorism runs rampant within and between communities of color, and as a result, one's skin tone may confer benefits with some ethnic/racial groups while proving disadvantageous with others. One multiracial woman, for instance, describes experiences of adulation and praise for her light skin when among African Americans, though at the same time, she feels skin color discrimination by Asian Americans. Moreover, colorism crosses Asian ethnic groups and typically privileges lighter-skinned Asian ethnic groups over their darker-skinned counterparts (for example, privileging East Asians over South/Southeast Asians), and several contributors describe the hierarchies among Asian ethnic groups based on skin color and its implications. One woman, who (as she says) "embodies the stereotype of an Asian American" because of her light skin, evades much discrimination in America as compared to her darker-skinned Asian American counterparts. Thus, through their essays, the writers in Part II show that privilege can be situational and fluid, conferring advantage in some contexts, while simultaneously disadvantaging them in others.

In Part III, "Aspirational Whiteness," the essays address the value placed not just on light skin but on whiteness itself, and the meanings attached to whiteness in Asia and in America. Through their narratives, the writers reveal that some Asian Americans strive for whiteness because, for them, it is equated with American assimilation and success, upward mobility, and sophistication, and the authors in this section describe the different ways in which they attempt to access whiteness in contemporary American society. Whitening products are one strategy to obtain whiteness, though for darker-skinned South and Southeast Asians, whiteness may be comparatively more elusive. According to one contributor, fellow South Asians may access whiteness digitally through the use of light-skinned emojis to represent themselves on social media. Another writer notes that in lieu of whiteness, some darker-skinned South and Southeast Asian Americans aspire to the American stereotype of "the Asian"—the light-skinned, successful East Asian—which, at least according to her, is "the next best thing."

While previous sections explore the privilege of light skin and the value placed on whiteness, Part IV, "Anti-Blackness," addresses the anti-black sentiment that exists in America, in Asia, and among Asian Americans. Here, authors describe the ways in which anti-blackness rears its head in their lives, and its connection to colorism. Within their communities, just as in the United States, blackness is juxtaposed in direct opposition to whiteness and is associated with a litany of negative stereotypes. Their experiences reveal that anti-black racism is intimately entwined with an aversion to dark skin in their Asian American communities, and they write about their own experiences with anti-blackness in their respective cultures. One contributor, for example, describes how anti-black narratives inform creationist stories in Pakistani culture (i.e., religious stories of how God created the races), and others in this section explain what anti-blackness means for them personally as a multiracial Asian/black American or mother of a multiracial Asian/black child.

In Part V, "Belonging and Identity," authors describe how their skin color affects their perceptions of belonging and sense of identity with their Asian American communities. Skin that is perceived by others as "too light" or "too dark" influences whether they feel as though they fit in with their ethnic group. One woman, white-skinned with blonde hair and born with albinism, explains how she feels "invisible" to her Indian American community, while another woman describes how her dark skin often precludes acceptance by others in her Chinese American community. Other Asian Americans make assumptions about the race and ethnicity of the authors included here, and in some of the essays, writers describe their frustrations when not recognized as members of their ethnic communities. According to one woman, her multiracial background, her ambiguous phenotype, and the relentless barrage of "What are you?" questions have given her the sense that she is not "*really* Asian." For these women, their bodies defy ethnic/racial stereotypes—as constructed by Asians, Asian Americans, and the American media—and through their narratives, they challenge these one-dimensional, narrow images. Accordingly, they argue that there is "more than one way to look Asian."

The final selection of essays in Part VI, "Skin—Redefined," features women who write about their journey towards self-acceptance and their embrace of their skin shade. They describe colorism in their lives (as in Part I) and, most importantly, they challenge the "light-skin-is-beautiful" mantra, often in direct defiance of mothers, grandmothers, friends, and society in general. For most of the women in this section of essays, this has been a decades-long process of acceptance and reclaiming of their skin; one woman writes, "The color of my skin will no longer define me." Another writer delves into some of her more painful experiences growing up with dark skin, though as an adult, she looks back to her "road of healing" and her evolving perception of her own worth and beauty. Another describes the "reprogramming" that is, as she describes it, a "constant work in progress," and all the women in this section describe how they are challenging the messages of their youth. For two of the women in this section, this is a labor of love for the next generation—their daughters.

Rather than being predetermined by me (as the editor), these six categorical themes grew out of a careful analysis and reading of the essays—even of those essays that did not ultimately make it into this collection. The words within each contributor's essay ultimately guided the overall organization of the book, and each essay reflects the fundamental theme of its assigned section. Readers may observe some degree of overlap between themes in the essays, as colorism is complex, and these essays reveal that, for many women, these six themes are connected in intricate ways. Additionally, each collection of essays begins with an introduction that describes and unpacks the theme of the section.

The Contributors

This collection includes personal narratives by Asian American women aged twenty-two to sixty-two of varying ethnicities, including Filipina (six women), Indian (five), Chinese (three), Pakistani (two), Vietnamese (two), Cambodian (one Cham, one Khmer), Japanese (one), Bangladeshi (one), and Pacific Islander (one). Two women describe themselves as multiethnic—one as Chinese/Filipina and another as Taiwanese/Chinese. It is important to recognize that the term "Asian" is a social construct that refers to those who have ancestry in Asia or the Asian subcontinent. I rely on current federal classifications of race (currently used by the US Census and defined by the Office of Management and Budget in 1997), which formally define "Asian" as "a person having origins in any of the original peoples of the Far East, Southeast Asia, or the Indian subcontinent including, for example, Cambodia, China, India, Japan, Korea, Malaysia, Pakistan, the Philippine Islands, Thailand, and Vietnam."[116] This racial category, like others, is not based in biology, nor rooted in shared physical characteristics (e.g., certainly people of India look different than those from Japan); rather, it is a socially constructed category employed to lump together diverse groups of people for political purposes. In fact, my Indian father did not think of himself as Asian when he first immigrated to the United States, and even now, I am not sure he sees himself as such; for many South Asian immigrants, such as those from India, Pakistan, and Bangladesh, for example, only after years exposed to American race politics might they identify as Asian or Asian American. Nonetheless, I rely on this definition as a practical tool with which to delineate whose stories would be included in the book. Though varied in culture and physiognomy, the women included (or their ancestors) come from a similar region of the world, even if that expanse is quite large, and together they share the cultural embeddedness of skin-color discrimination.

In addition to the varied ethnic backgrounds of the contributors, five identify as multiracial—as Japanese/white, Japanese/black, Chinese/black, Chinese/white, and Korean/white. For multiracial

Asian women with black or white ancestry, colorism can be particularly pronounced, and their stories add further nuance to our collective understanding of colorism. Their white or black ancestries are tied to a plethora of stereotypes and hold meaning in both Asia and the United States, further complicating onlookers' interpretations of their skin shades. All contributors are also American citizens and were born and raised in the United States, with the exception of two women—one is a Japanese citizen but has been a US resident for seventeen years, and the other is Indo-Canadian but has lived on and off in the United States for more than twenty years.

Despite the variability in the backgrounds of the contributors, there are two notable commonalities that traverse the experiences of the majority of the women included here. First, though it is rarely revealed in their essays, it is likely that most, though not all, of the contributors are heterosexual. Because colorism is often intertwined with marriageability (i.e., light-skinned women are advantaged in the marriage market), the male gaze is, at times, implicitly invoked in stories about skin color. Some women feel objectified by men because of their light skin, or, conversely, shunned by them because they are dark. In fact, Joanne Rondilla and Paul Spickard's work suggests that there is considerable pressure for women from a heteronormative perspective; one respondent in their 2007 study, a Cambodian American woman, describes the lyrics of a popular Cambodian song: "The man in the song sings out and he says that 'You're dark and you're not that attractive because you're dark.' Then the woman goes . . . 'Yeah, I'm dark but I could be a good wife.'"[117] Light skin acts as currency in the marriage market, and consequently colorism is deeply embedded in heteronormative culture and remains a calculable asset in heterosexual relationships, especially for women. The woman in the song is perceived by the man as unattractive because of her dark skin, and she attempts to counteract his appraisal by telling him that she could be a "good wife" to him. To what extent LGBTQ people feel this pressure from potential partners remains unknown, though certainly this is an area ripe for inquiry.

Second, the majority of the contributors are middle-class. Their class status is particularly important given the potential protection it confers; privileged backgrounds arguably mediate their experiences with skin-color bias and, to some extent, lessen its impact in job and marriage markets. Dark skin is assessed as a liability in Asian cultures, though those with high status may find that their education, high-status occupations, and money offset its weight. Though they are not immune to colorism (as their stories clearly reveal), readers should recognize that women from less privileged backgrounds may have more pronounced adverse encounters with skin-color discrimination. This fact cannot be overstated. The intersectionality of skin shade and social class undoubtedly affects the experiences of Asian American women.

Despite these shared commonalities, the women included here vary in ethnicity and, for some, race. They range widely in age. They are mothers, daughters, sisters, undergraduate and graduate students, writers and storytellers, scholars, and activists—all with diverse interests, occupations, and life stories. For more information about each contributor, biographies of each are included at the end of the book.

A Final Note

This project was a labor of love, and perhaps the most personal project that I have worked on to date in my professional career. Skin-color discrimination is a contentious issue in many Asian American communities (including mine), as well as in many other racial communities across the United States and around the world. This book was challenging to write because I worried throughout the process of writing and editing that I was "airing dirty laundry"—exposing something that many are not particularly proud to openly talk about—especially with those outside of our communities. Many of us, as scholars, as activists, and as Americans more generally, may be open to discussing white supremacy and racial inequality in America, but we may be more hesitant to talk about the bias that happens in our own communities and sometimes even within our families. However, colorism parallels racism in many ways, and we must be willing to bring it to the surface, name it, point it out, and most importantly, talk about it with each other and others.

As a mixed-race woman, I also struggled with how much to include of my own personal story because I grew up, to some extent, on the periphery of the Indian community. I was raised in a multiracial family, in a white suburb, and primarily attended predominantly white schools. For these reasons, I was shielded in many ways from colorism. Also, because of my light skin, I am privileged in America and in the Indian community, and I did not want my experience to take up too much space in the book or take away from other women's voices—especially from women who have been the most disadvantaged by colorism. Having said that, however, I wanted the book to be a wide platform to give voice to diverse women—including those of varying skin shades (light and dark), different Asian ethnicities, and even varied racial backgrounds. Because of my own multiracial background, it was particularly important for me to include the stories of multiracial Asian women because I knew that their experiences would add further understanding to the politics of skin color.

Finally, I thank every woman who contributed an essay to this collection. Sharing personal stories is not easy, and even more difficult is writing about our families in ways that do not always cast the most flattering light. Even for me personally, I struggled with how much to share and how much I had a *right* to share, given that some of my stories involved not just me but also my close family members. No doubt, each contributor had to make difficult decisions about what she felt comfortable sharing with the world and what she would leave out. I hope that when reading the book, readers recognize the vulnerable position that each woman put herself in (and sometimes her family members) in order to tell her story. Each woman is bold and brave, and I am thankful for their contributions—all of which are beautiful, powerful, honest, thoughtful, and, most importantly, graciously allow us an intimate view into their lives.

To each woman who contributed to this book, *thank you.*

Part I

COLORISM DEFINED

What is colorism? In this initial collection of essays, Asian American women introduce the concept of colorism as they have experienced it in their own lives. Through their personal stories, they explain, one, how and where they learned the social significance of their skin color (and other physical characteristics, such as eyes and nose shape); and, two, the underlying meanings attached to these physical features, both in their Asian ethnic communities and in the United States more generally. In many Asian American communities, just as in many parts of Asia, light skin and Eurocentric traits indicate high social class, wealth, and intelligence. In their respective ethnic communities and in the larger United States, these same traits are also considered markers of beauty and femininity for women, and the writers in this section describe the pressure to conform to these colorist ideals—especially as females—first as young girls and later as women.

Sometimes the pressure for light skin stems from mass media and sometimes from family, friends, and peers. Catherine Ma, Chinese American, remembers learning very young about the value of her light skin when an uncle pointedly asked her, "How does it feel to be the prettiest?" As a child, she learned quickly that her skin shade has value and is linked to others' appraisals of her beauty. Sambath Meas, Khmer American, learned about colorism both from mass media and from extended family. When she visited Cambodia, billboards, print ads, television commercials, and song lyrics communicated a uniform message—that light skin is superior to dark. Even day-to-day interactions with extended family taught her the value of her light skin, such as when a female cousin in Cambodia complimented her with, "You're so white; you're so pretty."

As in Sambath Meas's case, the pressure on females for light skin arises from many places—and often from other women. For some in this book, colorist beliefs are learned from those women closest to them, such as their female friends, female cousins, aunts, and even their mothers and grandmothers. Traits that diverge from Western norms of beauty (such as dark skin, creaseless eyelids, and flat noses) are deemed unattractive, and mothers and grandmothers, to take two examples of the most influencing figures, who have grown up with the same colorist burdens, place pressure on their daughters and granddaughters to lighten their skin or to modify other aspects of their bodies to conform to prevalent beauty norms. Perhaps it is not remarkable that mothers and grandmothers, at least in some cases, lead the charge when it comes to passing colorist beliefs from one generation to the next; they want their daughters and granddaughters to thrive and be successful. They want them to marry well. They are acting within the confines of social norms that have so clearly defined to them what is considered to be beautiful, and they draw on these norms when they buy their progeny skin-whitening creams and soaps, when they instruct them to stay out of the sun and under the protective cover of umbrellas, or when they repeatedly remind them to wear sunscreen each time they leave the house. They did not create colorism, but they have learned to operate within it and understand the value of doing so.

At times, pressure from women in the family can be particularly intense and has the potential to cause significant friction between generations. For instance, Rhea Goveas, Indian American, writes of a contentious exchange with her mother over her recently sun-bronzed skin and her frustrations with her mother's colorist beliefs. Miho Iwata, Japanese and light-skinned, describes the persistent pressure from both her mother and her grandmother to "preserve" and protect her skin shade. Though she expresses resentment over the pressure, she admits that she occasionally applied sunscreen and whitening creams because she wanted to fit in with her "[female] peers, older female colleagues, and overall cultural expectations attached to young women in Japan." It is women who are most influenced by colorist beliefs, though women, too, play a key role in transmitting the message that light skin is superior to dark.

The essays in this section also reveal potentially conflicting definitions of beauty in Asian America and in the United States—especially as it pertains to skin color. While tanned skin is seen negatively in the authors' Asian ethnic communities (as it is in Asia), it is viewed more positively in the larger United States. Arguably, the American tanning culture eases the pressure on Asian American women to seek out and maintain light, white skin, allowing them more flexibility in skin shade than those in Asia. Rhea Goveas, for example, describes an argument with her mother at a department store counter over makeup foundation when her mother insisted she buy a shade lighter than her recently tanned tone. Mindful of the mother-daughter struggle unfolding before her, the white saleswoman at the counter interjects, "We like all types in America. We like a bit of color. It's okay to have a tan," suggesting that America, indeed, has more relaxed skin-color norms as compared to those in India. Likewise, Miho Iwata observes that while light skin is "integral to the concept of beauty and femininity in Japan," people in America tend to be more indifferent about her tanned complexion, illustrating that cultural context is important when it comes to colorism.

Divergent beauty norms in America and Asia imply that, for Asian-descended women, colorism is less of an issue in the United States than it is in Asian countries, though a closer look reveals that there is perhaps a limit to American "broad-mindedness" when it comes to skin shade. Tanned skin is undoubtedly more accepted in the United States than in Asia, and this is readily apparent in the lucrative skin-tanning market in America, where millions of dollars are spent yearly on tubes of tanning lotions, sunless spray tans, and tanning beds (as I suggested in the introduction, even I am not immune). Indeed, sun-bronzed skin is considered attractive in the United States, though at the same time, dark skin certainly remains highly stigmatized and negatively stereotyped. Americans with dark skin are typically characterized as unintelligent and lazy (to name two stereotypes of many), and JeffriAnne Wilder, in a study of attitudes towards different skin shades, finds that even in America, "the majority of the terms for dark skin are loaded with negative connotations."[1] Perhaps there is a fine line between sun-tanned skin and dark skin—tanned skin (especially that which is temporary) is considered beautiful, though dark skin is stigmatized and devalued.

Moreover, identifiable physical features, those features that diverge from Eurocentric norms, are racialized in America, and because of this many Americans of color, including Asian Americans, are routinely perceived as non-American even if their families have been in the United States for generations (see Mia Tuan's analysis of Asian Americans as "forever foreigners"). Consider what comes to mind when you think of an "American." For many, the image is probably that of a light-skinned, Caucasian person—an image held by many Americans, but also a common stereotype shared by many outside of the United States. As a child (before I knew better), when asked about my racial/ethnic background, I always responded matter-of-factly with, "I'm half Indian and half American"—and when I said "American," what I really meant was "white" because I subconsciously equated the two. Similarly, Paco Mathew, a multiracial American Peace Corps volunteer, found while working in Africa that the stereotype of Americans is that "they must be blonde-haired and blue eyed. It was like anyone not fitting that description must not be American."[2] Ethel Nicdao, Filipina American, similarly recognizes the narrow stereotype and observes that because Americanness equates to whiteness in many minds, her brown skin makes her "a foreign object" in much of America. She also describes a summer trip to Taiwan, where she was told that she did not "look American," which cost her a coveted job teaching English in Taipei. She observes that "to many Asians (as with many Americans), American means white."

The American-equates-to-whiteness stereotype is particularly problematic for those whose physical features diverge from whiteness, and Ethel Nicdao recognizes that while white Americans may compliment her on her "nice tan" (a compliment she probably would not hear from other Filipinxs), she argues that their flattering compliments "ignore the realities, complexities, and consequences" of her brown skin versus their white skin. Skin shade and physical characteristics that diverge from Western norms may not always indicate unattractiveness (as they do in many parts of Asia or among Asian American communities), but they certainly indicate "otherness," and several women in this section write about their personal struggles with this reality while living in America. Their dark skin and almond-shaped eyes, to name two examples, have led to ridicule, contempt, rejection, marginalization, racial slurs, harassment, and sometimes even physical attacks. Tanzila Ahmed, Bangladeshi American, writes of the disdain she felt from others growing up, including from her white classmates, because of her dark skin. Three women in this section write of being targeted for racial slurs (this is also the case for other women throughout the book)—"Hey Ching Chong" or "You stupid fucking Chink"— sometimes by fellow white schoolchildren and occasionally even by white adults. Catherine Ma, for instance, describes how white children mocked her eyes while she was growing up (something she also sees happening to her young children even today), and she suggests that this disparagement has long-lasting effects for some Asian Americans, including women who, as she contends, "go to extreme measures to change their features (their eyes, their skin, and their bodies) to match a Western, Caucasian standard."

Though beauty standards differ somewhat in American and Asian cultures, perhaps attitudes towards skin color are not really so different after all. Dark skin and non-Eurocentric features may be perceived negatively in most parts of Asia, though they can also be alienating and isolating in white-dominated American society. In the final essay of this section, Bhoomi K. Thakore, Indian American, writes about her hopes for her light-skinned multiracial daughter growing up in America—in particular, that her skin color will not cause her the same disdain, judgment, and rejection that she herself experienced from other Indians and Indian Americans, and from Americans more generally. Bhoomi grew up in America feeling unattractive, stigmatized, and invisible because of her dark skin, and she hopes that her daughter's experiences will be different. Her essay, like others in this section, highlights the problem of, one, skin-color bias within Asian ethnic communities, but also, two, the burden of racialization in American society. As a result of both of these factors, dark skin and non-Eurocentric facial characteristics can be doubly challenging for those of Asian descent living in America.

1

Wheatish

Rhea Goveas, INDIAN AMERICAN, 22

I grew up in a progressive immigrant household. Although both of
my parents are Indian, they come from different faiths and different
regional-linguistic groups. They didn't have an arranged marriage.
In fact, they had a very standard love story (at least by Western
standards): they met at work in Mumbai and fell in love. Their
relationship made many people, both in their families and in their
communities, very apprehensive—at that time it was very unusual
for a Hindu (like my mother) to marry a Christian (like my father).
I suspect this is why they eloped, and once they arrived in the
United States, they were able to establish their own marriage and
lives in a new and more tolerant country. This narrative of tolerance
and progressiveness framed my family life. All the "divisive nonsense" (as my father would say) from the old country didn't matter.
Religion, language, class, caste, race, traditional gender roles, even
skin color: those things do not matter to progressive people. And
since we are progressive people, they don't matter to us.

Though skin color didn't matter in my family (at least theoretically
speaking), I somehow learned all of the vocabulary for skin color. I
knew I was "wheatish"[1] and that this was a good thing. I knew that
when my younger brother was born, everyone in the family was so
happy because of his light skin and light eyes. Even today, everyone
marvels at his baby pictures: "Look at him! Like a little *white* doll!
So sweet! So handsome!" I also knew that as he got older, started
playing soccer, and gradually got darker, some family members were
very disappointed. But I know that since he is a boy, he is given a lot
of slack for getting too much sun and not maintaining his skin tone.

It is not the same for me. Because I am a girl.

I know that everyone's mom nags them to put on sunscreen, but I don't know anyone who gets scolded for not wearing a hat *at all times* when playing outside. As a child, I was also not immune to the occasional snide comment about how I was "ruining" my skin after playing outside in the sun, but luckily I didn't receive daily harassment to apply lightening cream, as did some of my other Indian friends—dire warnings of what would happen lest they become too dark.

I have been "blessed" by my run-of-the-mill complexion—not too light, not too dark. Despite the genetics of my darker Manglorean father, my brother and I inherited light skin from my north Indian mother. Due to this happy accident of genetics giving me a desirable skin tone and my unhappy condition of being born a girl with all the beauty expectations this carries, I learned very early that it is my job to protect what I have. The older I get, the more I notice little references to my skin color and the more I feel pressure to keep my skin as light as possible.

My father is quick to tell me that this is nonsense. He loudly proclaims that none of this matters to him, that both his children are beautiful regardless of their skin tone. I believe him. My mother is a different story. She says skin color does not matter, but is quick to comment on how "pretty and fair" someone is or to slather herself with "luminizing" creams or homemade turmeric masks to lighten her skin. She occasionally exerts this pressure on me—persuading me to get facials or to try new "brightening" creams with her. Occasionally, she buys me expensive products to "clean up" my skin or beautify my face.

On one such occasion, she took me to the mall for the purpose of trying the new Chanel Vitalumiere Aqua Foundation. My mother had purchased some for an event and absolutely loved it. I never object to getting fancy new makeup, so off we went to the Chanel counter in the Bloomingdale's at our local mall—my mom, her friend, and myself. We got to the counter and my mom told the elderly blonde lady that I wanted the foundation.

"Alright, dear," the blonde Chanel lady smiled down at me. "Why don't you take a seat and we can color match you."

So I sat in the chair and allowed her to dab foundation in various brown tints on my cheek. The first one she tried was too light.

"Hmm, this is a teensy bit too light, I think," the Chanel lady observed, angling my face towards the light so she could get a better look.

"Yeah, I agree," I said. The Chanel lady turned to select another shade from the display.

"Don't worry, she isn't normally this dark," my mother interjected—a little too quickly, I might add. "She has been traveling quite a bit and got too much sun. When her skin is back to normal, she will be much lighter. You can give her a lighter shade."

I sensed where she was going with this and attempted to head it off at the pass. "My skin is normal, Mom. I'm only a little bit more tanned than I usually am. It's not like I am going to drastically get any paler."

"No, no, no. You can be much, much lighter than this. I've seen you in the winter," my mother insisted.

I opened my mouth to reply.

"You know what, *Beta*," my mom's friend interjected. "You should do a face mask of *haldi* and yogurt.[2] It helps lighten the skin."

"I know about that," I snapped, getting prickly. I shot a furtive look at the blonde Chanel lady, wanting this conversation to end. "I hate those masks. They smell awful. They don't even work. And I don't need to use that crap. My skin is fine."

"I promise you they work." My mom's friend was insistent. "And it is all natural. They look a bit funny, yes, but they work. I've been doing *haldi* masks for years."

I felt their critical eyes on my face, taking in my sun-bronzed skin. I remembered feeling that same gaze from my mom two weeks earlier when my parents picked me up from the airport after my recent trip to Spain and Portugal. My mother had turned around to scrutinize me in the back seat of the car as we were driving home. "You got some sun. You are looking really brown," she had said. There was a ringing accusatorial note to her voice. I suddenly wondered if taking me makeup shopping was her way of telling me to "fix" my skin.

"It's really not so bad, Rhea," my mom wheedled. "We can do one at home if you want. It will definitely help your skin. It won't lighten it. It will just even it out. Make it look cleaner. Back to what it should be."

"My skin does not need help," I said loudly, suddenly irritated. I no longer wanted this overpriced foundation.

They didn't get it. It's not that I hate face masks. I love face masks. I love most skin care products. I just will not do a face mask for the purpose of lightening my skin. I was acutely aware that the lady at the Chanel counter was listening as she fiddled with the foundation samples.

"Sweetie, you are overreacting. We aren't saying anything bad about your skin. We are just suggesting ways to make it better," my mom responded in a conciliatory tone.

"Don't worry, honey," the blonde Chanel lady said loudly and suddenly, squeezing my shoulder, startling me. "We like all types in America. We like a little bit of color. It's okay to have a tan." She pursed her lips and shot my mom and her friend a disapproving look.

After that it was awkward, so we quickly extricated ourselves.

The blonde Chanel lady made me a foundation sample in the darker shade that matched my current skin tone. As I turned to leave, she gave me a smile of solidarity. I did not return her smile. I wondered if she would tell the other cosmeticians later about the backward Indian customers who came to her counter.

Shame and fury coursed through me. How dare my mother make us look ignorant and backward in front of this random salesperson? How dare she *be* so ignorant and backward? I honestly wasn't sure what upset me more—my mother or myself. Where was her progressiveness now? But perhaps the worst part was that, despite all my bravado, her criticism hit home. I felt small and ugly and dark in that moment.

I tried to bring it up to my mom later in the day, but she blew me off as she always does when I try to talk to her about stuff like this: "Rhea, you are always so dramatic. I wasn't trying to make you feel bad because you have a tan. We were just makeup shopping. Let it go." I knew that if I told my dad, he would just get angry with my mom for perpetuating "all that nonsense," but it wouldn't really change anything. I felt like telling someone, but who should I tell? If I told my white friends, they would be horror-struck. They would have nothing but thinly veiled criticism and wide eyes. "But your mom seems so nice"; "That's nuts, why would she do something like that?"; or "That's so racist. I had no idea color mattered so much to Indians." I did not want the same judgment I had felt from the blonde Chanel lady.

It seems innocuous, but it's not. It's yet another standard that I cannot meet for something I can't really change, regardless of all the *haldi* masks I apply to my face.

2

Too Dark

Miho Iwata, JAPANESE (PERMANENT US RESIDENT), 42

Iro no shiroi ha shichinan kakusu.

White skin makes up for seven [physical] defects.

Growing up in Japan, my grandmother often told me this old Japanese proverb. She was very concerned about my dark complexion—particularly in comparison to my older sister's white skin. While my sister's skin just turns red and then back to white after any long exposure to the sun, I tan easily. And while my sister preferred to stay indoors, I spent much of my childhood playing outside. Despite the unwanted attention to my dark skin as a child and having the understanding that it could be viewed as a "deficit," I had little opinion about it, and I continued to enjoy playing outside. This, however, would soon change in my midtwenties when I moved to Southern California for college, while continuing to have ties to my family and friends in Japan. Indeed, I learned that my skin attracts different reactions from different audiences.

Cultural preference for white skin in Japan has existed for many years, and it has a gendered dimension; white skin is a particularly important trait for Japanese women. Light skin has long been integral to the concept of femininity and beauty in Japan, and as early as the eighth century, court women used white powder to lighten their faces to appear more attractive. This deeply rooted preference for light skin was further fueled by exposure to Western cultures and their glorification of white skin. However, since young girls are not yet concerned about their appearance to the opposite sex (for dating and, later, marriage), pressure for white skin has little relevance for them. So other than my grandmother's words, I received few comments about my skin. I, like my friends, enjoyed playing outside and going to swimming pools and beaches—often without sunscreen. And I loved my dark skin.

As I grew older, my dark skin became more problematic—for others. I began to face pressure from my family and friends to perform white-skin-preserving and -promoting practices, although I still enjoyed outdoor activities and loved my tanned skin. In Japan, students enter high school at the age of fifteen. My high school required that every student become affiliated with a club, and since I was not very athletic, I first considered joining a club that involved some sort of indoor activity. However, I met a guy representing the swim club, and he told me that they were looking for not only swimmers but also managers. Since I loved being outdoors and near water, I decided to join the swim club as a manager. I spent many after-school hours and endless summer days by the pool, often joining the swimmers in the pool to stay cool. Consequently, I was always tanned, and my mom and friends would make negative comments such as "You are too dark"; "You will get aging spots when you get older"; "You should put on sunscreen lotion." I despised their remarks, though admittedly I did begin using sunscreen and whitening lotion—at least occasionally. I was not motivated by a desire for lighter skin (I loved my tan!), but I was motivated to perform "being a proper girl" in the Japanese high school context.

As a young adult in Japan (as a junior college student and later as a full-time corporate worker), I started to pay more attention to my skin. I was not particularly focused on whiteness, though I began to feel pressure to wear makeup every day. In fact, for women not to wear makeup outside the home is considered "intolerable" in Japan, and even today, my now seventy-year-old mom applies makeup each day. Feeling the pressure to conform to the norm, I began investing in facial skin care and makeup products, and as with my mother, applying them became my morning routine. I wanted to fit in with my peers, older female colleagues, and overall cultural expectations attached to young women in Japan, although my practices concerning skin lightening were limited. However, since I spent the majority of my time indoors, my skin remained light, and during this time, it was much lighter than in my youth.

My environment changed drastically at age twenty-six when I moved to Southern California for school. I was, for the first time, exposed to racially and ethnically diverse groups of people around me, and I developed a diverse group of friends while in college. Meanwhile, as an international student, I was not allowed to legally work in the United States, which gave me a lot of leisure time to visit the beach with friends; this resulted in very dark tanned skin. I loved being tanned year round, and I even felt more close to my darker-skinned friends. I remember one time sitting next to an African American student, and my arms were darker than hers.

However, my dark skin was challenged by different sets of audiences. Due to the cultural preference for white skin, many Asian and Asian American friends frequently shared their alarm about my dark complexion. I remember some of them asking me why I liked to go to the beach and "risk" getting tanned, or why I did not wear sunscreen. This negativity would follow me across the Pacific when I visited my family and friends in Japan. There, my very tanned skin was seen as "deviant," particularly given my age. When I was a little girl, my dark complexion was somewhat acceptable. However, having dark skin as a woman in Japan is seen as very problematic. My mom would make comments such as "You are already old, so you should take care of your skin"; "Tanning will give you more 'aging spots' and your face already looks dirty with *shimi* [a Japanese term for dark spots/freckles but it literally means 'stains']." My peers would also make comments about my dark skin, and some of them tried very hard to convince me to stay out of the sun and to make sure to wear sunscreen all the time. Soon, I began to find that my positive self-image about my dark skin was under constant attack in Japan.

My appearance would also solicit questions from strangers, most often in public places, about whether I belonged in Japan. I pheno-typically look Japanese, but my dark complexion confused them. I think that many saw me as a foreigner, since they couldn't fathom the idea of a Japanese woman with dark skin. One afternoon, I was eating alone at a café, and I sensed that the server was acting strangely toward me. After she asked what I wanted for lunch, she realized that I was indeed a Japanese (my fluent Japanese speaking ability was a clue for this!). She became more friendly and, with a puzzled look, asked, "Why are you tanned this much?" On other occasions, I have noticed people move away from me in public spaces—such as public transportation. In Japan, people often avoid those who look foreign, and their behavior signaled to me that they perceived me as a foreigner and that my presence made them uncomfortable.

After graduating with my bachelor's degree, I moved to Connecticut for my graduate work and later to Maryland for a professional position, which again gradually changed my skin tone; my skin lightened due to little exposure to the sun in the Northeast. Since then, while I have been in the United States, people have been indifferent about my skin tone, and some people have even made positive remarks about my *shimi*, my freckles. Meanwhile, my folks in Japan continue to make negative comments about my skin whenever I visit, particularly about my "age spots," since I so brazenly ignored their dire warnings while living in California. Over the years, I have noticed how people around me interpret and react to my changing complexion, and their appraisals are largely influenced by my gender, place, and age. There are different sets of cultural expectations about my skin tone associated with my gender as a female, my age as a marriageable-age female, and the society that I happen to find myself in—whether in Japan or in the United States. However, despite the different views of my skin color, my self-image and confidence have not changed much.

I love my skin.

3

Sang Duc Ho

Catherine Ma, CHINESE AMERICAN, 46

In the early 1970s, I emigrated with my family (my parents, sister, grandparents, aunts, and uncle) from Kowloon, Hong Kong, to the United States. As I was growing up among a large family of immigrants, skin color was something that was mentioned in passing, but as a young child, I never really understood the significance of my family's words until I became an adult. Compared to my two sisters, I am the lightest in skin color, and as a child, my uncle once asked me, seemingly offhandedly, "How does it feel to be the prettiest?" My aunt quickly shut down that conversation before I even had a chance to answer, but that was my first direct encounter with colorism.

Chinese culture tends to be very focused on outward appearances. Many Chinese sayings have a "lookism" quality to them with a focus on the importance of being beautiful (or "*sang duc ho*," which translates to "born good looking" in Cantonese); this means having light skin, double-lined eyes, and a thin (but not too thin!) body. I benefit from being light-skinned, though my husband likes to tease me during the summers because I tan easily, and he jokingly calls me a "farmer." In Chinese culture, class distinctions are often based on one's complexion, with the farmers (or working-class people) being darker in complexion because they work long hours outside in the sun, while the upper class remain inside and are thus paler in comparison.

Eye shape is also important. I never fully understood the differences in how Chinese people regarded eye shape until I met my husband. He commented on my "double-lined eyes," and when I asked him what he meant, he explained that double-lined eyes (those with a fold of skin on the eyelid) are desirable as they make Asian eyes look bigger, and hence, more Westernized. I recall, as a child, that my grandparents would say that a person had "*moong ju ngan*" (squinty, pig eyes) or *shu ngan* ("rat eyes"). Both terms depict negative characteristics of either being lazy like a pig or sneaky and untrustworthy like a rat; my grandparents believed that people with those eyes could never be trusted. A colleague who is Asian recently expressed her anger and frustration with her father-in-law, who commented on her daughter's small eyes—he suggested that his granddaughter should not smile because it made her eyes look even smaller. And when my cousin gave birth to her baby girl, my aunt mentioned how lucky her baby was to have such big eyes.

This attention to physical appearance is not uncommon in many Asian families and manifests itself in other ways as well. When my daughter was a toddler, my mother said she was getting fat. Being a first-time mother who took every criticism about my child person-ally, I told her very pointedly that if she couldn't restrain herself from voicing those types of comments, we wouldn't visit her any more. The irony is that I, too, was body shamed as a child—though for being too skinny. Family members always wanted me to eat more, and when I wouldn't, they complained about how thin I was. Their criticisms brought me to tears more than once. My mother and aunts repeatedly told me that if I didn't finish my rice, I would end up marrying a husband with pockmarks or acne scars on his face for each piece of rice left in my bowl, or remind me of all the starving people in China who would love to eat my rice. Eventually, my response to their constant nagging was to tell them that they should send my leftover rice to all the starving people in China. Years later, after three pregnancies, my mother told me I was getting fat, even though I was only a size four. I was snarky and responded, "I'm not fat, but you are getting fat."

I grew up in the 1970s in New York City, where other children often made fun of me for being Chinese. They made squinty eyes and "ching-chong" noises. Even today, racism persists. Before the start of each Chinese New Year, I take time out of my busy sched-ule to go to my children's school to teach about Chinese culture and hand out treats. Last year, I went to my son's seventh grade class, and two of his classmates made those squinty eyes when I spoke about Chinese history. Their teacher didn't see this, but I did. I was infuriated. I notice that one of the first things some people do to make fun of Asians is to mimic and mock our eyes. Such racist behavior has long-lasting effects, as many Asians undergo drastic procedures to make their eyes bigger. For me, this is the ultimate sign of self-hatred, as Asian women go to extreme measures to change their features (their eyes, their skin, and their bodies) to match a Westernized, Caucasian standard.

Knowing this, I have tried to raise my children to be proud of their Asian characteristics and to take pride in their Chinese identity—something I find challenging to do as I raise my children in the United States. As a new mother, I remember scouring the Internet for beautiful Asian dolls for my daughter as a way to normalize Asian features for her. I wanted her to see dolls that looked like her (I couldn't find Asian dolls in the toy stores at that time); however, I was disappointed that all of the dolls were light in complexion, a reflection of a commonly held Asian standard of beauty that I had wanted to challenge. My generation doesn't have to perpetuate the same prejudices I grew up with. Parents can influence how their Asian children grow up in the United States by preparing them for prejudice in the real world, and by giving them the necessary tools to encourage self-love and acceptance in the way they look. By sharing and talking openly about our experiences, we can break the cycle of self-hatred, teach our children to value who they are, and resist Asian and Western society's narrowly defined standards of beauty. As in Asia, we also live in a "lookist" culture, but encouraging a strong sense of self-confidence can be a formidable tool to combat colorism, both in the United States and in our Asian American communities.

4

You're So White, You're So Pretty

Sambath Meas, KHMER AMERICAN, 44

While Europeans tend to associate tanned skin with leisure time, globe trotting, sportiness, and social status, Cambodians associate it with backwardness, unattractiveness, and low class status. Upon my first week of arrival in Cambodia, the greeting my parents and I received from my cousin, Vanny, was, "You're so white; you're so pretty." First of all, referring to Asians as white might sound utterly ridiculous to Westerners. Secondly, such shallow adulation bothered me. Growing up in the United States, we are taught that it is wrong to judge people by their skin color, never mind comment on it. There is nothing wrong with having white skin, but in the United States, we usually don't go around openly glorifying how pretty white skin is while, at the same time, degrading dark skin. In Cambodia, however, a common greeting is, "Hi. You're so white; you're so beautiful. I'm dark and ugly. I wish I had beautiful white skin like yours." Or, "Ew, you're so dark." Thirdly, if we have to define our skin color, my parents and I are not even white, we are *sra'em*, which simply means "tan" in the Khmer language.

Upon hearing Vanny's partiality to white skin, I turned to look at my parents with disappointment. They gave me a "don't-blame-your-naive-cousin-it's-the-Cambodian-way" look. "She is a victim in all of this," they later reminded me. I didn't buy it. To me, she was as much responsible for perpetuating this shallowness as anyone else.

"For goodness' sake, she's a teacher," I said.

"It's Cambodia. That doesn't mean anything," said my father. Well, okay then.

Vanny, with her skin like caramel and eyes like lotus petals, was so conditioned to see attractiveness in white skin when she was growing up that she is now blind to her own beauty. She often complains about being dark.

"You're beautiful the way you are," I reassured her.

"But I'm dark," she said, ashamed.

I said, "We're all born with different shades of color and we're all beautiful, each in our own way. As long as you wash your body with soap and your hair with shampoo, you'll be clean, healthy, and beautiful. Skin color doesn't determine your beauty, wealth, and intelligence. Regardless of what others say, you shouldn't let it. Look at your two sons; look at those big, ebony eyes. They're gorgeous and smart kids."

Her big, dark eyes glazed over as though she didn't hear a thing I said. "They're dark. If only they had white skin." At this point, my eyes rolled to the back of my head.

I got the same sentiment from another cousin. When I complimented him on his children, his response was, "I wish they had white skin like their mother." His wife's face perked up and beamed with pride. I turned to look at the little four- and five-year-old kids. They just sat there with doe eyes. The denigration of dark skin starts very young.

Unfortunately, my cousins are not the only ones who buy into the "white-is-pretty" and "black-is-ugly" perception. As more high-rise buildings are constructed and roads are paved, Cambodians seem to have become even more self-conscious about their skin color. Country folks, instead of sporting their straw hats or *krama* (checkered scarves), are now donning cap-scarves that cover their heads and faces, only showing their eyes.

My father's cousin said, "Back in the day, we used to be able to tell each other apart and refer to each other by name. Now, if my buffalo or cow has gone missing, I don't even know who I am calling out to, to ask. They're all covered up from head to toe." And if you peeked into their bathrooms as I have, you can see whitening products for their faces and bodies.

Pale-skinned people, especially city dwellers, generally display an air of superiority about themselves, as seen at social events, temples, restaurants, and malls. They walk much taller, their noses stick higher in the air, and their demeanor is anything but inviting. Their children, too, are boosted with an air of self-confidence bestowed upon them since infancy.

Friends and neighbors gather to admire light-skinned babies, no matter how unsightly they may be, as if they are the "chosen ones." For me to witness this was like watching Rafiki, the wise old baboon in the film *The Lion King*, holding Simba aloft to anoint and show him off to the population of Pride Lands. These "white" babies are generally spoiled, coddled, and handed from one person to the next, showered with kisses and lavished with praises: "Whose heavenly baby is this?" and "Who is this smart and gorgeous little one?" I hear them say.

Dark-skinned people are often looked down upon by the pale ones, especially if the former is a peasant and ethnically Khmer.[1] They tend to be timid and fearful and kowtow to the light ones to the point of crawling and prostrating themselves before them. If their kids are dark, no matter how attractive they may be, they tend to be ashamed of their appearance. Not all dark-skinned people and white-skinned people act this way, but too many of them sadly do. The problem lies in Cambodian society. Its obsession with skin color is an epidemic of epic proportions.

Right out of Pochentong International Airport and Siem Reap International Airport, we were greeted with images of "white" Asians on billboards and posters plastered on store walls and windows. Even the faces and bodies of Apsara dancers, which represent celestial beings from Hindu and Buddhist mythology, were paler than ghosts. In most arts, human subjects are not only portrayed as having porcelain skin but also as lacking Khmer essence.

Modern musicians also pay homage in their songs to the beauty of white skin. On the radio, I hear the lyrics, "Your skin is white, you are beautiful, whose daughter are you? I love you" and "I am not beautiful, I don't have white skin like other women, but I am loyal and honest."

As for magazines, they are filled with air-brushed models with skin whiter than Caucasians. Even the so-called Cambodian supermodels consist of light, near-"white" Asian girls. For the one or two dark-skinned girls lucky enough to find their way into the glossy pages of a Cambodian fashion magazine, their bodies and faces are so thickly powdered they looked ashen, gray, and even clown-like.

For the handful of existing Cambodian channels, movies, and music videos, dark-skinned people are rarely shown, let alone leading characters. Television hosts and hostesses consist mostly of white, light-skinned Asians. Commercials for whitening products dominate the airwaves and run around the clock—each time, promoting the confidence-boosting, superiority, and beautifying qualities of porcelain white skin. They are generally Khmer-dubbed commercials from Thailand, Japan, Korea, and other light-skinned Asian countries. The top three most memorable ones go something like this:

1. A young Thai woman is sitting on a bench reading a book. She discovers a good-looking man smiling at her. Self-conscious of her not-so-white skin, she goes home and dabs her face with whitening cream. The next time she sees the young man, he pulls her bench closer to his. Her skin shines white, and the two longingly gaze at each other as though they are the two happiest beings on earth.

2. A white-skinned Japanese flight attendant steps down from the jet bridge to be greeted by a dark-skinned Japanese flight attendant who admires the whiteness of her skin. The dark-skinned flight attendant asks the light-skinned flight attendant how she got her skin to be porcelain white. The woman tells her the brand of whitening cream she uses. The next time they see each other, they both look brightly white. They beam with pride as they walk shoulder to shoulder, heads held high.

3. A tall, svelte Asian woman steps out amid the crowd and her trench coat bursts away from her body, revealing her bright white skin that is wrapped in a scant, tight, purple mini dress. With an air of pride and jubilation, she parades herself among the young men and women who are awestruck by her stunningly bright, white body.

Pale skin is so glamorized in Cambodia that it is demoralizing. I get it. As someone who lives in the United States, I have more freedom to be myself; it is easy for me to parachute into the motherland every other year and be irritated with those who valorize whiteness and try so hard to fit into the shallow ways of mainstream Cambodian society. They are the ones who have to live with the daily prejudice and discrimination.

Very briefly, I got a taste of such prejudice and discrimination as my own skin began to darken under the scorching sun of Cambodia. Grocery and restaurant owners would not look at me or talk to me and had their employees, whom they publicly chastised and denigrated, tell me the prices. They threw my change at me, and turned their backs on me as if I were beneath them. Interesting. When my family first came to the United States, in grammar school particularly, a group of kids—especially boys—taunted me, harassed me, pushed me around, and beat me up. They routinely called out to me, "Hey, Ching Chong!" while they pulled up their eyes to make them look tight and slanted. They made weird sounds under the pretense that they were speaking to me in my native tongue. Yet, here I was, in the motherland, being treated with contempt by the very people who would have been ridiculed just like me in the Chicago of the early 1980s. Oh, the irony.

Vanny confessed that she felt prejudice and discrimination when she first left the countryside to study in the city. "Light-skinned girls normally hung out together and shunned dark-skinned girls," she said. "And they made fun of us because we spoke with a country accent." Having felt that, I thought that she might have learned from it, but instead, I find her giving in to Cambodian society in full force; perhaps she cannot escape the pressure even as an adult. She does everything to fit in: whitening her skin with a poisonous chemical and straightening her hair with harsh chemicals that smell so bad that her husband once jokingly told her to sleep in another bed.

For goodness' sake, even monks, who are not supposed to be concerned with superficialities or attached to material things, whiten their skin!

I have asked around about why Cambodians are so obsessed with having pale skin. The answer: It's common among Asian cultures to find light skin more alluring and attractive. Light skin means a person comes from a wealthy family—that he or she spends most of the time indoors and works less than others. Light-skinned people live sheltered lives. Light-skinned girls have more chances to marry, and an increased likelihood of marrying into rich families. Meanwhile, dark-skinned people are associated with the lower class because they must work most of their lives, often under the blazing sun. People seem to be proud of not having to work (or work as much as others), and thumb their noses at people of lower classes.

Some even feel offended by me questioning their quest for light skin. "It is our freedom," they say. Is it really a freedom of choice when people don't know all the facts and risks surrounding whitening products? Are they really acting on their free will? Or are they being brainwashed by the sophistication of mass marketing? Moreover, just because certain dark-skinned people voluntarily prefer light skin to their own, why should the rest of us, who are comfortable in our own skin, have to put up with this "light-skin-is-beautiful" nonsense?

5

You Have Such a Nice Tan!

Ethel Nicdao, FILIPINA AMERICAN, 47

Within the context of the Asian diaspora, my experiences of colorism are not unique. In fact, much of what I describe is rooted in the social science literature, both historic and contemporary, on the acculturation of Asian immigrants to the United States and other Western countries. But my stories of learning about and distinguishing differences in shades of skin color began in the Philippines more than four decades ago. I was born in the tropical climate of Luzon, the largest island in the Philippines, and the sun's rays were my constant companion. Under the bright and often blazing sun in the province of Pampanga (approximately eighty kilometers northwest of Manila), my chosen playground was the outdoors. My memory bank is full of childhood adventures around our property and bike rides in our subdivision. Unlike my lighter-skinned older sister, who spent most of her time indoors as a bookworm, I enjoyed outdoor adventures that added another shade of brown to my skin. And since this was the 1970s when words such as "skin cancer" or "sunscreen" were not part of my vocabulary (and certainly uncommon in the Philippines), I mostly cared about following my mother around the yard as she tended to her plants. I loved climbing trees, riding my bike in the neighborhood, creating make-believe games, and foraging for fruits that filled nearly half the acreage of our property: coconut, bananas, *guyabano*, *saresa*, guava, *santol*, and *macopa*. I was too young and oblivious to recognize that lighter skin was preferred and valued.

I recall hearing from others the Tagalog phrase *"ang itim mo!"* (you're so black/dark). The direct translation to English sounds rather insulting, but it is usually said in jest—though it wasn't meant as a compliment either. As a child, I also learned terms like "mestiza" and "mestizo," which refer to Filipinos with mixed ancestry. The message, in part due to three hundred years of colonization by Spain, followed by another century of American colonization and neocolonial domination, was this: Being mestiza/mestizo is equated with lighter skin, a sharper nose bridge, and Eurocentric features, and hence is associated with beauty. To my mother's credit, she never prevented me from playing outdoors, nor did I feel inferior because I had brown skin. As I was growing up, she would often tell me, "Beauty is in the eye of the beholder." The message of "light is beautiful" was the sentiment of others, and not of my immediate family.

Before I turned nine years old, my playground drastically changed. As with many stories of migration, my family immigrated to San Francisco in September of 1979 for better life opportunities. The move to America created a dramatic cultural shift on so many levels, including the way I viewed being a Filipina. The focus shifted away from my brown skin, due in part to San Francisco's cold and foggy climate, which kept me shrouded in layers of long-sleeved shirts, jackets, and pants. Rather than skin color, other (previously nonracialized) aspects of my physicality took center stage. At nine, I was the recipient of unwanted criticisms about my accent (despite speaking grammatically correct English), my flat nose, and my round face. Eventually and unintentionally, my Filipino accent disappeared. But downward social mobility and not being white increasingly began to influence my formative years of growing up in San Francisco. My race and ethnicity, along with my social class, suddenly mattered in a way that they never had before.

As renters in the 1980s, we often moved to several of the city's ethnically diverse neighborhoods (e.g., Glen Park, Excelsior, Ingleside). The image often touted of San Francisco is one of diversity—as a microcosm for the rest of the country—though this idealistic image masks its extreme social class divide and racial residential segregation. As a teen, I recall being dumbfounded on several occasions when a white person called me a derogatory name ("You stupid fucking Chink!") and wondering to myself why he had mistaken me for the wrong Asian ethnicity. On another occasion, while I walked along Ocean Beach, a white man yelled to me, unprovoked, "Go back where you came from!" In my naiveté, I thought to myself, "I live in San Francisco, so where should I go?" Clearly, I had yet to understand the meaning and consequences of being Asian in America.

Racial and ethnic identities became more pronounced in high school. My school had a predominantly African American student body with only a handful of white students, and the divide between racial groups was obvious. Still, I was only beginning to understand the reasons behind these divisions. In college, race was compounded by social-class differences. Although I only traveled seventy-four miles northeast of San Francisco for school, UC–Davis was a different world, though college life did not shield me from prejudice or colorism. While working on campus, I remember a comment made by a student: "You have such a nice tan!" While intended to be flattering, her compliment ignored the realities, complexities, and consequences of my brown skin versus her white skin. For example, the summer after my junior year, my classmate and I were selected to attend an international summer seminar in Taipei, Taiwan. There was a total of six US delegates; all were white except for me. While we were in Taipei, there was a temporary job opportunity to make some quick cash by teaching English to locals. My blonde American friend was immediately hired. When I expressed interest in the job, I was told I did not "look American." To many Asians (as with many Americans), American means white.

It was not until the fall quarter of my junior year that I discovered courses in Asian American studies and sociology, which helped me make sense of social inequities based on race, class, gender, and sexuality. Much has been written about Filipinos and their colonial mentality to explain the value placed on light skin and anything American (brand names, for example). Others argue that it is not about reverse ethnocentrism or reverence for our colonists (and all things American or white), but rather the association of dark skin with the lower classes of Filipino society. Regardless of the reason, those with mestiza/mestizo features are still celebrated and highly regarded in the Filipino community. Skin-whitening and bleaching products remain alarmingly popular and in high demand, despite documented harmful health risks.[1] As a teenager, during one of my summer visits back to the Philippines, I tried one of these skin-whitening products. Papaya soap was the craze at the time, and I was attracted to the orange soap bar, and its sweet scent reminded me of the fruit. I was curious and tried it, but was not immediately convinced of its efficacy. After a few uses, I stopped. Perhaps it was partly my laziness: *Where am I going to buy this product back in the United States? How long do I have to use this to see results? Do I have to scrub hard?* I was not committed to the time and effort required for this whitening experiment. And because no one was pressuring me to use the soap, I stopped.

Obsession with skin color is not unique to Filipinos (or to Asians more broadly speaking). Studies also show that among blacks and Latinos, light skin affords social, economic, educational, and health privileges and advantages. There is evidence, too, that lifetime experiences of micro-aggressions and discrimination for those with dark skin have negative effects on physical and mental health. And colorism extends beyond skin phenotype; physical and facial characteristics are also important and tend to be the first markers of race and ethnicity. There are numerous examples of micro-aggressions related to my race, gender, and sexual orientation—I have been teased about whether I eat monkey or dog, frequently told that I speak English well (without a foreign accent), and encouraged to find a good husband and have children. And I have come across non-Filipinos who, to relate to me through language, blurt out curse words in Tagalog as if it to impress me. I cannot imagine approaching someone and telling them I know English by dropping F-bombs.

One of my former students once told me matter-of-factly that he knew I was Filipino because of my flat nose. I don't believe his intent was malicious, but his words were not meant as a compliment either. I explained to him why his comment was inappropriate, though I understand that we are all socialized to associate physical attributes with racial and ethnic groups, and we are taught to value certain characteristics as the ideal standard of beauty, especially for women. In America, this means slim frame, well-proportioned body, long hair, large breasts, and light skin. Cosmetic surgery is the norm nowadays in Asia, the United States, and worldwide, including making one's nose bridge more pronounced (rhinoplasty), double eyelid surgery, breast augmentation, Botox injections, and so on. Certainly, there has been a movement towards challenging and redefining traditional standards of beauty, for example, Dove's "real beauty" campaign[2] and increasing representation of plus-size women in magazines and advertisements. But mainstream media, including digital and print, continues to promote narrow definitions of beauty: thin bodies and light, white skin. The glaring omission of people who resemble me in magazines, on television, and in movies is so blatantly obvious that on the rare occasions when people of my race or ethnicity are featured, there is cause for celebration. I find it refreshing and validating when Filipinos/ Filipino Americans are positively represented in the media. Or represented at all.

While some physical and facial features can be altered, my skin cannot. Even today, my brownness still makes me a foreign object in parts of the United States, and is most evident with stares and questioning looks of "What are you?" and "Why are you here in my neighborhood?" However, my brown skin has also served as valuable cultural capital. I can pass for other Asian ethnicities, and even as Native American. While conducting ethnographic fieldwork in the western part of New Mexico as a doctoral student, I must have passed as Native because I was often greeted with "Yá'át'ééh" (hello in Navajo), and Navajos often assumed I spoke their language. I blended in easily, and one Navajo family "adopted" me into theirs. A genuine friendship formed, followed by regular invitations to their home and sweat lodge, and to participate in their family ceremonies. It was comforting to be welcomed into their family community.

My perspective on race and brownness is largely informed by personal experiences and my profession as a sociologist. Now in my middle age, I can emphatically declare that I fully embrace my brownness and queerness, and the intersection of my social identities. In doing so, I am not ignorant of the ongoing assault towards women, specific racial and ethnic minority groups, the poor and working classes, and the LGBTQ community. Pride in our own skin should be intrinsic, but we do not live in a postracial America. Prejudice rarely stays contained within people's attitudes, and sometimes leads to blatant discrimination and acts of violence. In fact, considering the 2016 presidential election that has emboldened many to spew hateful rhetoric, especially around race, sexual orientation, and immigration status, my response has been immediate and assertive. Together with my allies from all shades of color, I am empowered and remain steadfast in using my voice simultaneously to speak out against injustices and to change the discourse on race, especially given countless news headlines that are indicative of the kind of toxic racial landscape that we now occupy. When countries populated by black- and brown-skinned peoples are singled out, and Haiti and Africa are referred to as "shithole countries" by a sitting American president, and the insistence to build a physical, divisive wall on the US-Mexican border pervades the news, I know that shades of color matter. I have the voice to challenge not only dominant racist ideologies but also all "shades of prejudice." Being a queer, brown, Filipina American breast cancer survivor anchors me, as it should, because these are some of the most salient characteristics of my authentic self, and I have no desire whatsoever to alter shades of my nut-brown self.

6

Brown Arms

Tanzila Ahmed, BANGLADESHI AMERICAN, 38

Bing-Bong. I heard the doorbell ring, and I ran barefoot up to the door, stopping just short of it. I knew I wasn't supposed to open the door without Mommy, so I slyly moved the curtain by the door to see who was standing on the porch. It was Uncle and Auntie, standing at the door patiently. Uncle was in a brown tweed jacket and Auntie was wrapped in a delicate silk sari. I quickly scanned their arms. There they were—gift-wrapped packages in their arms!

Mommy came rushing out of the kitchen, scolding me, "Why didn't you open the door? You know Uncle and Auntie!" I shied away bashfully, hiding behind the *ahchul* of Mommy's sari as she opened the door wide. "*A-salaam-walikum,*" she said. "*Ashaan, ashaan!*" she exclaimed, ushering them to come inside.

"Say *Salaams* to Uncle and Auntie," she demanded of me through an embarrassed smile. I continued to hide behind her sari, refusing to greet them.

"Bhabhi, she's grown up so quickly. Where are your other girls?" Auntie stroked my hair while peering around me into the house. She handed me a flat, square gift before wandering off into the house in search of my little sisters.

A flat, square package. I knew by the shape what this was. My heart sank. Another Little Golden Book for my shelf. I was eight years old and too old for these childish books. I had hoped that the long, rectangular-shaped box would be for me, but I knew it was going to my middle sister. She always got the best gifts from the aunties and uncles.

Sure enough, I peeked into the living room to see Auntie helping my middle sister unwrap her gift—it was the long, rectangular box. My sister was five years younger than I, with round cheeks and hazel eyes and dark brown hair—she always looked to me like a Cabbage Patch Doll. Her skin and hair even matched the Cabbage Patch Dolls I saw in the store. I never saw a doll that looked like me in the store—my hair was too black and my skin too dark.

My sister ripped at the gift wrap excitedly. It was a Peaches and Cream Barbie! From behind the wall, I could see that the Barbie doll had long blonde hair, fair skin, and a beautiful billowing peach gown. She looked so sparkly and pretty. "Bhabhi, you shouldn't have. She's too young to play with a Barbie doll! She's only four years old," Mommy hesitated.

"But it looks just like her, I had to get it. Just look at it. She looks just like this Barbie doll!" Auntie doted and fussed, while pinching my sister's cheek.

I looked down at my *Hansel and Gretel* Little Golden Book. My sister wasn't even old enough to play with Barbie dolls. I played with my Aerobic Barbie doll and Day-to-Night Barbie doll every day. She always got the best presents.

As Auntie and Uncle left that night, we went to the foyer to say goodbye. Uncle lifted up my middle sister into his arms. She always loved to be carried. She had her arms around Uncle's neck and a pacifier in her mouth. "Take care of this one extra specially," Auntie said to my parents, patting sister's hair. "Her skin is so light and *forsha* [light-skinned]! Keep her out of the sun. She's going to be so pretty when she grows up."

I looked down at my brown arms, wondering if I would ever be pretty when I grew up.

≈

My mother's forearms were wide, and the skin on the back of her arms was fair—what Rishta Aunties (matchmakers) would refer to as "wheatish." She wasn't particularly vain about the color of her skin—unlike the other aunties who invested in sunscreen and whitening cream. I noticed how these aunties would remark about Mom's skin color sometimes, often with envy in their voice. But Mom didn't care—she was running around raising three girls and keeping our family together as we constantly moved across country due to dad's work. I would often wrap my forearms around hers and compare our skin color. My dad's arms were bonier and darker—the kind of brown that resembled day-old chai—and his skin was more webbed with the creases of skin that are weather worn. As a child I'd compare my arms to theirs side by side—I wasn't as fair as my mother but I wasn't as dark as my dad—I was just brown.

My parents met on their wedding day in Dhaka, Bangladesh, in 1978—Mom said she wasn't interested in meeting my dad before the wedding because she was going to see him all the time after they got married. "What was the point?" she had said. Dad's family had sent her seven proposal requests, and at the age of twenty-three, she finally gave in because he was an engineer in Los Angeles. And maybe in America, she thought, she could pursue her master's degree. Of course, pursuing her degree didn't happen, because by the time she got on the flight to move to Los Angeles to be with my dad, she was already four months pregnant—with me. Five years later my sister was born, and two years after that, my youngest sister was born.

Dad eventually stopped being able to get engineering jobs, and our family experienced downward financial mobility. For the last fifteen years of my mother's life, she worked in a booth at an airport parking lot to make ends meet. It was a low-paying Teamster job, but because it was union, our family had health care. She'd come home from work with a forearm farmer's tan—her left arm repeatedly leaving her booth to collect money from cars only to become darkened by the blazing Southern California sun. When she'd get home in those later years, she'd talk tiredly about how brown her arms got, how hot the sun was. She would roll up her sleeves and stretch her forearm out in front of my face to show me the color of her skin now—both in awe and in sadness. She was less concerned about her vanity by then; for her it became more of a mark of how hard her life had become.

≈

I didn't really think about what color I was until I started preschool. When we drew portraits of ourselves, everyone used peach crayons to color their skin—I wanted to, too. "That's not what color your skin is," the blonde-haired, blue-eyed girl sitting next to me said. "Your skin is *brown*. So you use the brown crayon." I looked down at the brown Crayola crayon that she had placed in front of me. It was so dark. It looked nothing like my skin. It looked like the color of poo.

I started sulking, and the teacher came over to ask me what was wrong. I told her I wasn't the color of the brown crayon, but I wasn't the color of the peach crayon: so what color was I supposed to color myself? We laid out all the skin-colored crayons in front of me—brown, peach, raw umber, apricot, sepia, burnt sienna, and even tan. I tested out all the colors on my piece of paper, and we decided that the tan crayon would work the best.

≈

"Mom, we're going to play in my room!" I screamed while galloping up the stairs with my new neighbor friend, Margaret. We were eight years old, and she had come over to play Barbie dolls with a backpack full of dolls. I was excited to play with all of her fancy dolls—my middle sister had broken off the heads and permanent markered all over most of my dolls. The only one I had been able to salvage was Aerobics Barbie in the blue leotards, and that's because it was bendable in the hands of a four-year-old terror.

Margaret and I dumped out all of our dolls on the carpeted floor of my bedroom. Her collection was impressive—she had all the expensive Barbie dolls with the flouncy dresses and big, blonde, curly hair. She also had a couple of Ken dolls, which my Mom refused to buy for me—they were key to playing house. She had all the multiple outfits and the hot pink Barbie convertible. My set of dolls looked meek in comparison. And my mom wouldn't buy me clothes for my dolls and would instead sew me simple summer dresses using the scraps of leftover cloth from her sewing projects.

"Let's play house," Margaret said, bossily. I reached for a Barbie with beautiful long blonde hair and a bright pink dress. "You can't play with *that one*. You can play with this one." She grabbed the blonde doll out of my hand and threw me a brown doll.

"Why?" I said, confused. When I played Barbie with my other friends, it never went like this.

"Because you're *brown*. So you can only play with the *brown* Barbie dolls." I looked down at the doll in my hand—it was an old-looking Barbie doll, with a pointed chin and painted sleepy eyes. The color of the plastic skin was what Crayola might call burnt umber. The brown hair had a bob cut and weird bangs. It looked like a vintage doll from the 1960s—I'd never even seen a doll like this in any toy store.

I looked at the pile of Barbie dolls in the middle of the room. They were ALL peach-skinned Barbie dolls. By that logic, I was too brown to play with any of them. I sulkily reached for my Aerobics Barbie doll from the pile.

"You can't play with that," Margaret bossily snapped. "Only *I* can play with that one. Her skin is peach like *mine*."

The rest of that play date, as Margaret played with all the pretty Barbie and Ken dolls with the fancy outfits and convertible cars, I played in a corner with the brown-skinned doll, dressing her in hand-sewn dresses.

When she left that afternoon, she left behind the brown-skinned Barbie doll at my house. She didn't want it anymore.

7

Hopes for My Daughter

Bhoomi K. Thakore, INDIAN AMERICAN, 35

As I write this, my daughter lies sleeping next to me. I occasionally take breaks to stroke her cheek or run my fingers through her hair, amazed and truly in love. When I found out that I was expecting her, I couldn't even imagine how my life would change. Now, when she is almost three months old, I look forward to every day together.

One of the biggest wonders I had was what she would look like. With her mix of Indian, Vietnamese, and European ancestry, it was literally a toss-up. But when she arrived, I could see a little bit of everything in her. I was so happy to see how beautiful she was: her thick black hair, almond-shaped brown eyes, and full lips. She got the best of her mommy and daddy. I also could not help but be thankful for her light-brown complexion—one that marks her as just-minority-enough, but will not stigmatize her as much as my dark complexion does me. I know that life is challenging for everyone, but hopefully no more for her because of the color of her skin.

For my daughter, I have many hopes:

I hope that my daughter will be more accepted by her extended family than I was. Growing up, I knew that my family loved me unconditionally, but it only felt like they loved me because they loved my parents. My cousins would play with me, but even at a young age I could sense that the connection was not entirely there. Like me, they grew up understanding that Indian society favored light skin. How could they love me if they didn't like the way I looked? Like them, I was pressured into using skin-lightening creams throughout my adolescence. Even today, I feel disconnected from many of them. I hope that my daughter will be more comfortable with her relatives, and always feel their full love and support.

I hope that my daughter will come to know her Indian heritage more than I did. My mother was sensitive to her own skin discrimination in India, and she did not want her daughter, who was much darker, to suffer. Even in social settings with my parents' Indian friends, the children would treat me differently. So, my mother kept me from children's activities at the Hindu temple, from Bharatnatyam dance classes, and in general from the Indian American community. She made the choice to isolate me, rather than have me experience the isolation from them. This resulted in a true disconnect from my Indian identity. I hope that my daughter will be embraced by her communities and develop a strong identity, with whichever group she chooses to align herself.

I hope that my daughter will see herself represented in the media much more than I did. As I grew up in the 1980s and 1990s, the only character that represented my ethnicity, to me and to others, was Apu from *The Simpsons*—heavily accented and overtly foreign, which even today symbolizes the ways in which people mock me. Beyond this caricature, there were no representations that looked like me or reflected my experiences as the child of Indian immigrants. The representations of women that I saw were also limited, with virtually all of them adhering to the same Western beauty ideals (light skin, light eyes, light hair), and serving as a reminder that I did not look like them. Today, these representations have improved to a degree, but the Eurocentric beauty ideal and whitewashed characters remain strong. I hope that my daughter will not be influenced by these stereotypes and images as significantly as I was.

I hope that my daughter will not be stigmatized in school as I was. Because of the class status of my parents, I exclusively attended private schools where racial diversity was very limited. As I was surrounded by mostly white students and white teachers, my brown skin made me stand out and, at times, triggered experiences of overt discrimination. For example, soon after my father died, a substitute middle school teacher ridiculed me in front of the entire class for a "messy work space." Since I had had no prior interaction with this instructor, and my workspace was not any messier than any other student's, I felt intentionally targeted. A few years later in high school, I was asked by my history teacher to read out loud an excerpt from the textbook written in Swahili, presumably because she assumed that my dark skin meant that I was African American. I was embarrassed as I struggled with the passage in front of the class. Today, I understand that these experiences were intended to single me out. I hope that my daughter will be judged by her merits, not by her perceived identity or skin color.

I hope that my daughter will have an easier time making friends than I did. I have many memories of being excluded by groups of girls, and being judged when I took the initiative to try to join them. I always wondered what was wrong with me. I didn't understand it back then, but I know now that their behaviors were simply a reflection of what they were taught—that I was not "one of them." To them, I did not matter, and I was not worth getting to know. I felt invisible. Ultimately, I know that my daughter is still brown, and she may have experiences like this. But, I hope that her environments will be much more diverse, and that, because of her lighter shade, she will not be viewed with the same disdain that I was.

I hope that my daughter will find love sooner than I did. In the same way that teachers and peers judged me for my dark skin and "different" appearance, so too did the people I liked. I put myself out there with confidence, only to be rejected over and over again. When I got older, many of the people I dated told me frankly that I was good enough "for now," but not good enough to bring home to their parents. I now understand what they meant when I look back at whom they dated after me, and with whom they eventually partnered and had children. I sought out love for many years, until I was much older and found my partner, who sought me out. It was worth it in the end, to have this family, but it did not come easily. Regardless of whom my daughter chooses to love, I hope that she will not be judged by anything more than her personality and what she has to offer to someone else.

I hope that, unlike me, my daughter will have the ability to be whatever she wants to be when she grows up. In graduate school, I was made to feel that my contributions were not as good as my white peers'. I struggled in classes with professors who did not give me the same attention as they gave to them, and I was less successful as a result. I worked hard, only to struggle even more on the academic job market. Despite my brown skin, I struggle with being seen as not "diverse" enough for jobs in my area of expertise, which is race and ethnicity. As an Indian American professional, I am often not seen as someone who has experienced discrimination and micro-aggressions. As a result, some people think that I am unqualified to speak, teach, or write on these subjects. In a racialized black-white social system that surrounds me, my very real experiences are often negated or trivialized—especially by whites. Ideally, I do not want my daughter to experience any of these struggles, and I hope that her exposure to them is much more limited.

Above all, I hope that my daughter does not have a life as hard as mine. In our society, everyone is judged by his or her physical appearance and ascribed an identity based on it. Dark-skinned people are neither seen, nor recognized, nor taken as seriously as those born with light skin. We remain invisible in a society that values a beauty ideal that does not look like us. My entire life, society has told me that my dark skin means that I cannot be beautiful.

Fortunately, my daughter is much more beautiful than I.

Part II

PRIVILEGE

Light skin is privileged over dark. The growing body of research on colorism among African Americans, Latinx populations in the United States, and Asian Americans reveals that one's shade of skin is linked to educational attainment, employment, occupational status, income, wealth, physical health, mental health, and marriageability, as well as perceptions of intelligence, social class, trustworthiness, and attractiveness.[1] In a 2017 piece titled "I'm a Light-Skinned Chinese Woman, and I Experience Pretty Privilege," written for *Teen Vogue*, Rae Chen describes the skin-shade privilege that she experiences in China and in Canada; in both contexts, strangers often tell her she is pretty, and then typically follow the compliment with a remark about the fairness of her skin. She writes, "Whether I'm in Canada or China, I hear an echo every time my fair skin is complimented. There's always an implication that someone else's dark skin is being simultaneously policed, knowingly or not. My echo has always been my sister, whose skin was a beautiful, buttery tan color growing up. . . . Whenever one of our aunties, friends, or acquaintances saw us together and complimented my fair skin, they were also tacitly implying because her skin was darker, she was less notable."

In this section, authors examine their privilege, or lack thereof, based on their skin color. For some, their skin is a social liability and stigma, but for others, like Rae Chen, it is an enviable asset. Rhea Manglani, Indian American, for example, learned from her mother at a young age that she is "blessed with beautiful skin," and she writes about her personal experiences with light-skin privilege. For her, privilege means "compliments, never criticism" of her skin, and growing up in "blissful ignorance" of the struggles of her darker-skinned South Asian classmates. As scholar Peggy McIntosh writes in her pioneering work on race privilege titled "Unpacking the Invisible Knapsack," privilege is often invisible to the privileged, and those born into privilege typically live in a state of obliviousness to their unearned advantages. Many like Rhea, who have light skin, may be unaware of the privileges that their skin confers, while those with dark skin do not have the same luxury of ignorance. Society repeatedly reminds them of their skin color and its associated stigma.

Rosalie Chan, Chinese/Filipina American, similarly describes her light-skin privilege, and how her skin is an "asset" in parts of Asia, but also in the United States. In the United States, she is perceived as foreign, but she understands that because of her light hue, she is seen as "nonthreatening" as compared to fellow brown-skinned Asian Americans for whom racial profiling and discrimination are more common—often due to Islamophobia. Rosalie recognizes that colorism privileges lighter-skinned Asian American ethnic groups over those with darker skin, and Julia Mizutani, multiracial Japanese/white American, similarly describes the colorism that exists across Asian ethnic groups. As a self-described "hafu" (a Japanese term often used to describe someone who is multiracial and "half" Japanese), she experiences light-skin privilege in her Japanese American community and in the United States, though she also recognizes that Asian ethnic groups differentiate themselves from each other on the basis of skin color, further privileging her because she is of Japanese ancestry. According to Julia, Japanese Americans have "shunned" darker-skinned Asian ethnic groups, such as Indians, Filipinxs, and Cambodians, "to access social benefits connected to whiteness."

Notably, discrimination between Asian ethnic groups is seen in Asia as dark-skinned Asian ethnic groups face discrimination in East Asia. Filipinos in Korea, for instance, report significant discrimination, "from taking a taxi to renting a house and landing a job," and even frequently encounter pointing, disrespect, and derisive language in public spaces.[2] Even in America, colorist thinking has fashioned a hierarchy among Asian American groups, whereby those ethnic groups with lighter skin (i.e., East Asians) are relatively more privileged than those with darker tones (e.g., South and Southeast Asians). Perhaps, this stems from prejudices rooted in Asian ethnic cultures, but perhaps it also derives from biases found in the larger US culture whereby light skin is privileged over dark.

In American mainstream media outlets, for instance, "brown Asians" are often invisible as compared to East Asian ethnic groups, and E. J. R. David, professor of psychology at the University of Alaska, argues that South and Southeast Asians are often excluded from television, magazines, and newspapers in favor of lighter-skinned East Asian groups such as Koreans, Japanese, and Chinese.[3] Perhaps this is the case because lighter-skinned Asian ethnic groups are more palatable to the white masses than those whose ancestries originate in places such as India, Cambodia, the Philippines, or other parts of South or Southeast Asia. Asian/Asian American visibility in American media is already quite low as they are typically underrepresented, though Asian Americans with dark skin are nearly absent altogether. In 2016, for example, the *New York Times* released a video about the experiences of Asian Americans, though the newspaper was widely criticized for privileging the perspectives of East Asians; the voices of South and Southeast Asians were nearly absent, though they compose approximately half of the Asian American population.[4] In an open letter to the *New York Times* in response to the video, David writes that "even though this is 2016, people still don't understand that #BrownAsiansExist," calling out the paper for marginalizing South and Southeast Asian Americans to the point of invisibility.[5] In 2018, the film *Crazy Rich Asians* was heralded as a "watershed moment for Asian representation in Hollywood" for its all-Asian cast, though critics noted that South Asians were conspicuously missing from the story. This is curious given that the film was set in Singapore, where nearly 22 percent of the population is either Malay or Indian. One critic asks, "Where are the brown people?" and argues that while the film is the first in twenty-five years to feature an all-Asian cast, it "presents a single version of Asia that is 'palatable' for Hollywood audiences."[6] Would audiences embrace a darker-skinned Asian cast? I have no definitive answer, though their current invisibility in American media suggests no.

Even looking beyond disparate representations in American media between light- and dark-skinned Asian Americans, hate crimes towards South Asians in the United States are reportedly on the rise. Asian Americans, as a whole, are frequent targets of verbal harassment, brutal attacks, and even murder, probably because their attackers perceive them as "other" or as perpetually "foreign" due to physical characteristics that set them apart from the white majority. South Asians, in particular, may be further targeted because of, one, their brown skin color, which makes them relatively more visible in the American population, and, two, larger anti-Muslim sentiment in the United States, which stigmatizes anyone who looks stereotypically Middle Eastern. Since the 9/11 terrorist attacks, Islamophobia has been particularly intense in the United States, and South Asian Americans have been targets of racial profiling (in airports, for example) and, at the extreme, brutal violence. In fact, the first victim of a retaliatory killing post-9/11 was a brown-skinned Indian Sikh, Balbir Singh Sodi, who was shot and killed while pumping his gas in the days immediately following the 9/11 attack.[7] Though Asian Americans are collectively marginalized and, at times, on the receiving end of racial bias, some Asian ethnic groups may be more or less privileged than others because of their skin shade. Because dark skin is stigmatized, brown-skinned Asian American ethnic groups find themselves marginalized in Asia, within the Asian American community, and in the larger United States.

Finally, authors in this collection of essays reveal that privilege is shaped not only by one's particular shade of skin but by, one, the context in which one is viewed—whether in the United States, Asia, or another part of the world—and, two, the ethnicity and race of the audience(s) before them. For instance, though colorism is global, region of the world matters. Sonal Nalkur, Indo-Canadian, recognizes her privilege in Indian circles (as well as in India and Saudi Arabia) because of her light shade, but she also understands that this privilege dissipates in American and Canadian contexts, where people of color have historically been relegated to second-class citizenry. In the United States, in particular, she contends that the "bar for being 'non-white' is very low" and privilege more elusive for her, even though her skin is light. Finally, Brittany Ota-Malloy, multiracial Japanese/black American, observes that her privilege is heavily dependent upon her audience. She describes her experience of colorism as a "magnetic repulsion" wherein her perceived skin color "produces messages that are in constant conflict with each other." She writes that colorism is a problem among Asian Americans and African Americans, and the politics of skin color in both of her racial communities live within her. Her dark skin disadvantages her with Asian American audiences, though the same shade benefits her in the black community. In short, skin-color privilege is not straightforward or intrinsic, but rather is situational and fluid, conferring advantages upon those of Asian descent in some contexts, while simultaneously disadvantaging them in others.

8

Blessed with Beautiful Skin

Rhea Manglani, INDIAN AMERICAN, 22

I am a light-skinned, South Asian woman who has spent most of my life not having to think too much about skin color. As I was growing up, family members would comment about how "fair" I was, and my mom usually beamed with pride. I never paid much attention to the color of my skin because it generally garnered compliments, never criticism. I didn't see myself as different from the other Indian kids I grew up with, and, certainly, I didn't think that I looked much different from most of the white or Latino people in my neighborhood. I rarely felt like an outsider. I merely thought my skin tone was "normal" and nothing remarkable. Because of my own light-skin privilege, I was blissfully unaware of the struggles that some of my classmates faced in their own communities.

Of course, my blissful ignorance did not last forever. In middle school (my school was about 80 percent Asian), an Indian friend of mine would slather on sunscreen every day after school and say something along the lines of, "Rhea, I can't end up *kali* [black]" and offer me sunscreen. I used to gleefully reject her sunscreen and talk about joining a new sports team to get tanner. Upon meeting one of my South Asian friends in an after-school program, I thought she had a striking beauty to her—sharp eyebrows, a thin nose (that I was jealous of), big boobs (that I was even more jealous of), and an air of confidence that high-school-me couldn't muster. But there was something off about her face. I realized that the eyebrows I admired were drawn on and her skin color was splotchy. That's when I realized that she had been bleaching her skin. It shocked me to my core. The following year another friend, who is Filipina, shared with me that she also used to bleach her skin. I was ill equipped to talk to her about any of this and simply nodded along as she complained about her family's obsession with fairness. It made me think of my mother's words to me: "You're blessed with beautiful skin."

During my college years, my classmates shared stories of their aunties calling them "ugly," or their parents not letting them play sports for fear of darkening their skin. A family trip to India to visit extended family further opened my eyes. I noticed that commercials for Fair & Lovely, a skin-lightening cream, routinely played on television (much like the number of weight-loss commercials I see in America). I was amazed by the spectrum of lightness that the commercial endorsed; the lightest shade the product promised was a good shade or even two lighter than my own! Even I, someone who has lived largely unaffected by colorism, found that these commercials hit an insecurity that I didn't realize that I had.

9

Shai Hei

Rosalie Chan, CHINESE/FILIPINA AMERICAN, 23

"Wear sunscreen," my mom said. "You don't want to *shai hei*."

"*Shai hei*" means, literally, "to dry until one turns black." In Asia and among Asian diasporas worldwide, smooth, light skin is the ideal. Those with dark skin are seen as coarse, ugly, low class. When I would return from the pool in summers, my mom would irritably eye my tanned arms and legs. "Your skin has become too black," she'd say. When we looked at Christmas photos, she'd say, "Look at how white your skin was in the winter. Don't stay in the sun too much." This is how I learned that dark skin is shunned in my community, while light skin is seen as a marker of beauty. In fact, I am not a dark-skinned Asian American. I'm of Chinese heritage—my mom from Taiwan, and my dad from a Chinese family in the Philippines. Because of my Chinese ancestry, I have light skin, and I find that the color of my skin is an asset both in Asia and in the United States.

When I visit my family in the Philippines, I often feel out of place, though admittedly privileged—because I am an American, but also because I am light-skinned. Lighter skin implies high class, education, and the privilege of staying indoors while the darker-skinned masses work in the streets and darken under the tropical sun. On Filipino TV, all the celebrities have pale skin. Every other commercial is a cream that promises to lighten or whiten Filipino skin, making one's skin as white as the beloved celebrity flashing a wide smile on screen. When I go to the beauty aisles in stores, I see endless shelves of whitening products. I've also noticed these products in other parts of Asia. When I travel to Taiwan and China, I see the same commercials for skin-whitening products and face masks, even though the population typically has light skin. When I studied in China, I was warned that some brands of body wash and face wash in stores have bleach in them. Chinese women are conditioned to value light skin, and they go to great lengths to whiten their skin, even if it means using products with dangerous chemicals.

As in Asia, colorism is prevalent in the United States. My Asian American friends often use face masks and makeup to lighten their skin. They go through daily face-washing rituals to ensure that their skin stays smooth and light. Despite colorism in the United States, these cosmetic products come not from the United States but from Asian countries like South Korea, Japan, and India.

I also find that colorism is rampant in the United States beyond Asian American communities. Colorism affects most communities of color in America (e.g., black, Latino) and even affects how these groups view each other, including how they view Asian Americans. In the United States, for instance, people (white and otherwise) typically have a one-dimensional image of Asian Americans. When people talk about Asian Americans, I find that they are usually referring to those who look just like me: Chinese, light skin, black hair, almond-shaped brown eyes—completely erasing those who diverge from this image, such as darker-skinned Asians. When they encounter Asian Americans who don't match their stereotype (for example, someone from Southeast Asia with dark skin and round eyes), they are often confused, trying to comprehend the "anomaly" before them.

These one-dimensional images held by most Americans often stem from American media. Asian Americans are rarely represented in television and film, but when they are presented, they are whitewashed or uniformly light-skinned. There's a long history of Asian whitewashing in film, dating back to the era of silent film when white actress Mary Pickford played the Asian lead in *Madame Butterfly* (1915), but whitewashing continues in modern-day movies as well. In 2013's *Star Trek into Darkness*, British (white) actor Benedict Cumberbatch was cast as the villain Khan Noonien Singh—an Indian character. In the 2015 romance film

Aloha, Emma Stone (a white actress) plays a mixed-race character, Allison Ng, who is supposed to be of Hawaiian and Asian heritage. And in the 2017 movie *Ghost in the Shell*, Scarlett Johansson (another white actress) portrayed Major Motoko Kusanagi, who was originally written as a Japanese character. In all of these cases, Asian characters are whitewashed for white audiences. Even when those of Asian ancestry play Asian characters, they are almost always light-skinned (e.g., Lucy Liu, Daniel Dae Kim, Sandra Oh), and in many cases, multiracial with European ancestry (e.g., Ryan Potter, Jordan Connor, Katie Chang, Sonoya Mizuno). In 2016, the *New York Times* published an online video about Asian Americans sharing their stories about the racism they face every day, yet most of the commentators were East Asian and light-skinned. The voices of darker-skinned Asians, such as those from South/Southeast Asia, were excluded, even though Filipinos and Indians are the second and third highest percentage of Asian Americans, respectively, and despite the fact that they arguably have important stories to tell given the value placed on light skin in the United States.

Because I embody the stereotype of an Asian American (i.e., light-skinned, East Asian), I understand that I benefit from colorism in the United States. When Asian American organizations are formed, I know that they will include me. They will call themselves "yellow power" or "yellow peril," not realizing that they are excluding darker-skinned Asians who may self-identify as "brown." When I walk down the street or drive in my car, I do not get racially profiled as do some of my brown Asian American brothers and sisters. In 2015, a fifty-seven-year-old dark-skinned Indian man, Sureshbhai Patel, was beaten and partially paralyzed by Alabama police; they had been called by a neighbor reporting the "suspicious" behavior of a "skinny black man" lurking in the area—he was taking his morning walk. And while people may see me as foreign because I am Asian, they do not see me as dangerous. When I go to the airport, I do not experience the effects of Islamophobia and undergo extra security checks like those with brown skin.

I move through space under the gaze of people who think I'm foreign, but also nonthreatening. I listen to what my mom says.

I still wear sunscreen and protect my skin. But when I hear the words "*shai hei*," I cringe. In the Asian American community, in our attitudes and in our language, we demonize darker skin, and we need to do better. In the United States, we also need to do better. Vilifying dark skin must stop.

10

Whiteness Is Slippery

Julia Mizutani, MULTIRACIAL JAPANESE/WHITE AMERICAN, 24

Sprawled on the couch in the warm home of a close friend, I was scrolling through music videos with her two children when the younger of them, Nolan, bounced up and began to teach me some of his dance moves. Nolan's curly, dark hair bounced on his forehead in front of his eyes as his lanky nine-year-old body shuffled across the living room's wooden floors, showing me what the "white boy" dance looked like. I laughed and blurted out that white people don't dance like that. Nolan turned to me incredulously with wide eyes and a slack-jawed mouth, "Wait . . . are you white?"

I had never been asked that question before in my life.

The definition of who is considered white is one that has shifted and varied over the course of this country's history, dependent upon time and place, and rooted in the calculated decisions of those in power to subordinate people of color. My father is Japanese, and his heritage was visibly passed on to me through my shock of black hair that sticks out thick and straight, and my facial features that render me ethnically ambiguous, but ethnic nonetheless. White men, whether through court systems, media, or law, are the ones who decide who is white, and I have never been mistaken for a white woman by any white man.

To Nolan's credit, he isn't white either, but both of us have white mothers, and it was in that moment that he understood we shared something. We are mixed. We are the in-betweens. Not quite one and not quite the other. We often identify according to how the world sees us, while painfully aware of the part of us it doesn't see. Society tries to box us into one race, though we are sometimes seen as "racial imposters" by members of the racial groups to which we belong. We are not black enough or Asian enough. Yet, we are not white enough either.

Whites often perceive us as "exotic," and we are fetishized by those who wish to investigate "the unknown" through their sexual exploits. We receive comments about our hair, our eyes, our skin, and comments on the "jungle fever" or "yellow fever" our parents must have had. Strangely enough, the fetishizing bleeds into Asian communities as well, except it is due to our white features.

≈

As an Asian American woman who is part white, I have Asian facial features that render me unmistakably East Asian, but have light skin and double eyelids and features that many of my Japanese friends do not have. Because of my appearance, I am treated differently than my full-Asian friends since colorism is a prominent part of many Asian communities, and my privileged treatment for simply existing proves this point.

Whether I am traveling in Nepal, Thailand, Korea, or Japan, I see ads for creams that bleach and whiten skin and for facial plastic surgery meant to whitewash Asian features. My light-skin privilege gives me special treatment in these countries. I know that I am treated differently than my darker-skinned Filipino, Indian, and Japanese friends. I see it in the way that sunny days bring out umbrellas, and I see it in the funny looks I am given when I stroll down the streets soaking up the sun. I hear it from the *o'bachans* and *obasans* and *halmonis* and *ajummas* (aunties and grandmothers) who wag their fingers at me for not properly preserving my pale skin. I see it in the multiracial Asian-white models used to promote skin-care products. We are just Asian enough to be identified as Asian, yet we have features and light-skin privilege that consumers might wish to have. In the beauty industry in Japan, we are called "*hāfu*," meaning "half" or "mixed," but usually referring to those of us who are half-white. Beauty magazines have articles called "How to Look like *Hāfu*," which really means, "how to look part white." It is poisonous to Asian women being constantly told that lighter skin is beautiful, and that their standard of beauty should be someone who looks like me, someone who was born to a white mother.

The phenomenon of colorism is not only found within each of our communities, but it is also used *across* Asian communities. As a Japanese American, I understand what it is like being both the oppressed and the oppressor. My ancestors have been both imperialist occupiers of large swaths of Asia, as well as forced into internment camps in America by a president's executive order. Identity is complicated, and we can often hold multiple contradicting ones at the same time. While Asian Americans were segregated, just as African Americans and other people of color were before *Brown v. Board of Education*, we are now often a part of the effort to resegregate schools by fighting against affirmative action and throwing our black and brown counterparts under our proverbial bus. The Japanese community has, at times, also shunned our darker-skinned Asian American counterparts from South/Southeast Asia (e.g., the Philippines, India, Cambodia, Bangladesh, and Laos); we differentiate our own skin from theirs to access societal benefits connected to whiteness.

But whiteness is slippery, we must never forget. We mustn't forget that the white man defines whiteness, not us. We must remember that the definition of whiteness has shifted and changed with the turning tides, and that we must not be swept up in it. We mustn't forget the one-drop rule, or the Supreme Court cases of Takao Ozawa or Bhagat Singh Thind, of Japanese and Indian ancestry, respectively, who were ineligible for US citizenship because the Court (read: white men) decreed that they were not white.

When writing about Bhagat Singh Thind, a US Army veteran who sought US citizenship a few years after his honorable discharge, Justice Sutherland wrote that "intermarriages . . . produc[ed] an intermingling . . . destroying to a greater or less degree the purity of the Aryan blood" and that "the average man knows perfectly well that there are unmistakable and profound differences" between Asians and white people.

Nowadays, some Americans may shudder at such statements. Those same Americans may look at someone like me or like Nolan and believe we are the look of "progress" and that racism will be erased once we all become mixed. With mixing, our skin colors will blend into a honey-tinted tone, and racism will be defeated. Yet, this fantasy doesn't consider the colorism that runs rampant within and between communities of color. Takao Ozawa and Bhagat Singh Thind tried to attain privilege by proving their whiteness, and it may not stop us mixed-race, lighter-skinned folk from using our privileges at the expense of others.

Personally, I regard with suspicion the idea that we can fuck our way out of this country's racism and white supremacy. I am skeptical that we honey-tinted people can defeat racism while colorism continues to thrive within our own communities. We, the ambiguous mixed-race folk, must choose whether we will be an erosion of white supremacy or a buffer for it.

≈

Nolan doesn't understand most of this yet. His nine-year-old mind is starting to wrap around the idea of what being a person of color means in this country. He is just starting to understand what being seen as a black man may mean for him in the future, as I am still learning what being an Asian woman means for me. Having a conversation about his light-skin privilege, about the colorism that exists within our own communities, will add yet another layer of complication to his identity. Understanding that colorism is yet another hurdle in the journey to end white supremacy is difficult for grown adults to grasp, let alone a child who is told by others that his identity represents racial progress.

For now, we continue dancing and shuffling our feet across the floor.

11

Regular Inmates

Sonal Nalkur, INDO-CANADIAN (CURRENTLY RESIDES
IN THE UNITED STATES), 41

The guard's frisking was firm and aggressive. Across my waist,
under my bra, between my legs, her command announced a
complete disinterest in the body parts she handled. She dumped
out the contents of my purse, asked me to put my cash in my
pockets, and silently put handcuffs around my wrists. She asked
me my name and my birth date, then pointed me to a red corner
on the floor so I could have my picture taken. Looking down at her
clipboard, she asked if I was a US citizen.

"No."

"That's the first time I ever heard anyone say no! What are you?"

"Canadian."

"I mean . . . what's your race?"

"Indian."

This was my first encounter with the American criminal justice
system. As an academic, I know that most scholarship offers
evidence that "race matters," especially if a person is a black male.
But there isn't much published on the arrests of brown-skinned
South Asian women. Until my arrest, I had never had a serious
traffic violation, nor been particularly interested in the color of my
skin. As a South Indian, and fair-skinned at that, I understood that
my skin color affords me privilege over black men in the criminal
justice system. Yet, here I was.

A few months before my firm frisking, I had been pulled over for
running a stop sign in Georgia—on a quiet road just outside the
university campus where I work. I wasn't speeding in the ten-mile-
per-hour zone, but my driver's license, which I had to renew every

four months because of the way my work visa had been arranged, had expired—carelessness on my part. The incident would result in my first time in court, where I would stand before a very busy judge who asked me a litany of questions while sifting through a large stack of paperwork before him. I was surprised when he announced the eight-hundred-dollar fine, one hundred for rolling through a stop sign (did I *actually* do that?) and seven hundred for driving with an expired license in Georgia. I was even more surprised when the judge called me back to the stand to tell me that I had committed a "finger-printable" offense. I later learned that "finger-printable" actually means that you're being arrested. For driving with an expired license.

≈

The guard who opened my cell door didn't say anything when she unlocked my handcuffs and closed the door behind me. The exhausted young woman sitting beside me near the pay phone, whose hair and nails showed traces of having been glamorous the night before, told me that she had turned herself in at 9:00 a.m. for the same thing. Neither of us knew how long we'd be in the jail, but she said her friend told her that they do fingerprints first thing in the morning.

I sat for about three hours, staring down at my toes, then back at the wall, and out the glass window to the offices, and then reluctantly back to the ticking clock in the hallway. At one point, there were five of us. The woman in the corner opposite mine was Tessi—she was in for trespassing. "I'm not trying to stay here," she said. She and some friends had been sleeping over at her brother's place. "The property manager came in and called the cops on us since we weren't on the lease," she said. The cop had pointed a gun at her brother. "My brother said, 'if you're gonna shoot me, then kill me.' He's been shot before, so he ain't trippin.'" She told me that DeKalb County takes about eight to twelve hours to release people. Gwinnett County was so much faster, she recalled. "Yeah, my brother put his hands up and surrendered immediately. Neither of us had taken out our guns or anything. There's no reason for me to be here."

The woman beside me called someone on the pay phone who told her that he didn't have money to come get her. It sounded as though he was giving her some advice because she was listening intently. She was telling her friend about the male inmates who infrequently passed by our cell: "These regular inmates keep walking around, peering in like they gonna eat us." We all laughed, and she continued, "I ran into Teresa and Jaz on my way in here . . . uh huh. Yeah, my mug looks cute. I look cute today." She giggled like a little girl, but was probably more like twenty-four. "Uh huh, yeah . . . we all black in here, except one girl. But she ain't white neither."

≈

The first time it really hit me that my skin color mattered was when my South Indian high school friend advised me to date Indian boys exclusively because, at the end of the day, white boys would only see me as brown. It was the first serious dating advice I'd ever received, and it was the first time someone explicitly told me I was not white—something I knew, but nothing I had ever really considered. Knowing your skin color is one thing, but knowing that your skin color matters to everyone around you is another. Years later, while teaching kindergarten in Saudi Arabia, I discovered that, in some places, I was not brown either. I was teaching Arab four-year-olds the letter "B" one day, and when I asked, "What is this thing in my hand?" they screamed, "Book!" When I asked, "What is that thing on the shelf?" they screamed, "Basket!" When I asked, "And what is the color of my skin?" they all screamed, "White!" There hadn't been any doubt in any of their minds, and yet they had now injected some doubt in mine.

≈

All of us in the cell were trying to keep our attention on one officer who was busily walking back and forth. Eventually, the officer rushed in to tell Tessi that she'd be getting out, that she would get to go home today. "That's right," Tessi announced as she sat up straight and folded her arms. Another thirty minutes later, the officer came back and called me out and pointed to a wall where I could stand and wait for my prints. Sometime later, it was another officer, then fingerprints on a scanner, then fingerprints with ink, then mug shots. After more sitting around and waiting, I was escorted out by a warm and cheerful male cop.

"Your wrists are so tiny, just let me know if these fall off!"

Several hallways later, he removed my cuffs, "Alright, let me get you set to go. Wait. What's the origin of your last name?"

"Indian," I said. And that was it.

≈

The reactions from my colleagues and friends that evening told me the experience was equally unfamiliar to them:

"That is the craziest story I've ever heard! You're kidding me, right?"

"Will they deport you?"

"Are your mug shots public?"

"Could this affect future job prospects?"

"Did you at least get a few selfies in? Haha—wait, can you take your phone in?"

"I'm so sorry you had to go through all this! Let me know if you need anything."

"I told you to hire a lawyer! Next time you should listen to me. I'm telling you . . . the difference between rich people and poor people in America is: lawyers."

Some of them were so nonchalant, but from that day on, I drove with my hands clenched on the wheel, always making full and complete stops, and always having checked—ten or twelve times a day—that I had my driver's license with me.

≈

When asked "what I am," I often tell people I am "Canindian," hyper-aware that while I was born and raised in Canada, I am seen as Indian. I am aware of the Queen's power, the power that built the British Commonwealth, the power that subordinated Indians for hundreds of years and relegated us to second-class citizens in our own country. But in an independent India, I am also aware that my light skin color gives me privileges and makes me relatively closer to the white man in status than my darker brothers and sisters. In other parts of the Commonwealth, including Canada, my color undoes that privilege, reminding me again that true citizens are white.

Like so many with privilege, I often forget that I have it, until I don't. After all, my experiences have taught me that the bar for being "nonwhite" is very low in America—for a woman of color becomes a criminal forever the moment she enters the criminal justice system, no matter how she got there. And a brown-skinned foreigner is suspect every time she crosses a border, no matter how brown. Last month, I was crossing the US/Canadian border with my visa reapplication materials in hand. The US government requires original documents of my professional qualifications, so I had my PhD diploma rolled up in a case as I always did. I also had my parole paperwork and arrest release documentation.

"So, I see you have this arrest," the border patrol officer said after having asked a series of questions about the nature of my work in Atlanta. "You know, you shouldn't be driving around without a license. That's just plain irresponsible."

"Yes, sir," I responded with some shame.

"I mean, you're a professor, for goodness' sake! You should know better." He raised his voice. As fear began to well up in me, I reminded myself that he was just doing his job. He paused and went through my paperwork and then looked at his computer, and then back at my paperwork. "Running a stop a sign . . . well, that is just plain reckless." He shook his head. "So, when was the last time you were in Saudi Arabia?"

"I believe it was about three years ago," I said, not expecting the question and, to his chagrin, unclear of my exact travel dates.

"Ma'am, it's a simple question. And if I can't trust you to answer that, I just don't see how you can be trusted. It's clear you are unfit to be in this country." I felt a hard lump tightening in my throat. My mouth was dry and I said nothing. He took out a large metal stamp and slammed a visa in my passport.

"Are you sure you should really be here?"

There hadn't been any doubt in his mind, and his words had now injected some doubt in mine.

12

Magnetic Repulsion

Brittany Ota-Malloy, MULTIRACIAL
JAPANESE/BLACK AMERICAN, 29

Some of us are born sun-kissed. That's me. As a biracial Black and Japanese woman, I often present as racially ambiguous, but obviously as a woman of color.[1] I have a tan complexion year-round, and in the sunniest summers my skin often turns a shade of deep caramel. My experiences with colorism manifest as a magnetic repulsion (two equal forces repelling each other), wherein my perceived lightness or darkness produces messages that are in constant conflict with one another.

I understand colorism to be rooted in anti-Blackness around the world. The underlying message that "lighter skin is better skin" inherently disadvantages Black people and others with similar dark skin (e.g., dark-skinned Latinos, South Asians). Within the American Black community, light skin is privileged; those with light skin have received certain privileges since slavery, such as indoor work on the plantation and, later, relatively more access to dominant American cultural institutions than their darker-skinned counterparts enjoy. Within Asian (and Asian American) communities, light skin is similarly privileged, cherished, sought after, and often connected to perceptions about social class. The politics of skin shade in both of these communities live in me. However, the messages that I receive about my skin color from these communities are often conflicting—like a magnetic repulsion, both disadvantaging and privileging me at the same time.

≈

Growing up in a primarily Black family in Southern California shaped my experiences with race and colorism. My father was born in Nagasaki, Japan, and he immigrated to America in the late 1980s. My mother, a Black woman, comes from a large family of varying shades. Great-grandma was the lightest of us all, cousin Deon and my sister Jasmine fall within the median, and cousin Dana's skin is rich obsidian. Mom often paired our fried chicken with rice, taught me to count to ten in Japanese, and ensured that I had both the African and Japanese collectible Barbies. Beyond these efforts, my upbringing was culturally Black, and while my Japaneseness was not always seen, my Blackness was more readily visible. Though I recall my mother's attempts to make sure some Japanese influences were present in my life, I've never known what it means to be an Asian woman. And for much of my life, the only other people I have known of Japanese ancestry have been my father, twin brother, and Traci, a classmate in school. Soom, the Asian woman who owned the local Black beauty supply shop, was the first Asian woman to show any interest in me. She gave me free barrettes with each visit to the shop.

Racialized experiences in my life produce messages with great polarity, particularly with women from the racial communities to which I belong. My interactions with Asian women typically render me invisible, wholly unseen. With these women, the news that I too am Asian is, more often than not, met with surprise. With wide eyes, I am asked, "You are Japanese?! And what?" or "How Japanese are you?" To these women, something doesn't add up, and these experiences remind me that I don't look like other Japanese women. A few years ago I visited my partner in Shanghai, China, where he'd been assigned to work. We'd stopped by his office so I could meet his supervisor and peers. After the initial introductions, the Asian women in the office surrounded me, poking and prodding. His supervisor asked, "Is this how your hair grows?" as she tugged at my wild, curly strands. I felt the distance between us in that moment and, in the pit of my stomach, an aching pain because inside of me there was a Black woman silently pleading with her, "Please don't touch my hair." On the train ride back to the hotel, I was surrounded by advertisements for skin-lightening products on billboards and magazines. I did not encounter, during my two-week trip, a single person who looked like me.

In a graduate-level class in Wisconsin, an Asian American peer complained that we'd had too much sun this year. She was upset that her children were getting dark because they have "such beautiful pale skin." When I commented that dark skin is beautiful, too, she interrupted me to add, "It's an Asian thing." In that moment, this Asian woman did not see me as Asian, while at the same time insulting my own tan skin. She looked right through me, rendering me invisible as an Asian American woman. Apparently, I am too dark to be Asian, too dark to be Japanese. I am seen as an "outsider."

Interactions with Black women can also be complicated. While I am generally seen as Black, my Blackness is, at times, challenged. My knowledge about and experiences within Black communities support me in these challenges, and, when all else fails, a photo of my mother will usually do. In my freshman year of college, I attended a retreat with other scholars of color. In a discussion about the use of language as a form of oppression, I spoke about how the words "bitch" and "nigga" have been reclaimed by women and Black people, respectively, as colloquial expressions of love for and validation of one another. A Black classmate stood up to express her disappointment that someone who is not Black would use the N-word in the conversation, while she looked directly at *me*. This was the first time I had to explain myself, and it was the first time that I felt my Blackness challenged. This experience caused me to consider my Black and Japanese identities and how they converge in me.

While I sometimes feel frustrated in those moments when my Blackness is questioned (especially since this is the reality I grew up in), I also understand that other Black women, including my own mother and monoracial Black sisters, experience Blackness differently than I do. Like many other Black women, I spent much of my early life pressing and flat-ironing my hair to get it bone straight. In college, however, I began wearing my natural curly texture, doing little more than adding conditioner. I quickly learned that my natural hair is accepted everywhere and I am complimented at least once a week; by comparison, many Black women are stigmatized for their natural hair, often worn in tight curls, afros, and braids.

And recently, Shea Moisture (a company that markets a wide variety of beauty products to women—primarily Black women) faced backlash for their advertising campaign, which featured two white women and one light-skinned, loose-curled Black woman. Prioritizing Eurocentric traits, even in the Black model, neglected the millions of Black women whose features diverge from this image (women whose support serves as a foundation for the company's success). As a graduate student in Wisconsin, I participated in a dialogue with other Black women about the ad. One woman asked the group to raise a hand if they had ever used Shea Moisture products, and most of the women in the room raised a hand. Then she asked that we raise a hand if we felt represented in the Shea Moisture ad. I was the only woman to raise a hand. Shea Moisture's hair products are centered on loving natural hair, a prominent issue in Black hair care. But the campaign's absence of dark-skinned, kinky-haired women, who felt Shea Moisture's products were for them too, if not mainly, was a slap in the face. The ad campaign reflected the whitewashing of the brand, and when it comes to representation of Black women in media, women like me, with lighter skin and "good hair," are prioritized and privileged.

Throughout my life, messages about my skin color have been contradictory—with equal and repelling forces from Asian and Black communities, communities for which skin shade and colorism are especially deeply rooted and contentious. Anti-Blackness is pervasive in Asia and in the United States, and in both Asian American and Black American communities, light skin is privileged over dark. My relatively darker skin marks me as an "outsider" among Asians and among Japanese Americans. Because of my darker hue, I am not seen as Japanese, and I am perceived as "less beautiful" by a culture that idealizes light, white skin. But this same skin, my sun-kissed shade, is viewed differently in the Black community. While I am disadvantaged by dark skin among Asians and Asian Americans, I understand that I am privileged by light skin in the Black community. These experiences with colorism repel me towards and away from my own racial identities. They impact my ability to build lasting relationships with and to see myself in my racial peers. As I engage with others about colorism, I am constantly learning how people perceive each other, themselves, and me. Through this learning I am able to position myself as a purposeful actor in experiences where colorism is at play and maximize my impact in redefining what is known about biracial Asian/Black women and skin-color privilege.

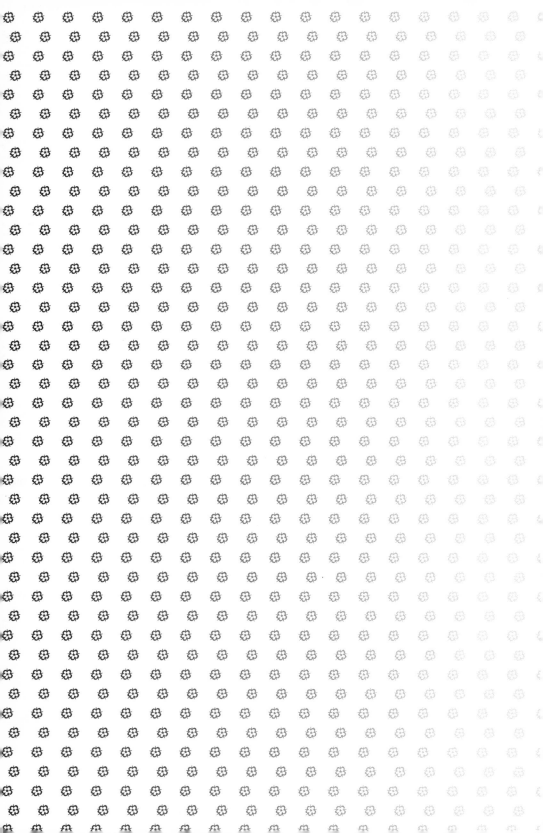

Part III

ASPIRATIONAL WHITENESS

"Do you wanna be white?" In 2014, Korean skin-care brand Elisha Coy posed this very question to American consumers (particularly to Korean Americans) on a billboard in Koreatown, Queens, New York. Positioned alongside the provocative question was an East Asian model with light, near-white skin and a picture of the product she was advertising—a tinted moisturizing cream for women with so-called skin-whitening properties. The ad was heavily criticized for its blatant racism, though at least one critic wondered whether it was merely a case of "lost in translation."[1] Nonetheless, the ad raises important questions: Are whitening products marketing pale skin or are they peddling the promise of whiteness itself? Is colorism about privileging light shades over dark, or about venerating racial whiteness?

Colorism among Asian Americans is not always about so-called white worship—that is, unbridled adoration of all things Caucasian and Western. In many parts of Asia, skin-color discrimination existed long before any significant contact with Europeans, and in Japan and China, for instance, the preference for light skin has existed for centuries and arguably has to do with social class, not race. In a 2018 *New York Times* article, Andrea Cheng examined the motivations underlying a recent spike in Asian American women bleaching their hair blonde. According to Cheng, not all Asian American women go platinum with the desire of "mirroring Western beauty ideals," but rather dyed hair is an expression of their creativity, personal style, and individuality, and a rejection of the "old fashioned femininity norms" of their parents' generation. Blonde hair is a personal choice; clearly, white women dye their hair blonde all the time, and their motives are not psychoanalyzed under the proverbial microscope. Laura Miller, a professor of Japanese studies at the University of Missouri–St. Louis, further argues that "what they see in Asia, especially in Japan and Korea, is a lot of hybridity and playfulness with hair colors and styles" and adds, "When Asian-Americans bleach their hair, they may not have in mind white Americans, but rather Asian celebrities such as Moga Mogami or Hyo-yeon Kim."[2]

Moreover, whether Asian American women really want to be white is a contentious and hotly debated question, and Rondilla and Spickard argue that there is "overwhelming evidence" that they do not want to look or be white, but rather they want to look like wealthy, upper-class Asians.[3] For some Asian ethnic groups, however, particularly those whose histories are deeply entwined with and shaped by European imperialism, value is perhaps placed not simply on possessing light skin (or light hair for that matter), but on white-ness itself. Whiteness, for some, is held out as a goal—something to which to aspire.

In this section, Asian American women reveal how colorism in their ethnic communities and in their families *is* connected to the idealization of and, in some cases, desire for whiteness. Traits con-nected to whiteness are valued because whiteness itself is valorized and glamorized—perhaps not surprising given the long history of European colonization in some parts of Asia, such as in India and the Philippines. European rulers held power and privilege over their Asian subjects for centuries and for the oppressed masses, white-ness became a symbol of status and sophistication. According to sociologist C. N. Lee at the University of Massachusetts at Amherst, "European colonization of non-white countries in Africa, Asia, and Central/South America elevated European history and culture, including the physical appearances of whites as a racial group. This solidified Europeans' position at the top of the political, economic, cultural, and military hierarchy on a global scale. As their culture spread, frequently by means of physical conquest, racially-based standards of beauty came to include light-colored hair and eyes, and perhaps most importantly, light skin."[4]

This is evident even today in postcolonial Asia in the "white is right" mentality held by many Asians, wherein all things Caucasian and Western (including but not limited to physical appearance) are held up as superior to all things local. As described in the introduction, for example, Caucasian models are often employed to advertise products to Asian peoples across Asia, and author and editor Elaine Y. J. Lee writes about her experiences growing up in Seoul, South Korea, reminiscing that "I'd been all too used to passing by Korean billboards with blonde, blue-eyed couples modeling, say, my dad's preferred domestic brand of golfwear. My eyes had grown so accustomed, passive and immune to Western foreigners modeling Asian brand apparel that I hardly even noticed."[5] She continues, "Fair-skinned foreigners not only appear in fashion apparel campaigns, but also in magazine editorials and even television commercials for household products. This applies to many countries across East, Southeast and South Asia, including Japan, India, Thailand, South Korea, China, and Singapore."[6]

In fact, a 2011 study of race in advertising found that in China and Malaysia (just as in the United States), the vast majority of mannequins were white and most of the models used in advertisements were Caucasian; this was true especially for fashion ads, but also for a wide range of ads marketing cosmetics, eyewear, shoes, jewelry, and even electronics.[7] Other studies have found that most clothing ads in Taiwan and Singapore feature Caucasian models,[8] and most of the models used in ads in women's magazines in South Korea are Caucasian.[9] Perhaps the use of Caucasian models for Asian brands simply represents Asia's attempt at racial diversity and inclusion, though, notably, black models or those of other races are relatively rare.[10] For instance, a study of ads in Korean women's magazines found that more than 70 percent of the models were Caucasian, while less than 1 percent were black.[11]

The adulation given to Caucasians and Western beauty norms can be further observed in the ways in which white women are placed front and center on platforms specifically intended to showcase Asian beauty. Recently, *Vogue India* featured Kendall Jenner, Caucasian, as the cover model for their tenth anniversary special

Figure P3.1. Chinese woman walks past a billboard featuring a Caucasian model in Beijing, China. Source: Shutterstock.

edition issue, and *Vogue Japan*'s fifteenth anniversary cover starred Caucasian model Miranda Kerr. Regarding the latter, style blogger Eliza Romero admits that she finds it difficult to believe that "Japan, with its own prosperous fashion and modeling industry, couldn't find a single Japanese model to grace its cover."[12] Likewise, many found it frustrating and highly improbable that no Indian woman among the more than millions in India and around the world could be found to represent Indian beauty in an Indian-based fashion magazine on its anniversary cover. One person tweeted in response, "Were ALL the Indian women unavailable??" as the magazine faced considerable backlash, criticism, and accusations of

Figure P3.2. White-appearing mannequins dressed in saris in front of clothing store in Varanasi, India. Source: Shutterstock.

"whitewashing," something that is all too common in Asia (just as it is in the United States).[13] Perhaps globalization and the spread of Western beauty norms through mass media are part of the problem, though undoubtedly, the impact of colonization continues to bear down upon the psyches of many in Asia, as well as much of the Asian diaspora, including Asian Americans.

Noor Hasan, Pakistani American, argues that desire for light skin among South Asians cannot be divorced from the "impact of European colonization" and, likewise, Agatha Roa, who identifies as Pacific Islander American, writes that colorism within her own Filipino family is firmly tied to colonization by Spain and the United States. Her mother was born in the post–World War II Philippines where she learned that "everything in America was syrupy sweet" if you were white. For her mother, as perhaps for other Asian Americans raised in colonized or postcolonial countries, whiteness (the racial group, not simply light skin) is equated with beauty, but also status and ascension up the social ladder. Noelle Marie Falcis, Filipina American, similarly describes her mother's aspiration for whiteness because, as Noelle contends, she suffers from a "colonized mentality" and believes that whiteness is the key to success in America. According to Noelle, her mother learned the value of whiteness in the postcolonial Philippines, where "the indoctrination for Western, Eurocentric traits as preferred was introduced, enforced, and solidified." Notably, Noelle recognizes that the desire for whiteness is not solely about Caucasian beauty norms but about all things Western, including European language (rather than native tongues) and Catholicism, which was introduced to the region by Spain (as opposed to their ancestral spirituality). She further contends that her mother's veneration of whiteness was additionally compounded with her migration to the United States, where the image of American success also looks overwhelmingly white.

As in many parts of Asia, whiteness is esteemed in American society and is equated with financial success, social mobility, and assimilation. Even the American Dream was and is a white one. Historically, people of color were "excluded from its promise" through racist exclusionary practices[14] such as Jim Crow laws, which reserved the best schools and public amenities for whites; restrictive covenants and outright violence, which kept people of color out of white communities; federally backed housing policies that denied home loans to people of color; and even US citizenship laws, which originally granted citizenship only to free white males. By the late nineteenth century, US citizenship would be extended to African Americans, though it remained elusive to immigrating Asians until the 1950s. In two landmark Supreme Court cases, Asian immigrants fought for US citizenship, and they did so by claiming whiteness. They recognized that if they could be classified as white, they could obtain US citizenship and hence the full protection of the law and all of the rights of American citizens—this meant the right to vote, own and lease land, serve on juries, and hold public office. In *Ozawa v. the United States* (1922), a Japanese immigrant, Takeo Ozawa, hoped to persuade the Court that the Japanese, by virtue of their light skin, were white. A few months later, Bhagat Singh Thind, an Indian immigrant and former US serviceman, made a similar plea in *Thind v. the United States* (1923), though in his case he did not argue for whiteness based on shared skin color, but rather he claimed that Indians shared common ancestry with Caucasians. Despite Ozawa's and

Thind's requests for racial reclassification, the Supreme Court ruled against them both, arguing that despite their light skin (as in the case of Ozawa) or so-called shared ancestry (as argued by Thind), they were not white. In the case of Baghat Singh Thind, Justice George Sutherland stated, "It may be true that the blond Scandinavian and the brown Hindu have a common ancestor in the dim reaches of antiquity, but the average man knows perfectly well that there are unmistakable and profound differences between them today. . . . [I]t cannot be doubted that the children born in this country of Hindu parents would retain indefinitely the clear evidence of their ancestry."[15] Despite their failures in the Court, both cases reveal the desire for whiteness among some groups of color, including some Asian immigrants,[16] who quickly learned upon arrival to the United States the immutable value of whiteness in American society. To reap its benefits, they sought to be racially redefined as such.

Today Asian Americans are no longer fighting, as some once did, to be racially classified as white, but desires for whiteness among some Asian Americans may persist. Even today, the American Dream is arguably a white one—the images of white picket fences, suburban home ownership, and financial success are intertwined with whiteness itself. This is not to say that Americans of color do not dream of success in America; Asian Americans, like whites and other groups of color, also believe in the American Dream, and many immigrate to the United States in order to pursue that dream. In fact, collectively, Asian Americans have been stereotyped as highly successful, suggesting that the American Dream is their reality (perhaps more so than that of other racial minorities), though the uncomfortable truth is that there are wide economic disparities among Asian Americans. Some ethnic groups, such as the Japanese, Chinese, and Indians, have been described as "outwhiting the whites" in terms of economic success, while some Southeast Asian American groups who immigrated to the United States as refugees with few resources (such as Cambodians, Vietnamese, and Laotians) are trapped in intergenerational poverty; in fact, some of these ethnic groups lag well behind Latinx and African Americans in terms of socioeconomic status.[17] Because of the reality of uneven successes among Asian Americans, whiteness in contemporary America, as in postcolonial Asia and early America, continues to embody the American Dream and economic success, and for some Asian Americans (especially first-generation immigrants looking to assimilate and climb the social ladder), whiteness remains something to which to aspire.

This collection of essays explores aspirational whiteness as part and parcel of colorism for some (though certainly not all) Asian Americans, but also examines the strategies they use to access whiteness both in their real lives and in their virtual worlds— through, for example, skin-whitening soaps, bleaching creams, and even digital self-representation online. Whitening products may be a literal manifestation of Frantz Fanon's "white masks"[18] (as described in the introduction) as women modify their skin color to attain whiteness, though perhaps another expression of the desire to wear "white masks" occurs online (as described by Noor Hasan) as Asian American women utilize white-skinned emojis to represent themselves on social media. For some, skin-whitening products are not always effective or even desirable; therefore, digital whiteness may be a reasonable alternative.

A final note: For some South and Southeast Asian Americans, attaining whiteness may not be the goal, but rather they aspire to the American stereotype of the "light-skinned, East Asian"—which, at least according to Noelle Marie Falcis, is "the next best thing." She describes how, as a Filipina American, she once modified her skin and eyes in attempts to fit the East Asian physical stereotype because East Asians are held in high regard in the United States as compared to some of their darker-skinned Asian counterparts. Likewise, Joanne Rondilla in her analysis of colorism among Filipinxs writes that "people in the Philippines using skin lighteners is not necessarily a move towards whiteness or Europeanness; it is also related to looking East Asian or Chinese."[19] For some, East Asian beauty is valorized— "extremely pale skin, straight jet-black hair, and large, double-lidded, almond-shaped eyes"—but she reminds readers that this beauty is nonetheless defined "according to white standards"[20] as these characteristics represent the ideal Asian *in the eyes of whites*.[21]

13

Digital Whiteness

Noor Hasan, PAKISTANI AMERICAN, 26

Most of my friends are brown women. We have entered one another's lives through connections in communities, college, graduate and professional schools, the workplace, places of worship, and friends of friends. At twenty-six years old, I find that we are scattered all over the country and even the world. We reside in drastically different time zones, locales, and cultural contexts. To keep in touch, we communicate with each other in a variety of ways. Most often, we connect through social media platforms—frequently through Snapchat, Facebook, and Instagram—and express ourselves through countless posts, tweets, pictures, Snapchat videos, and emojis.

When Apple introduced racially diverse emojis in recent years, they made their way into our digital social marketplaces. The reactions of my friends varied—some were excited, others critical. Though the emojis are diverse in skin tone, other features (such as hair texture and eye shape) remained Westernized and Eurocentric. Some friends further wondered whether, now that social media platforms had given us the opportunity to attach our racial identities to our social communications, we were now culturally and socially obligated to use the newly created emojis. Some of us fought to see ourselves represented on the emoji keyboard, though perhaps this victory presents itself with unintended consequences—to openly attach our racial identities (and hence, divulge demographic data) to the material benefit of platform owners and advertisers unknown to us.

Despite these arguments, for me, it was a no-brainer to use the medium-toned brown woman emoji. Sure, she didn't have black hair like me, but her skin tone was consistent with mine—right in the middle of the spectrum—and, to me, her brown tone best represented my South Asian identity as a Pakistani American woman. Many of my friends use these emojis, and with the rise of Bitmojis, avatars that enable even more flexibility and personalization, there are seemingly endless ways to express moods, mindsets, feelings, attitudes, and activities through these tiny socio-digital cartoons.

What I never anticipated from the introduction of these digital expressions of identity was a significant shift in how I perceived people of color on social media—especially brown women. I expected that most South Asian American women would choose the medium-toned emoji to express themselves, though I was surprised to find that many opted instead to use the lightest-skinned emoji—a woman with light skin and black hair. Most surprising, the skin tone of this emoji is *even lighter* than what is presumably the archetypal American "white woman" emoji that is illustrated with faintly bronzed white skin and blonde hair. As I noticed more and more brown women, including South Asian actresses, beauty bloggers, and social media personalities, captioning their Instagram photos and Snapchat stories with the light-skinned emoji, I grew confused. *Don't you realize that you're brown?* I thought. Why would brown women opt for an emoji that is obviously unrepresentative of their actual skin tone?

I didn't understand why brown women—women who believe in racial justice, who disavow the impact of colonialism and prejudice on our society, who are "woke," who are liberal-minded, who believe in a fair and equal society—selected emojis that are not brown like them. Sure, the medium skin–toned brown woman emoji isn't everyone's skin tone. Maybe you are a little lighter skinned. But still, aren't you brown? Instead of opting for the emoji that reflects your racial identity, what informs your decision to swipe all the way to the left in the emoji selection pane and choose the lightest-skinned digital representation of yourself? Every time I see this happen on a social media platform, I cannot help but think—*why are you, a brown woman, opting for digital whiteness when there are options to express yourself with emojis that are more consistent with your racial identity and phenotype?*

I cannot divorce emoji usage from its underlying racial and cultural connotations. I think about the impact of European colonialism and preference towards light skin in our cultures. I know that when we walk into *desi*[1] grocery stores anywhere in America, we find shelves full of skin-lightening creams and soaps. I think about the historical South Asian aspiration to access whiteness in America and the precept of Western assimilation as an indispensable goal. When I witness brown women of South Asian origin choosing to express themselves with the lightest-skinned emoji that is available to users, these realities are undeniable.

As I consider these truths, I understand why brown women, some maybe subconsciously, opt for digital whiteness. Perhaps what we cannot access in reality, we appropriate digitally. These tiny characters hang off the edges of witty Instagram captions and make their way into the corners of Snapchat stories. These ornamental cartoons are expressions not only of our feelings but of who we are, who we want to be, and how we want to be seen. In opting for digital whiteness through the use of emojis, I find that even with new ways to communicate and express ourselves, we enter into these new digital marketplaces with the same old cultural baggage.

14

Mrs. Santos's Whitening Cream

Agatha Roa, PACIFIC ISLANDER AMERICAN, 39

Mrs. Santos's eyes dart from her iPhone to the white paste on top of her left hand. For ten minutes, the paste had been burning. A crust had formed soon after the baking soda/hydrogen peroxide solution dried, and she lifts her hand toward the camera for her viewers to get a closer look.

Mrs. Santos is older than most YouTube posters I've seen—in her late thirties and a housewife, perhaps. Her glossy, thick black hair is cut into a neat pageboy that swings when she talks and brushes past her shoulders. Her big, deep-set brown eyes reveal Spanish ancestry, and I can tell she is from the Philippines by her accent. She is on the paler side of olive skin and, although she's Asian like me, I can easily see that without sunscreen she'd suffer from sunburn in the summer. I am on the other side of the skin spectrum, and cannot fathom how Mrs. Santos could get any lighter without losing her natural yellow color.

She waits. Sitting on her carpeted living room floor, she repeats her disclaimer: "I want you all to know that I am not a medical professional," adding, "and I am not a nurse." She blinks her eyes, big brown saucers. Her deep-set eyes are such a desired look that many Chinese and Koreans attempt to emulate them by undertaking an epicanthoplasty, an irreversible surgical procedure. "Eyelids with a fold," I mutter, "that's what everybody wants."

I can't tell if Mrs. Santos is broadcasting from Vancouver, or Chicago, or Houston, and it is not her homemade recipe for skin-whitening cream that irks me. From cake soap to L-glutathione injections, the secret has been out of bathrooms and closets for years. Bleaching is on television, billboards, and magazine ads, and in the streets of New Delhi, on the store shelves of Tokyo, and in the Tondo slums in Manila. It's rapped about and commodified as Chinese Jamaicans sell whitening powders in the downtown markets of Kingston. The Internet has made it so we can all compare formulas, mock, or inquire with abandon.

The naïveté in her sing-song voice annoys me as she begins to rinse off the papery glue bandage from her hand, as if to demonstrate how magically easy it is to be white. The image dissolves, and next we see her in a kitchen that is lit just enough to allow viewers to see her diligently rinsing, rubbing her hand, conjuring a genie out of its bottle. She grabs a towel, and we cut to the final scene. She is overjoyed with the results, her plump, manicured yellow hands showcased before my laptop screen. With the zoom lens, the bleached hand is ready for all the world to see and admire. It has undergone a chemical reaction, with faint peeling at the edges where the burnt and unburnt skin meet. I'm fascinated and repulsed at the same time, and swallow a lump that forms in my throat.

"Ooh," she says, lightly flexing her hands as if there were hunks of shiny diamonds on her fingers.

"*Di ba?* [You see?] It's white! Look at the difference." The video takes a few seconds to fade to black, yet the sadness I feel for this stranger will linger on and piss me off.

Mrs. Santos is at her happiest when she looks least like herself.

≈

That epiphanic moment was paralyzing, and it brought back buried memories, and a need to disengage. Dealing with the complexities of colorism in my life has taken years for me to unravel in order to save my life. Whitening videos are wounds that can be revisited, reopened with ease on the Internet, and I'm often baffled by the reasons why I do it.

≈

It began with my mother. Her light skin was the product of a marriage between a young Basque soldier and my grandmother when

Spain surrendered the island, only to be colonized yet again by the United States. My *lola* (grandmother) was mestiza—indigenous and Spanish, living in the southern Philippines, so my mother, too, was born a mestiza.

What my mother never mentioned to me was that my great-grandmother descended from Austronesian tribes, and possibly from dark-skinned Borneans from Indonesia and Maoris from the Pacific. Was she ashamed of that? I don't know, but while I was growing up, the indigenous "dark" side was never mentioned, and I watched as my pale mother never went out in the sun. One day she told me that the pediatrician said I had sensitive skin, as if that would persuade me to stay indoors. Chasing me down as I ran along a Long Island beach, she would repeatedly tell me to get under some shade. I'd ask why, and she would state matter-of-factly, "*Kasi* [because], you do not want to be dark. Dark is bad."

I can't really blame my mother for wanting to be something she was not. She was a product of a post-WWII Philippines. While she was growing up, the country was a US territory, and my mother had moved from her small town of Antike to Manila to the north. I think of that period of her life as the "Holly Golightly" period— just like the Truman Capote film and book, *Breakfast at Tiffany's*, where the main character goes from country to city girl upon moving to New York City. My mother grew up in the technicolor age, watching Douglas Sirk melodramas, smoking cigarettes like an American eighteen-year-old. And as she watched *Imitation of Life*, she learned that everything in America was syrupy sweet and color-ful. If you were white.

≈

My mother loved the whiteness of New York in winter, dressing up in heavy coats to walk in snow. She loved the whiteness of the cold air that enabled her to see every billowing breath as a cloud as she walked to church. As I got older, we couldn't have been more different, and sadly, our relationship became toxic for me. Our mother-daughter relationship was further strained when I decided to drop out of school and move across the country.

I relocated to California and soaked up every single ray of sunshine I could. While living on Venice Beach, I surfed, and the only time I covered myself on the beach was in winter, to don a three-millimeter-thick neoprene wetsuit. I took up rock climbing, and spent my summers in Joshua Tree National Park and my winters camping in Yosemite.

Never once did I ever consider wearing sunscreen, not that I needed it because of the melanin in my skin. I saw it as an act of rebellion against my mother. I rebelled against her, against colorism, and against whiteness. I rebelled out of self-preservation. I knew I'd never comfortably fit into a traditional New York life, the kind she wanted me to have—the lives her immigrant, working-class white neighbors had. She wanted me to be like the daughters of Italian and Greek families, who were smart, got accepted into elite schools, and climbed the social ladder. I was a disappointment to my immigrant parents, who expected me to go on with my stellar SAT scores to be a lawyer, at the very least. I never told them about the letter from NYU asking me to "please reconsider attending" after I left. I couldn't wait to leave. I took a camera, the one I bought for a freshman photography class, and told the college I needed a break. Over the years my mother suffered hypertension, partly caused by stress. I knew she had a ton of internalized frustration, but her need to perpetuate our differences instead of seeking to understand them resulted in failure: Her only daughter ran away from her and her whitewashed dreams.

≈

Mrs. Santos's latest video shows viewers how to make a quick whitening facial mask out of lemon juice, sugar, and her favorite brand of disinfectant, called Oxigenada. She waves the half-empty bottle of hydrogen peroxide, a brand only available in the Philippines, at her audience. She says the formula is guaranteed to whiten skin in only thirty minutes.

Among YouTube viewers, an inverse correlation seems to exist. The lower the educational level and social class, the greater the desire to whiten one's skin via questionable means. The riskier the treatment, the more destitute (and, perhaps, desperate) the individual. One video I observed from Jamaica used untested, possibly carcinogenic chemicals that are made cheaply in China, regularly sold over the counter in Kingston, and banned in the United States.

I realize now that Mrs. Santos may not be a housewife. Perhaps she is the live-in nanny or the housekeeper. The frugality of her recipes now begins to make sense to me. I came to this conclusion after a conversation with a very distant cousin, Fernanda, who lives in Ibaraki prefecture, an upper-middle-class suburb outside Tokyo. I see pictures of her on Facebook. In one taken in her front yard, her vellum skin is shielded from the sunlight peeking through a Japanese maple tree. She has dark-skinned nannies for the children, and servants with kind brown faces and soft voices. I begin to see Mrs. Santos in one of these photographs—the shyness, the servitude in her polite, kind voice—and I suspect Mrs. Santos is nothing like a golf-playing suburban mom. Instead she's a part of the post-colonial mixed messages fed to her by skin-whitening soap ads, just as my mother was back in the day. If she were upper-middle-class, why would she be slaving in a kitchen, perfecting homemade whitening recipes? We all know she would have gone to a Vancouver spa to seek treatment from a licensed aesthetician. And the spa would be located around the corner from a plastic surgeon, the one who, with the utmost discretion, routinely performs double eyelid surgery on Asian women. It all comes full circle.

As upset as I am with Mrs. Santos, we are both Asian, and as in my relationship with my mother, I want desperately to believe that we're more alike than I originally perceived. We're alike in our Asian features, no matter how light or dark. We are beautiful in our brown skin, in spite of the insidious messages whitening-cream manufacturers and mainstream media may try to market to us.

15

Shade of Brown

Noelle Marie Falcis, FILIPINA AMERICAN, 27

I first learned of my supposed outward "deficiencies" when I was twelve. I have a vivid memory of standing in my grandmother's kitchen, where, by the table, she closely watched me as I played. When I finally looked up to ask why she was staring, her expression changed from that of intent observer to one of guilt and shame. Her mouth opened and she cleared the phlegm lodged in her throat.

"My *anak* [dear child]," she began, "You are so beautiful. It is a shame that you are so dark. No Filipino man will ever want to marry you."

At the time that this bit of abrasive news was delivered to me, I had not yet begun the process of understanding my skin tone and all its connotations. My best friend growing up was also Filipina, and she was just as dark as I—both of us a deep burnished brown, the color of the clay found in the Southern California desert around us. We grew up surrounded by Latinos and African Americans, and the few Filipinos whom we knew were also dark-skinned. Because of the regularity with which I saw dark skin, colorism was outside my experience. Due to this, my grandmother's words appeared more confounding than painful.

Later, her words would resurface with my mother—but in a more subversive, nonverbal way. My mother had always played an integral role in my hygienic routine. During my teens, she brought home cardboard boxes filled with Likas brand herbal soap—a papaya-scented soap that promised "SKIN WHITENING," the language unapologetically precise and explicit.

She would make me scrub myself *multiple* times a night to ensure that I had optimized the possibility for the whitest skin. It became our daily ritual, so normalized through sheer frequency that I did not recognize the routine for its insidiousness and the way it silently wove insecurity into my psyche. My mother believed that with this soap, we could erase the reality that I was a brown body living in sun-drenched California. She, like my grandmother, worried about my dark skin. While they were both endowed with pale skin, I inherited my father's skin—the type of skin shared by Filipino workers who labor in the fields under the relentless sun. I think my mother was ashamed of my skin; for in our culture, skin color is synonymous with social class. By one's shade of brown, social status is visually discerned and cemented.

As Filipino immigrants, my parents also worried that the color of our skin would complicate our transition into American society and, hence, our future financial success. Suffering from a colonized mentality, they believed that regardless of how my siblings and I dressed, how kind we rendered our faces, how stellar our academic profiles, or how many extracurricular activities we logged, none of this would ever be enough to erase what people would see first—the color of our skin.

This became motive to push us further; we had to do more, to do the best even, to differentiate ourselves from the other dark-skinned minorities in America. Our individual qualities that, rightfully, should have determined our successes remained invisible. Rather, what my parents saw were all the things that we were not, all the things that marked us as different from the "better" American children—those who were white, blonde, and blue-eyed.

My mother understood early on what qualities were needed to advance in the Western world. She recognized them because she had been taught them well before her arrival to American shores, back when she still lived in the Philippines. There, Western colonization already had a firm grip upon the island culture. The Philippines was colonized by Spain for nearly four hundred years, during which the indoctrination of preference for Western, Eurocentric traits was introduced, enforced, and solidified. This was not with beauty alone. To speak one's native tongue as opposed to Castilian Spanish indicated one's peasantry class; to practice one's ancestral spirituality was a direct offense to Spanish Catholicism and, in many cases, capitally punished; and one's outward appearance (skin color) dictated whether one belonged to the upper echelon of society or was from the *barangays*, or barrios. Filipinos watched those of Spanish descent (including mestizos, those with mixed native and Spanish blood) reap the rewards of society and ascend the social ladder.

To achieve upward mobility, Filipinos learned that all things native were inferior, while all things European were to be held in high esteem. Because the brainwashing of Filipinos started many centuries ago, my mother and grandmother already understood the value of whiteness long before they arrived to America.

The additional information they received upon migration only compounded this understanding. They saw first-hand the ugly ways in which dark-skinned people were viewed and treated in America—with contempt, condescension, and discrimination. Perceptions of danger, threat, and distrust were not lost on them, and rather than question the morality or verity of the stereotypes, my mother and grandmother worried that we would be lumped into the very same category. They wanted nothing more than to prove that we were outstanding representatives of the American citizen—mirrors to the successful white Americans who epitomized the United States; they wanted, essentially, the pinnacle of the immigrant dream, the portrait of American (white) success.

Thinking about my mother's struggle, I realize that it was not just that we couldn't be white but also that we didn't fit the next best thing: the "model minority" stereotype that held Asian Americans up as a "model" for other groups of color. This affluent "model minority" is often imagined in the United States as East Asian, wealthy, highly educated, and, most importantly, light-skinned— wealth and skin tone intertwined and seemingly inseparable. We did not look the part, so my mother struggled under the weight of this knowledge.

As I've grown, I've watched her struggle, and I have felt the weight of her pain in my own body. I remained unaware for so long of how I had begun to embody the same expectations, failures, and frustrations. In the way that my mother disapproved of her own body, I had begun to do the same. Growing up, I was constantly bothered that I didn't look like the stereotypical Asian. The bulk of my teenage years were spent trying to stay out of the sun and trying to do my makeup in such a way as to make my eyes appear more Asian—both actions being forms of visual modification. I actively went out of my way to befriend more light-skinned Asians and become more informed about East Asian culture, as if there were a way I could have integrated and hid myself into the "better" culture. I am more aware now of how I was performing a self-erasure, trying to minimize the parts of myself that were Hispanicized Filipino and make more clear the aspects that were aligned with model Asian appearance.

When I was in high school, I dated a Korean boy. In a moment of brutal honesty, he confessed to me that the relationship couldn't, and wouldn't, go anywhere. When pressed as to why, he evaded my question with a new one: "How could it?" He then launched into the passive, dismissive, yet inevitable truth that he was Korean and I was a dark-skinned Asian. How could he ever bring someone like me home?

"Could you imagine?" he pointedly asked.

The realization that I would never be the type of girl that a light-skinned Asian man could "take home" horrified me. It was something that I felt certain I had to correct even though I knew I could not erase my skin, my features, or my country's history. His words also highlighted another uncomfortable truth: the hierarchies that exist between Asian American ethnic groups regarding skin color and the taboos of light-skinned (often East Asian) groups dating and intermarrying with those from South, Southeast, and Pacific Islander Asia. Colorism is rampant within my own community, but also across Asian America, positioning Asian ethnic groups along their own social hierarchy and, at times, pitting them against each other. As I look back now, I cannot blame him for his words; he was, like me, chained by a culture steeped in colorism.

Even today, I often find myself locked in an internal meditation, sorting what beliefs are genuinely my own from what was culturally passed to me—both from my Filipino and from my American cultures. Growing up in America, I learned that I was not beautiful in a Western way—and through my interactions with other Asians, I learned that I did not fit the Eastern standard either.

Today, the voice of Asian America grows louder, and with growing diversity and multiculturalism in America, I am beginning to understand that our definitions of beauty matter.

Those young years of defining self-worth come and pass quickly, and who I am now is heavily informed by my struggles. What I once understood as markers of negative difference, I am now beginning to view with reverence. As America experiences the cultural shift of women and minorities becoming more persistent in voicing their discontent with the incongruities of equality sewn into the fabric of our society, I have become empowered by my uniqueness. We are still finding the language in which to address the ways we internalize cultural expectations and all the negative connotations that come with this, but with each step forward, we are becoming more aware, more empowered, more persistent.

As we go, I watch with delight the shifts that happen for me internally, erasing the things that I had once allowed to erase myself.

Part IV

ANTI-
BLACKNESS

When Ariana Miyamoto was crowned Miss Universe Japan in 2015, she broke unspoken barriers. She was born and raised in Japan and is a Japanese citizen, though she was no ordinary Japanese beauty queen—primarily because she was born to a Japanese mother and an African American father. Because of her racial background, her win garnered international attention, and many in Japan openly questioned her Japaneseness: "Is it OK to select a *hafu* [a half-Japanese person] to represent Japan?"; "Miss Universe Japan is . . . what?"; "Even though she's Miss Universe Japan, her face is foreign no matter how you look at it."[1] Her mixed-race background drew both interest and criticism, though Martin Fackler of the *New York Times* argues that "experts on pageants say it is precisely because she is half black that she has gotten so much attention" because her victory "overturned an unspoken hierarchy . . . in which those with lighter skin color have long been celebrated as the most beautiful."[2] Had she been part-white, she might have received similar criticisms, though the intensity of the backlash might have been markedly different. For many, and perhaps for Ariana Miyamoto herself, there may be no doubt that her blackness and dark skin were the primary issues of contention.

In the previous section, authors discussed colorism within the context of aspirational whiteness; in this section, authors explore anti-blackness and its connection to skin-color discrimination among Asian Americans. Anti-black sentiment exists in many parts of the world, including the United States, Asia, and Asian America, as blackness is juxtaposed in direct opposition to whiteness and is linked with a host of negative stereotypes and degrading racist tropes. While whiteness (and light skin) is often associated with superiority, intelligence, and beauty, blackness (and dark skin) is frequently linked to inferiority, lack of intelligence, backwardness, ugliness, and dirtiness. In addition to anti-black stereotypes, those of African descent also face blatant discrimination worldwide, including across Asia.

In India, for example, Africans are commonly stereotyped as "prostitutes," "cannibals," and "people snatchers."[3] In 2017, young Africans studying in Indian universities shared their personal stories of being targets of racial slurs, verbal threats, physical aggression, brutal assaults, and even mob violence. Nigerian chemistry student Zaharaddeen Muhammad spoke of daily verbal abuse on the streets of Greater Noida, near Delhi, such as, "Hey *Bandar* [Hey monkey]," and other Africans described endless stares and aggressive posturing by Indian locals, and general perceptions of feeling unsafe in public spaces.[4] A 2013 survey by the *Washington Post* found India to be one of the least racially tolerant countries in the world,[5] and widely reported racial attacks in recent years further reveal the deep prejudices specifically against Africans in India. In 2014, a mob of Indian men attacked three African university students in a Delhi metro station with fists and sticks, while shouting "Bharat Mata Ki Jai!" or "Victory for Mother India!"[6] In 2016, a twenty-one-year-old Tanzanian woman was stripped naked and beaten in Bengaluru by a mob of locals, purportedly as revenge for a car accident caused by a Sudanese man (under the assumption that because both were black, they must have known each other). While in the hospital, she told reporters, "We are now scared of every Indian around us."[7] In the same year, a Congolese national was beaten to death in New Delhi by a mob of men over a dispute regarding the hiring of a rickshaw; his friend said it was a "clear hate crime, with racial epithets repeatedly invoked."[8] Nimisha Jaiswal, a reporter based in India, warns, "Being black in India can be deadly."[9]

Anti-blackness exists in other parts of Asia as well—including China, which in 2018 banned hip hop, a music and dance genre rooted in African American culture, from television and popular streaming sites, as part of a crackdown on what the government deemed "low taste content."[10] Rappers, even Chinese rappers, were censored, and fans of the popular television show *Super Brian*, which is not hip hop related, watched as one contestant had his hip hop style necklace blurred out.[11] A few years prior, anti-black racism was evident in an ad for a Chinese laundry detergent deemed by some as perhaps the "most racist ad ever."[12] In the spot for the Chinese detergent brand Qiaobi, a beautiful Chinese woman playfully beckons a black man, splattered with paint, towards her. Once she lures him close enough for a kiss, she pops a detergent pod into his mouth and shoves him into the washing machine. When he emerges, voila! He is squeaky clean and rises from the machine magically transformed into an Asian man! The linkage of blackness with dirt is a reflection of broader anti-black sentiment, and the ad arguably a symptom of the deep prejudice towards black people in China and across Asia.

Some argue that the homogeneity and lack of diversity in some parts of Asia explain anti-black bias; perhaps limited contact with other racial groups is the real culprit here. A. Moore writes that those of African descent visiting China should not be surprised if they are stared at, or swarmed by locals snapping their photo, touching their hair, rubbing their skin, and asking them a litany of questions that "reflect their ignorance and lack of interaction" with black people.[13] However, while those of African descent typically face prejudice and discrimination, it bears notice that whites are often on the receiving end of praise, positive attention, and shows of respect, suggesting that lack of interaction is not the only explanation for anti-blackness. Asians in some parts of Asia have limited contact with both blacks and whites (as well as other racial groups), though the treatment of blacks is markedly different than that of other racial groups.

In Taiwan in 2008, one prestigious private school advertised on social media for substitute English teachers to teach four- and five-year-olds in New Taipei City. In addition to routine information about salary and location was a postscript inserted by the poster of the advert: "The school has informed me that it will not accept applications from people who are not from predominantly English speaking countries, or who are black or dark skinned."[14] The job requirement reportedly sparked outrage among the expat community in Taiwan after the ad went viral on social media. Though the ad is a clear example of blatant racism, a closer look at Taiwan reveals deep complexities in the treatments of blacks. Nicole Cooper, African American, blogged about her experiences living in Taiwan and describes them as *both* positive and negative. The majority of her interactions with locals have been positive and affirming. Though she stands out in Taiwan because of the racial homogeny there (she says that "being black in Asia is like being a unicorn"), she finds locals to be polite and sometimes even complimentary of her hair and skin. She admits, however, that when it comes to English-speaking jobs (especially in education), white employees are most preferred because a "white is right" mentality exists in Taiwan.[15]

Dave Hazzan, in a piece on anti-black racism in South Korea, takes a harsher perspective on racism there, observing that "one way or another, racism affects almost every foreigner in Korea [regardless of race]. But being black here is different. Whether African-American, African, or not even black but mistaken for it, experiences in Korea are tainted by the perception that blacks are lower than other races. Blacks are violent, unintelligent, and poor. Black Americans are not really American, and inappropriate teachers for Korean children. Africans live in a backward, single African country, consisting of little more than a jungle. Certainly these views are not universal, but they are commonly heard in Korea."[16] Hazzan reports on the struggles of black teachers in finding employment in Korea, their difficulty hailing taxis, their daily harassment in public spaces, as well as stories of Koreans refusing to share elevators or subway cars with them. Moreover, visitors to South Korea often learn that the "No Foreigners Allowed" rule for some bars and clubs generally means "no black foreigners," while white people "enter just fine."[17]

Sam Okyere, a Ghanaian television personality and arguably the most famous black man in Korea, speaks of his early experiences in South Korea before achieving celebrity status—people stared at him everywhere he went, taxi and bus drivers would not pick him up, and fellow travelers on the subway refused to sit next to him. Describing his more "innocent" interactions with Korean children, he says, "The little kids would come and try to lick your skin thinking it's chocolate. Some children when they see me they try to take a napkin and clean my skin. They think by doing so it's going to turn white or get lighter or cleaner."[18] Lack of interactions with black people partially explains the prejudices there, but so do persistent negative stereotypes of black people.

Moreover, anti-black racism is not simply a problem confined to Asia, but is also an issue found within Asian American communities. Some of the anti-black racism found in Asian American communities is transported over in the "baggage" from Asia itself as Asians migrate to America, though Asian immigrants also learn anti-blackness upon their arrival to American shores. According to writer Jezzika Chung in 2017, "As Asian immigrants work toward building successes in a foreign environment, they begin taking cues from the people they see as most successful. Because [of] America's historical oppression of people of color, these people are usually white. To many Asian Americans, whiteness often becomes equated to success, and all of the elements that have been conditioned to come with the paradigms of whiteness. One of those, historically speaking, has been anti-blackness." She argues that Asian Americans must recognize that the fight for social justice for black Americans is linked to their own struggles for equality and justice. Asian Americans may think of themselves as "better than" black people, though she reminds us that Asian Americans are frequently seen as "perpetual foreigners" rather than "true Americans."[19] Further, Kim Chanbonpin, a law professor at the University of Chicago, maintains that Asian American desires to move up the social ladder often center on anti-black racism and the belief that in order to move up the ladder, "they must step on the shoulders of Blacks and then not pull them up, but crush them heel to head."[20] Of course, they do not *have* to step on black Americans on their way up, but perhaps this is their perception in our race-based, competition-oriented, capitalist society.

Furthermore, racial stereotypes learned in the United States, both negative and positive, contribute to anti-black sentiment among Asian Americans. Black-white relations in America, with the legacy of slavery and Jim Crow segregation, have been particularly contentious, and negative stereotypes of American blacks abound. Anti-black stereotypes are broad and deep in American society, and routinely reinforced through mass media platforms such as American film, television, music, and even social media (certainly this list is not exhaustive). No African American, no matter how powerful, rich, or successful, is immune. Former US president Barack Obama, multiracial with black and white ancestry, faced a barrage of racist stereotypes spread through social media leading up to and during his eight-year presidency (e.g., they were frequently portrayed in ape- and monkey-like depictions), and his wife, Michelle Obama, was called "an ape in heels" by a sitting West Virginia mayor.[21] The association of apes and monkeys with American blacks is a longstanding racist trope in the United States and endures even today. Comedian Roseanne Barr's widely popular rebooted sitcom, *Roseanne*, was abruptly canceled in 2018 after a single season when she publicly insinuated on Twitter that one of Obama's former senior advisors, a woman with African ancestry, was an ape. Because of these negative stereotypes and dehumanizing characterizations, it should be no surprise that Asian Americans would want to distance themselves from American blacks.

Moreover, even a seemingly positive stereotype, such as the "model minority" stereotype often ascribed to Asian Americans, contributes to anti-blackness. The stereotype asserts that Asian Americans are highly successful economically in America and should be held up as a "model" for other minorities to emulate, including African Americans, though the stereotype is highly problematic and misleading. Journalist Chris Fuchs argues that the "model minority" stereotype masks wide economic disparities among Asian Americans (as described in Part III), and causes great anxiety and stress among second-generation Asian American children who are expected to live up to the image.[22] According to Suman Raghunathan, executive director of South Asian Americans

Leading Together (SAALT), the "model minority stereotype" is "not just a myth, but really a farce,"[23] and perhaps an intended by-product of the stereotype is its divisiveness among people of color. According to the stereotype, if Asian Americans can work hard and be successful, so too can black Americans; if blacks cannot achieve financial success, then (as the stereotype contends) there must be something wrong with them—laziness, lack of desire, or even lack of intelligence—while, at the same time, the stereotype glosses over several hundred years of institutional discrimination directed at those of African descent (e.g., slavery, Jim Crow segregation, and well-documented institutional discrimination that persists today). This narrative positions Asian Americans as a "better" racial group, while willfully ignoring Asian ethnic groups who do not fit the model minority stereotype; it also conditions those of Asian descent to see themselves as superior to American blacks and even blame blacks when they do not achieve comparable educational and financial success. Hence, what is intended to be a positive stereotype of Asian Americans (though deeply flawed and outright false) serves as a further catalyst for anti-black bias.

In a 2017 *Jet* article about anti-blackness among Asians and Asian Americans, contributor Tyrus Townsend further claims that anti-blackness is entwined with an aversion to dark skin. He writes, "The rejection of brown bodies seems to live within [Asian American] communities,"[24] which, I argue, is clearly problematic for African Americans, but also for those Asian Americans with dark skin. Perhaps the disdain for brown bodies, even their own, can be observed in former Louisiana governor Bobby Jindal, Indian American and brown skinned, who made headlines in 2015 when a portrait of him hanging in the state capitol portrayed him with white skin. One cultural commentator facetiously asked, "Was brown paint busy when they created this Bobby Jindal portrait?"[25] and Twitter users joked, "Who's the white guy?" and "Will they be releasing the colorized version?" Even Jindal himself, responding to the backlash, asked in jest, "You mean I'm not white?" though he downplayed the flap and described the criticism of the painting as "silly."[26] This was not the only time, however, that Jindal's skin was front and center; another self-portrait that hung in his office similarly appeared whitewashed, and some wondered if his skin in official government photographs had been lightened.[27] Perhaps Bobby Jindal's case is an anomaly, though research suggests that dark skin is reviled among Asian Americans and self-disdain, especially among those with dark skin, may not be uncommon.

In this collection of essays, women write about anti-blackness in their Asian/Asian American communities and how anti-black racism is closely entwined with the aversion to dark skin in their respective ethnic groups and in their own families. Sairah Husain, Pakistani American, writes about creationist stories embedded in Pakistani culture (i.e., stories about God's creation of different races), which, she argues, reinforce anti-blackness and colorism among Pakistanis and Pakistani Americans. Further, she contends that dark skin is equated with blackness and dirt, thus contributing to "self-hate [that] trickle[s] down from generation to generation." Wendy Thompson Taiwo, who is multiracial Chinese and black, writes about anti-blackness in American society and in her Chinese American community. She considers "what it means to be brown" in America, how anti-black racism is tied to disdain for dark skin, and how her dark skin and black ancestry have shaped her life. Blackness in America is tied to a host of negative stereotypes with which, as a multiracial woman, she must constantly contend. Finally, Marimas Hosan Mostiller, Cham American and mother of a multiracial child, wonders if her child, Asian and black, will experience life as a "perpetual outsider" because of her blackness and dark skin. She describes the anti-black racism she sees in her Cambodian American community and in the United States, and considers what this will mean for her daughter's future.

16

Creation Stories

Sairah Husain, PAKISTANI AMERICAN, 30

Galoshes splashing through muddy puddles, my older sister Aafia ran home from Bus 59 distraught and drenched. Her tears flowed faster than the precipitation that Monday afternoon.

"They said I'm too dark, Mamoo," she blubbered about her classmates' taunts. Mamoo attempted to decipher his niece's words through muffled, snotty slurps, and despite the challenge, he caught the gist.

Now my family wasn't unaware of or inexperienced with the racism directed toward people of color in the United States. They had had their fair share of it—twice or thrice was more than enough to understand the racial lay of the land. During the height of the first Gulf War, patients frequently associated my physician parents' "Husain" surname with the black sheep of our "family"— Uncle Saddam. Humor effectively eviscerates racism. Thanks, Jon Stewart, Trevor Noah, and 2 Dope Queens.

Back to the blubbering.

In an attempt to console his niece, Mamoo relayed to her a story that he had been told by his parents: "When Allah was creating us human beings out of clay, He had to bake us in the oven. The white people, you see, Aafia, Allah took them out of the oven too early. As for the black people, Allah burnt them. And us brown-skinned people? Well, Allah took us out of the oven in perfect time. We're juuust right."

Her pain alleviated from the kindergarten bullying, Aafia triumphantly strode into her classroom the next day with the story that shocked her classmates.

≈

"Everyone can see your thong tan lines!" Mumani exclaims. She is referring to the light, triangular marks left in the ruins of the surrounding blackened skin on my feet, not my ass. "How can you tolerate these stripes on your skin?"

My aunt's words were inspired by my vivid tan lines, her diatribe followed by orders to vigorously scrub my feet. It's telling, I reflect, that darkened skin from the sun's penetration is equated to dirt that can be scrubbed off.

But Mumani, like every human being, has context. She grew up in Hyderabad, a former princely state in India. I have never visited Hyderabad, yet it is part of me. Growing up, I've learned that colorism seems to comfortably coexist with the culture. As children, many of us were fed the overly simplistic story of a ruling elite Muslim class with "Arab and Persian blood," light-skinned, who invaded and conquered the "indigenous dark Dravidian race" of the Indian subcontinent; this historically inaccurate narrative continues to dominate the discourse on colorism and fosters divisions among us. But isn't fostering divisions among oppressed communities a goal of colonialism? Though I ponder—it is one thing to assign blame for our collective self-hate to the British. It is another to jettison all responsibility, while we, at the same time, perpetuate the colorism ourselves. Whatever explanation I can think of is deficient.

So there is context, but there is also the reality that feelings of self-hate trickle down from generation to generation. The "dirt" associated with tanning brown skin is real. For me, there is nothing wrong with my "black" toes. I look at my feet as I respond to Mumani, "But they're not even black."

Why is whiteness our standard?

≈

She proceeded with skillful intonation, gesticulating with drama and a forceful voice. Annette, a white-presenting Argentinian literature professor, came into the library reference area at my workplace with some questions. It also seemed as though she simply wanted to chat with my coworker and I about our cultural backgrounds, and she was reminded of a story: "God was baking human beings in His large creation oven. He took us out at separate times, so our skin was different shades. White-skinned humans were tossed in Europe, Brown-skinned humans in the Middle East, and Black-skinned humans were tossed in Africa."

Upon hearing that I too had a version of the story, Annette concluded her telling with, "What's your version?"

I led with, "It's super anti-black but . . ."

"This is how you ruin a story! You do not lead with a conclusion. Build it up. Let your listeners come to their own conclusions."

She came to that very conclusion.

≈

I reflect upon how racial harmony or solidarity does not exist within a vacuum; it is often oppositional to some oppressive reality. But what if the "oppressed" take on "oppressor" qualities? In my family, I'll say with certainty that we have absorbed anti-black sentiment as a legacy of colonial education.

My skin isn't light enough.

My hair is too curly.

And how do I make my lips appear less full?

American fashion magazines instruct their readers to wear dark lipstick to make full lips appear smaller. I comply. So while color- ism and all its ugliness can be inherited, what about individual accountability for these mindsets?

I call out myself first.

≈

The sun's rays warmed the skin under my sandals on a Friday morning this past September. My Venezuelan college friend was summoned to the Immigration and Customs Enforcement (ICE) Detention and Deportation Center for a random check-in to review her DACA[1] status. We walked briskly to the building, her breath shortening from anxiety. Why this check-in? This was the second one in the past year, and it must be due to the policies of our Orange-in-Chief (how did Allah go about baking him?).

Having left our cell phones in the car because they are banned in the center, we walked through the metal detector beep-free. The waiting room was icy silent, as immigrants (most of them, at least here, brown) watched the doors to the ICE offices swing open and shut, patiently waiting for decisions on their fates. After entering the office for the check-in, I sat with my friend opposite the stocky, lightly baked ICE officer with the buzz cut—a massive American flag and patriotic slogans emblazoned across his office wall. Staring at the huge red, white, and blue flag that for many symbolizes whiteness, I was reminded of the creation story of America, which prides itself on being "one Nation, under God, indivisible, with liberty and justice for all." So, what about my friend's potential deportation from a country she's known as home for most of her life? Just like Mamoo's creation story reinforcing colorism and anti-blackness, the creation narrative of this nation is a myth that similarly reinforces these mentalities.

When will whiteness not be our standard?

17

What It Means to Be Brown

Wendy Thompson Taiwo, MULTIRACIAL
CHINESE/BLACK AMERICAN, 36

When I was a little girl, I wanted to look just like my mother. Her brown laughing eyes were always in a partial squint—the kind of eyes my white classmates would mock my Asian classmates for having, their dirty pink fingers pulling down their eyelids—and her skin was the color of aged bone. I thought she was the most beautiful person in the world. She had arrived to the United States in 1974, a Chinese immigrant whose baby face hardly needed the rough scratch of red she drew across her lips or powdery dabs of blue and green shadow that she layered above her eyes to "make herself look pretty." Yet she would continue the practice, teaching me through each application that a woman must always make herself attractive to her husband or else he would leave. It was a private ritual between us: me sitting on the bed watching her apply makeup, and her gazing at her face in the mirror. And I would go on believing that a woman's appearance could keep her house intact until the day my father left her.

Growing up, it didn't matter to me that I didn't look like my mother until other people pointed it out. Then I was forced to explain myself and our relationship to those who were often demanding and rude in their inquiry. "Who is that woman?" they would ask me. "That's your mom? You're lying," classmates would accuse. On shopping trips to Oakland Chinatown, men and women behind counters and cash registers would force my mother to respond to their curiosity—"Is this your daughter?"—before extending her service or allowing her to collect her purchase. Constantly, strangers would question us—*How? How?*—searching for answers about our biological connection until I realized that their questions were less about understanding how we were related and more about policing racial boundaries and sexual transgressions—specifically, the interracial relationship of my Chinese mother and my black American father. This also meant that of all their questions asked, there was one unuttered question that troubled them the most: *Why would your mother choose to be with a black man?*

This particular question would trail me into adulthood, arising whenever I was with my mother. It was my body—visibly mixed-race and black—that revealed her sexual history and led others to assume my father's sexual dominance and my mother's physical ruin. It was my body that made Chinese people uncomfortable, disrupting their beliefs that Chinese people should only choose each other as intimate partners or, if they crossed racial lines, should do so only with white people, whom a history of racist state policies had disproportionally granted excess social authority, political autonomy, the highest property values, and the best financial credit. It continues to be my body, and reactions to it, that reveal the pervasiveness of anti-blackness within Asian America and among Asian immigrants who see blackness as undesirable; many would do anything to avoid black adjacency in the same country that treats blackness as a liability and black people as disposable. After all, anti-blackness remains at the core of American citizenship and requires that all immigrants assume what writer Toni Morrison refers to as a "hostile posture" against black people "at the Americanizing door before it will open."[1]

Finding myself routinely dismissed by Chinese people who told me that I wasn't *really* Chinese or who implied that my mother's desires and choices were shameful would convince me that immigrants of color who had been allowed through the "Americanizing door" would not hesitate to repay their hosts for entry, and that this repayment would be made through their complicity in the (re)production of social exclusion and state violence against me and other vulnerable black, brown, and indigenous people. At the same time, the evidence of my body and the anti-black harm it has experienced would convince me that there is nothing that my mother or anyone else could offer to settle the material and symbolic debt black people have had to pay and continue to pay for our blackness in a white-supremacist settler-colonial nation.

Like me, so many black women are forced to accept their lack of social power and diminished sexual desirability rather than recognize that powerlessness and devaluation are consequences of living in a racist, capitalist system that places black women at the center of under- and uncompensated servile labor, bodily and environmental degradation, systemic violence, and targeted disposal. Through European colonial expansion, New World slavery, and the creation of a racial regime in which whiteness equated with freedom and positive value, blackness became synonymous with generational enslavement and social death. This was followed by numerous local and legal attempts to police and defend racial boundaries, including the violent exclusion of black people from white neighborhoods and the criminalization of interracial sex in order to preserve the purity, integrity, and market value of whiteness. All of this would make clear that nonwhiteness, but especially blackness, was considered inherently threatening due to its potential to contaminate and degrade.

Thus, to be black and a woman in America is not only to carry the burden of history but to contend with a long litany of stereotypes: black women are inherently nurturing and therefore naturally suited for the care of others whose needs they put before their own, even at the expense of their own well-being; black women are less desirable and therefore desperate for the validation and companionship of men from whom they are willing to tolerate mistreatment, betrayal, and abuse; black women are masculine, aggressive, and loud, and must be put back "in their place," with force if necessary; black women are generally incompetent and therefore inadvisable to hire, retain, or promote, and if they happen to be in professional settings, it is solely because there was a need to fill a diversity quota; black women are disposable, and when they disappear, you will not even notice that they are missing, unlike the white girl abducted in Aruba more than a decade ago whose name and face you can still easily recall.

As a mixed-race black and Asian woman whose light brown complexion, ethnically ambiguous appearance (Asian-appearing eyes and long, dark, wavy hair), performance of middle-class whiteness, and academic credentials allow me to evade some of the more vile and pervasive public mistreatment and institutional abuses experienced by my black female counterparts, I am forced to consider the symbolic and material ways in which I benefit from colorism. With the ability to enter more easily into spaces that are predominantly white and exclusive, it becomes clear that my acceptance is conditional and dependent upon my ability to be unintimidating and assessable to white people: playing audience to their moral outrage and simultaneous lack of action regarding educational inequality or mass incarceration, listening earnestly when they explain why institutional racism isn't really institutional racism, being expected to acknowledge them for being less racist than other white people, and keeping a straight face when they allude to me making them feel comfortable because they perceive me as nonthreatening. But then again, given the history of this nation, how could I, a brown-skinned woman, expected to validate, reassure, forgive, teach, and love my oppressor, not have been in service to them?

Since moving into my thirties, I have felt increasingly weighed down by both the mundane (the ease at which a racist comment is slipped into conversation) and the sensational (witnessing second-hand the police murder of another black person). On days when it feels impossible to carry any more, I call my mother and tell her about the latest incident: a comment at work, a gaze at the grocery store, a body on the news, a phone call from my daughter's school. And while she tries to soothe me, she tells me repeatedly, "It's a white man's country anyway. What did you expect?" Perhaps I ex-pected to be the unique individual I was told I was throughout grade school by my white "color-blind" teachers who supposedly saw my character but not my race. Perhaps I expected to be free from the afterlife of slavery that continues to shorten and degrade black life, barring me and my children from the same degree of personal free-dom and material comfort that my white middle-class neighbors are afforded. Or perhaps it was simply the expectation of being affirmed in the arms of my parents: black, Chinese, emancipated, immigrant, hard-working, American-dreaming, house-proud people.

But because the reality of racism precludes my individuality, because the afterlife of slavery is all around us, because my parents continue to carry the weight of generational trauma and internalized shame, I find myself facing the world alone without my parents' arms able to hold the whole of me.

My mother, now a senior citizen, has been joined by an influx of affluent Chinese women who have moved into her suburban East Bay neighborhood and refuse to leave their near-million-dollar homes without their protective sun visors or parasols. I see them everywhere: getting in and out of cars in the 99 Ranch Market parking lot, jostling each other in line at the Taiwanese bakery, dropping off children at the local library. Like them, my mother has begun donning visors and applying sunscreen while giving me porous answers as to why: because she doesn't want to get sunburned, because she doesn't want any more wrinkles, because she doesn't want to get skin cancer. Beneath it all, though, what she doesn't say is that despite being my mother, she never wanted to look like me. No longer the child, I watch as a new ritual plays out between my mother and my youngest sister, whose complexion is lighter than mine. The objective has changed. It is no longer makeup, but hats to shield the sun from their faces and the application of sunscreen to prevent cancer and wrinkles, and perhaps most importantly, to prevent the slow creep of brown from spreading across the skin.

To be beautiful. To be desired. To be chosen. To be protected from predatory practices and racist policies. To safeguard one's children from structural harm and deliver them into elite private schools that promise increased social capital and high-paying futures. To be visible. To be treated courteously in the supermarket checkout line. To never answer to people's assumptions that you are the help. To have value. To be included in society's understanding of who is human and has a life that matters. Locked in their ritual, my mother and my sister won't tell me that these, too, are the reasons they protect their skin.

In learning how to value and hold myself, I have begun prioritizing my need to be abundant and loving towards myself and others, especially to my two young children, who will spend their lifetimes grappling with what it means to be brown-skinned black people in this country. I tell my children that the people whose ancestors created a racial system that elevated their own humanity while denying ours will see our skin and all that has been mapped onto it. They will judge us despite our punctuality and consumption of fair trade coffee and grass-fed meat. No matter how perfect our diction, advanced our degrees, and good our financial habits, none of these will save us from institutional harm or structural erasure. But against all of this, my children should never forget that they are valuable and that their value is quantified outside of existing capitalist measurements like work status, income level, and property ownership; their value exists beyond the racial measurement of whiteness.

As a people, we have been subjected to the cataclysmic destruction of our worlds, and yet we can point to the constellation of traditions that still live within us. As people, we have been pressed into all the corners of the earth as human tools of colonial and capitalist expansion, and yet we have found ways to continue shaping our children's dreams. We are music. We are bone—solid, fragile, living—one day to return to the earth. We are the length of our origin stories, unraveling. Exposed to sunlight, the cells in our bodies produce melanin, causing our skin to radiate with the rays of the star at the center of our solar system. Through this, we become heat, we become light, we become energy. I tell my children, *This is what it means to exist in this century, on this earth, in this skin.* To be at once the entirety of and more than the struggle of our people. To inherit life in a nation that was never designed to sustain us, in which we grow wild and unapologetic in the face of brutality and social death. *This,* I tell them, *from the collective to the cellular level, is what it means to be brown.*

18

The Perpetual Outsider

Marimas Hosan Mostiller, CHAM AMERICAN, 32

When my daughter was born I immediately fell in love. She
was beautiful. At birth, she looked just like me: a light-skinned
Southeast Asian American. As she got older, however, it became
apparent that she was going to look more like her father, who is
African American; her skin tone grew darker, her eyes became
bigger, and her hair began to curl. Even though she does not look
like me, she is beautiful.

We currently live in Hawai'i, which is somewhat insulated from
the growing racial strife in the continental United States. Hawai'i is
considered relatively more diverse because of its large population
of people of color, though most of the residents are Asian or white.
Native Hawaiians make up only 10 percent of the population,
and the African American and Latinx populations are minuscule.
Hawai'i also has the most multiracial people in any US state
(almost a quarter of the population); many are "*hapa*" (a Hawaiian
term), which commonly refers to those of partial Asian ancestry,
though the term typically refers to those with Asian/white backgrounds.[1] My multiracial daughter will fit in in Hawai'i as long as
her skin tone allows her to be seen as Asian, Polynesian, or *hapa*.
If her tone appears to be black, she'll be a perpetual outsider. I am
painfully aware of this and other cruelties that my daughter, who
is so innocent and full of life, will face in the world because of her
dark skin.

I know this because I also grew up in a community that preferred
light skin over dark.

≈

I am a light-skinned, second-generation Cham American[2] whose parents were refugees from the Khmer Rouge genocide in Cambodia in the 1970s. I grew up in a Cham Muslim community in Southern California surrounded mostly by Mexicans as well as Khmer and Cham folks from Cambodia. As kids from varying backgrounds thrown together by circumstances, mainly poverty, children befriended those outside their racial and ethnic communities, but each community inscribed its own racial and ethnic hierarchy that placed their own group at the top. Within my own community, I learned early on that there was a hierarchy based on skin color, ethnicity, and religion. In summer, when children tanned from swimming at the community pool, Cham children were often derogatorily called "Khmer" by older Cham folks; I quickly learned that the term "Khmer" was a euphemism meant to disparage anyone who was dark-skinned or not "full-blooded" Cham. In fact, some of my relatives who are not "full-blooded" Cham have been ridiculed as being Khmer (especially if they had dark skin)—even though they are not ethnically Khmer.

In the Cham Muslim community the hierarchy is: light skin over dark, but Muslim over all things. This is especially important when one seeks a mate to marry. My dad told me, and I have heard this from other folks in my community, "It's fine if you marry a *joo* [black] guy, as long as he's Muslim." Depending upon the tone of the word "*joo*," it can be an insult or term of endearment, but whatever the context, it always implies otherness.

When I visited my maternal aunt for the first time with my one-year-old daughter, my aunt called her "*mu joo*" (loosely translated: black girl). While her words reinforced my family's status as "outsiders" (because I married a non-Muslim black man), I wasn't offended; I understood that she meant those words lovingly as she scooped up my daughter, and hugged and kissed her. But I also know that her words also reflect the view that other community members may have about my daughter as someone who is an outsider: someone who is non-Muslim and non-Cham.

Why is there so much anti-black rhetoric within my community and other Southeast Asian communities? In Will Jackson's 2014 article "Beneath the Skin: The Reality of Being Black in Cambodia," people of African descent living in Cambodia discussed their experiences of racism given the "cultural preference for light skin" among Cambodians. Black skin is often equated with immorality, as one teacher of African descent discovered: "I remember I was in the market one day and I heard one woman say that because I have dark skin my heart is dark and I'm probably an evil person." Several black women also recounted stories of Khmer nationals being surprised that they were so attractive for a black person, and one woman remarked, "I get people coming up to me saying: 'Oh, you're pretty . . . but you're black. You're so dark.'" Others discussed experiences of overt discrimination, such as being charged extra fees for visas, or being blatantly rejected by an employer because of their dark skin. One individual also stated, "I did have an 'elite Khmer' acquaintance who asked if he could say 'n——er' around me because he says it all the time to his friends. I had to tell him no, obviously." Anti-black racism occurs regularly in Cambodia, probably because most Cambodians have limited contact with black people. Arguably, the majority of negative racially based encounters are rooted in a lack of cultural awareness, though perhaps anti-blackness runs deeper. For example, while Cambodians avoid black people because of perceived negative stereotypes, they conversely flock around white foreigners because they are viewed as wealthy (even if they are not). These interactions, or lack thereof, reveal that blackness is perceived as socially inferior to whiteness in Cambodia.

From my experiences, anti-blackness exists even among Southeast Asian Americans, and I've found that my community has a love/hate relationship with blackness. Southeast Asian Americans often seek out and culturally appropriate black culture (through music, dance, dress, lingo, slang) and easily say the N-word, but at the same time, avoid interaction with actual black folks. I was once at a party where some Southeast Asian Americans were throwing around the N-word without any regard. Someone apologized to me about using the word in front of me because my boyfriend (now husband) was black.

This experience reminds me of Dustin Tahmahkera's 2008 article "Custer's Last Sitcom," in which he discusses how whites and people of color culturally appropriate Native culture by "playing Indian."[3] The portrayal of Native peoples in popular media and sports produces and reproduces the stereotypical image of the red-faced, howling, savage, or noble Indian. Tahmahkera argues that people of color, too, have appropriated the "white man's 'Indian'" by accepting Native American stereotypes.[4] I argue that people of color have also appropriated the white man's black man. This appropriation submits itself to a stereotypical version of blackness—thus, the imaginings of black folks by Southeast Asians (as with whites) is one-dimensional and associated with ghettos, "ghetto" behavior, hip hop, and street talk. In these images, there is little to no diversity in American blackness. And just as some put on red face paint to play Indian, these party-goers put on the "face" of being black through unabashed cultural appropriation.

The irony is that, as children of refugees, many of us have experienced poverty and the ghetto, but due to adopting the white man's view of black people, many would be afraid to walk past my husband at night. Many would not guess that he was raised middle-class in the white suburbs of western New York, with two college-educated parents. Another irony is that as Asian Americans, the model minority stereotype posits that we are able to seamlessly transition to the "hills, out of ills of the ghetto hood," and for many of us, light skin is an elevator to higher socioeconomic status. Yet, my husband, many other black folks, and those with dark skin (including dark-skinned Asian Americans) will struggle under the weight of colorism.

As a light-skinned Asian American woman, I am privileged. That privilege is more readily visible to me because I am married to a black man. I understand that I am always seen as more approachable. When we finished graduate school, I got a job first. When we went apartment hunting together, we never got a call back on our application, but when I went alone, the application was always approved. Unlike my husband, I do not get the side-eye when I walk into a retail store with a large bag or followed around as I shop.

These are privileges that I have taken for granted. And these are privileges that I have become even more aware of since the birth of my brown-skinned daughter.

When my daughter was a few months old, I realized strangers cannot tell that I am her biological mother. Although we share many of the same mannerisms, we only share a few physical traits; she looks different than I. The weight of that realization sunk in; my daughter will not have the same privileges that I have. At some point in her life, she will be stereotyped, feared, viewed as a thief, or viewed as unfit or unworthy. I worry that she might look at what I have accomplished and, instead of seeing how my privilege eased my path, view herself as "less than." I worry that she might hate her black skin and grow to believe that only whiteness is beautiful. This terrifies me.

I feel that all I can do is show her that she is loved for who she is, inside and out. I hope that she grows up with the confidence to battle any adversity that she faces as a perpetual outsider, a dark-skinned woman of color in the United States. I am certain that it will be a difficult journey, but her father and I will be there to support her every step of the way.

Part V

BELONGING AND IDENTITY

During my first year of teaching, I met a young undergraduate who was Indian American. She had light brown hair, big brown eyes, and milky-white skin. In fact, her skin shade was lighter than my own as she held up her arm next to mine for comparison one day after class. Like my family, her family is from North India, where skin is typically light, though admittedly her skin shade is even lighter than most North Indians'. I knew that, like me, she is privileged in the community—her skin color is considered attractive and represents what many Indian women aspire to as they spread whitening creams onto their faces and bodies. But what I remember most were her words: "Indians don't see me as Indian. They think I'm white, and when I tell them I'm Indian, they don't believe it." I don't remember every word of that conversation, but I do remember that it ended with, "I don't do anything with the community anymore." For me, this raised several questions: What does it mean to be Indian? Korean? Cambodian? Chinese? Does it mean possessing the "correct" heritage or socially accepted quantity of ethnic ancestry, having the knowledge of the culture and language, or does it simply rest on how one looks? Probably all matter to varying degrees, but what happens when one's skin color diverges from the stereotypical image of the ethnic group? What if one is considered "too light" or "too dark" for one's Asian ethnicity?

In this section, women describe how their skin color affects their perceptions of belonging and sense of identity within their Asian American communities. In the African American community, studies show that light skin is privileged because it is linked to perceptions of intelligence and beauty, though on the flip side, light-skinned African Americans often find their blackness questioned, illustrating that possessing light skin comes with its own struggles. In particular, dark-skinned African Americans may challenge the authenticity and blackness of their lighter-skinned counterparts: "But you're not *really* black" or "You don't/can't understand what it's like being black." In my previous book, *Biracial in America*, biracial black-white women spoke about these challenges to their identities, challenges that often stemmed from black women, and one respondent, biracial and light-skinned, remarked, "I think when I was growing up, [black girls] just did not accept me as being a black girl. . . . I still think there are some instances where they don't see me as an authentic black woman, because they'll make a comment about how something was so hard for them, like getting a job or whatever. And I'll say, 'Oh yeah, it's not that way' and they'll say, 'Oh, it's different for you.'"[1]

This sentiment is similarly mirrored in the ways in which some Americans (black, white, and otherwise) question the blackness of light-skinned African Americans, many of whom are multiracial. Journalist and news anchor Soledad O'Brien, who has black and white ancestry but self-identifies as black, describes a situation when she found her blackness blatantly questioned in a very public way. Reflecting on an interview that she conducted with Reverend Jesse Jackson for CNN, she describes their interaction like this: "Even though I am not sure what [Jesse Jackson] is saying, I can tell he is angry. Today he is angry because CNN doesn't have enough black anchors. I interrupt to remind him, 'I'm the anchor of *American Morning.*' He knows that. He looks me in the eye and reaches his fingers over to tap a spot of skin on my right hand. He shakes his head. 'You don't count,' he says. I wasn't sure what he meant. I don't count—what? I'm not black? I'm not black enough? Or my show doesn't count?" She describes herself in that moment as angry and embarrassed and feeling "like the foundation [she'd] built [her] life on was being denied."[2] Jackson had literally pointed out her light skin to tell her that she was not black, openly challenging her racial identity.

The importance of skin shade is also seen in other groups, including light-skinned Mexican Americans who find themselves alienated or marginalized because of their skin shade. Margaret Hunter writes about the many advantages of light skin for both African Americans and Mexican Americans, which are clearly documented in the broader literature, though she also argues that "skin color has long been tied to notions of 'racial purity,' and in more recent contexts, has been associated with group membership and 'ethnic legitimacy.' In both the Mexican American and African American communities, dark skin is usually perceived to be more ethnically authentic than light. Women and men with dark skin are more likely to be seen and accepted as legitimate members of their ethnic groups. . . . Many light-skinned members of these groups, especially if they are multiracial, report feeling excluded from their ethnic groups and viewed as not 'Black enough' or not 'Chicano enough.'"[3] For those with light skin who find their ethnicity or race challenged, this can be confusing, emotional, and frustrating.

Likewise, Asian American ethnic identities are tied to skin color. Skin that is deemed "too light" by others may thwart recognition, acceptance, and inclusion by fellow Asian Americans, and because of these challenges, Lori Tharps recognizes that light skin is not always the "universal prize." She adds, "Yes, there is skin-color hierarchy in which those with lighter skin rule from the top, but most people don't want to be a different color; most people just want to belong to their assigned group. They want to fit in. They want to be recognized members of their community."[4] As Margaret Hunter contends (above), this may be especially problematic for those who are multiracial—in particular, for those with white ancestry. Anne Jansen, who is multiracial (Chinese and white), writes about her feeling growing up that perhaps she "wasn't *really* Asian" as others repeatedly asked, "What are you?" She describes herself as light-skinned, as "ambiguously ethnic," and as "the question mark in a room full of periods."

Feelings of marginalization may also affect those who are not multiracial, given that for Asian Americans, light skin does not always stem from white ancestry. Many Asians have light skin, as

Asians show wide range in skin tone, though nonetheless possessing light skin may be challenging within some Asian ethnic groups—particularly South and Southeast Asian groups, for whom dark skin is relatively common (such as for my student within her Indian American community). Kim D. Chanbonpin, Filipina American, was born to Asian parents, though she has light skin. She describes being repeatedly miscategorized because her skin tone does not align with the stereotypical image of Filipinxs. She writes of "infuriating" though fairly common experiences when her knowledge and connection to Filipinx culture are ignored, and she wonders whether, if she were darker, people would see her as Filipina.

Kamna Shashri, Indian American, also has light skin—very light, in fact. She was born with albinism, a rare genetic condition in which there is a deficiency in melanin production and hence a lack of pigment in the hair, eyes, and skin. Because of her white skin and blonde hair, Kamna describes feeling "invisible" to fellow Indians. Though she was born to two Indian parents and feels deeply connected to her Indian culture, she describes her frustration when not recognized as Indian. She questions whether she is "white" or in fact a "person of color," drawing attention to the overly simplistic ways in which we racially classify each other. Though there has been little written about the psychological effects of albinism, many with albinism face questions of "Where do I belong?" and feelings of marginalization.[5] According to Dr. Murray Brilliant, the director of the Center for Human Genetics at the Marshfield Clinic in Wisconsin, "Human beings define race as an important factor in identity. It's very important for people to have a group identity and albinism can complicate things."[6] This may be especially true for those who are members of ethnic or racial groups that typically have dark skin.

Kamna, in her essay, also interrogates light-skin privilege and asks, "Is lighter always better?" Some living with albinism recognize the privileges they receive as compared to darker-skinned family members (because they are often assumed to be white), though for Kamna, the answer is no, challenging what she sees as the commonly held narrative of colorism itself, as she observes that "even the ideal of fair skin has a limit." Her light, white skin does not privilege her—at least among Indians; in fact, she argues that it paints her as "less attractive" in her Indian American community and makes her "less physically able to blend into the South Asian circles." Her essay provides a counternarrative to essays in Part II, which rest on the assumption that light skin equals privilege. Perhaps this is not always the case.

Moreover, unlike African Americans and Mexican Americans, for whom dark skin is positively linked to authenticity and ethnic/racial legitimacy, dark skin among Asian Americans is more complicated. Asian American women may feel their identities questioned and feel like ethnic outsiders because they possess light skin, but they may also encounter similar experiences because of their dark skin—especially if their skin diverges from stereotypical skin-tone norms of their particular ethnic group. Because having skin that is "too light" or "too dark" can be problematic in Asian American communities, colorism operates somewhat differently for this racial group as compared to others—at least when it comes to perceptions of authenticity and belonging. Erika Lee, Taiwanese and Chinese American, for example, describes how her dark skin often raises questions about her ethnicity and marginalizes her within her Chinese American community. Because light skin typifies Chinese Americans, dark skin confers no benefit to her. She writes about her frustrations when people assume she is adopted or question her Chinese background, and she asserts that "nobody deserves to feel like a foreigner in her own culture."

Finally, Cindy Luu, Vietnamese American, describes feeling as if she does not "belong" in the Vietnamese American community because of her dark skin shade and physical features, which diverge from what she perceives as the archetypal image of Vietnamese women. She writes that Vietnamese women typically come in "one size and color," though she describes herself as "six inches too tall, three cup sizes too busty, and too dark." She has tried to conform to Vietnamese norms by dieting, exercising, binding her breasts, and wearing her makeup "a shade too light," yet she constantly wondered, "Was I pale enough for others to stop mistaking me as belonging to other ethnicities? Was I finally pretty enough to belong as a Vietnamese woman?" She describes the sheer exhaustion she feels when trying to keep up with others' expectations, providing a peek into the psychological and physical toll that colorism takes on many Asian American women.

For all the women included in this section, their skin shades and bodies defy ethnic and racial stereotypes and, through their narratives, they challenge what they perceive as one-dimensional, narrow images of Asian American women. For some, their skin is deemed "too light" for their Asian ethnic group; for others, "too dark." Accordingly, they collectively argue (in the words of Erika Lee) that there is "more than one way to look Asian," defying the overly simplistic physical stereotypes of their diverse ethnic groups.

19

What Are You?

Anne Mai Yee Jansen, MULTIRACIAL
CHINESE/WHITE AMERICAN, 36

I am used to the question. I know the look: people searching
my features for matches, finding few that correspond. It is
confusing to some people to look at me.
—Alexander Chee, *Edinburgh*

When I was growing up, there was a dusty thrift shop about a
mile from my house where my best friend and I would go to find
groovy clothes, curious knick-knacks, and used books. The shop
was a converted house, and one of the small rooms in the back was
chock-full of books, their spines broken and their edges worn from
all the hands that had turned every one of their soft pages. Once a
week, it was Dollar Book Day: pack as many books as you could fit
into a paper grocery bag and they were yours for (you guessed it)
one dollar. It was my favorite day of the week.

Usually I'd load up on books by Tom Clancy and John Grisham,
Agatha Christie and Stephen King, but one day, I found two books
by Amy Tan—*The Joy Luck Club* and *The Kitchen God's Wife*. This
was shortly after *The Joy Luck Club* had come out on VHS, and I
excitedly tossed both books into my bag. Afterward, we ambled
over to Houston's Liquors down the street for some Red Vines and
beef jerky before walking home in the hot summer sun.

That night as I lay in bed, I began reading one of Tan's books. I
was always an avid reader, but this was the first time in my life that
I read a book and saw my family in it. I was amazed to realize that
books could be about people like us; the possibility had simply
never presented itself to me. But every time a character added "Ah"

before another character's name—a kind of cultural prefix I knew by heart—I could hear one of my aunties calling my name. When the younger generations attended Chinese school on Saturdays, I thought of my cousins, who did the same. *That's my family*, I thought. *There are others like us!*

It was my first exposure to Asian American literature, and it was *magical*.

I grew up in California, but not in one of the large urban centers that so many Asian immigrants and their Asian American families call home. My home town is located in a rural area, in a town best known for a restaurant serving split-pea soup and its proximity to one small town renowned for its horse ranches and another small town settled by Danish immigrants (the result: amazing pastries and an annual festival called Danish Days). Oh, and Michael Jackson's famous Neverland Ranch was less than twenty miles away. In this cluster of small communities, surnames like Petersen and Martinez were far more prevalent than names like my mom's maiden name: Lam. Aside from one Filipino family who lived in our neighborhood for a few years, my sister and I were the only Asian American kids at our school (and many people read my sister as white because she's much more fair-skinned than I am).

When I was in seventh grade, a Chinese family moved to town; their son was in my grade, and everyone expected us to date (we didn't) because we were the only Asians around for miles. I had access to Asian American culture through my boba tea-drinking, Cantonese-speaking, manga-reading cousins scattered throughout the Los Angeles area, but my daily reality was set in a place where I was asked to do a presentation explaining Chinese New Year to my fifth grade class because nobody else had ever heard of it.

To complicate matters further, I always had the sense that I wasn't *really* Asian, but hadn't heard the term "Asian American" yet, so I just felt a little fraudulent all the time. I'm not sure it would have helped if I'd had access to that concept anyway, because even within my mom's family (who hailed from Hong Kong) we were unique: My mom was the only one of all her many siblings who married a white guy, making my sister and I the only mixed-race kids among our numerous cousins. We were also the only ones who didn't speak fluent Cantonese or eat Chinese food most days of the week.

Because I lived in this rural area with no other Asians in sight and only two restaurants (the Mandarin Touch and China Panda) to remind locals that Asians even existed, it shouldn't come as a surprise that people had trouble figuring out how to read me. I inherited my mom's rich olive skin and ability to brown under the constant sunshine; I also got her full lips, high cheekbones, and dark hair, but I got my dad's nose, bone structure, and double eyelids. Everywhere I went, I was faced with the same question: What are you? The kids at school, local shopkeepers, teachers, and tourists alike all had the same question. *What are you?* As if they couldn't know how to interact with me before they knew what made my skin the color it was, my face the shape it was.

Most people were surprised to find out I was half Chinese; in the context of Southern California, my dark hair and tan skin led many to assume I was Chicana. The Chumash Indian Reservation was only a few miles away, so some people thought I was Native American (an assumption that was, tellingly, most often made on days when my mom had braided my hair). I've been on the receiving end of my fair share of racist remarks, but not a single racist encounter has accurately targeted any of the various bloodlines I actually carry within my body.

The result is that I've never had the opportunity *not* to think about the color of my skin. When others look at me, they seem compelled—by curiosity, discomfort, or something in between—to ask me that most tired of questions: *What are you?* Too dark to be wholly white, too pale to be brown, I've come to understand that I'm ambiguously ethnic, and there's something about that ambiguity that makes people want more information.

When I went to Hong Kong in 1996, the consensus was that I wasn't Chinese enough to be a local, but I wasn't white enough to really count as white. While I was vacationing in Italy in 2012, a street vendor outside the Duomo stopped me to ask if I was

Japanese, insisting that I sure looked like I was despite my negative response. As I enjoyed the beach in Hawai'i in 2016, a number of shopkeepers told me they'd assumed I was Native Hawaiian—a local like themselves. Everywhere I go, my skin appeals to strangers like a good mystery just waiting to be figured out, solved, answered so they can nod their heads with finality—*I figured as much*—or, occasionally, render some kind of judgment, as in the case of one especially confounding encounter where the news of my mixed racial background was met by an earnest and enthusiastic, "Good for you!"

These intrusions, innocuous as many of them are, have caused skin color and phenotype to be a constant presence in my life. I'm never allowed to forget that I'm confusing to the eye, or that others seem to feel entitled to the personal details of why my skin is the color it is. That they feel that information should be public knowledge. That I am expected to explain myself in order to unburden them of their desire—their oft-professed *need*—to know exactly what I am. (Never *who*, always *what*.)

Perhaps it's unsurprising that I ended up studying US ethnic literatures. When I initially applied for PhD programs, I planned to study postcolonial literature; I intended to focus on Hong Kong. However, within a year I had discovered US ethnic studies. It was like Amy Tan all over again, only this time I wasn't seeing my mom's family—I was seeing myself.

After my first quarter of the PhD program, I went home for the holidays. Shortly after my arrival, I sat at the kitchen counter having a cup of tea (with cream and sugar as the British take their tea, a vestige of colonialism that followed my mom over from Hong Kong) and talked with my parents about my new course of study. I gushed about the books I was reading, the ideas I was learning, the courses I was taking. I shared the new direction my dissertation was headed in, feeling that anticipatory tingle a really exciting idea fills me up with. And then my mom asked me a question—a simple, obvious, important question: *Why are you focusing on multiethnic literature—why don't you focus on Asian American literature since you're Asian American?*

I had no ready answer. At first, I was so surprised by the question that my mind went blank; I just sat there with my hands around that lukewarm cup of tea, my parents' curiosity turning my mind inside out. Then I began to realize how obvious the answer was to me, and how not obvious it was to my parents, whose love forms the truth of my racial roots. Sure, on paper I'm Asian American. But my lived experience hasn't really been a typically Asian American experience. Growing up in California, I was presumed Chicana; when I moved to Ohio for grad school, I was just plain confusing (most of the encounters I had there indicated that anything between black and white was illegible); now, living in western North Carolina, I'm most often mistaken for Cherokee due to the proximity of the Qualla Boundary. My skin color has led others to bring race to my attention on a regular basis. Misdirected racism (no less harmful for its inaccuracy) has broadened the scope of my understanding of and interest in the far-reaching and often intertwined effects of colorism.

For my whole life, others' questions and comments about my skin have left me to wonder about those interactions long after my interrogators have satisfied themselves. Why did a friend's well-intentioned schoolyard remark—*I didn't even notice you weren't white!*—leave me feeling so dejected? (Because honorary whiteness isn't such an honor after all.) Why did a (white) dermatologist's insistence that I don't need to get my skin checked regularly—*since it's so dark*—despite a family history of skin cancer irk me so much? (Because evidently our medical industry hasn't bothered to figure out how skin that's not white works.) Why did a fellow bus rider feel it was acceptable to pop my ear bud out of my ear and ask me—*because you're soooooo beautiful!*—what my "heritage" is? (Because my ethnic ambiguity bugs strangers enough for them to feel justified in violating my personal space to demand that I explain myself.) As a result, my professional life has shaped itself out of the questions I take away from each of these encounters, leading me to want to understand how skin color functions in the United States today and to teach others to think critically about their own relationships to race and colorism.

In my personal life, I find myself thinking about these issues with increasing urgency because I recently had a child. She is one-quarter Chinese and three-quarters myriad shades of whiteness, and she has inherited her father's (and my father's) fair skin and light eyes. When we go to the park, I wonder who will pose the question so many of my friends in interracial marriages have been confronted with: the nanny question. (When you're discernibly not white and are toting around a white-passing baby, it's common for strangers to assume you're the child's hired caregiver rather than his or her biological parent.) More troubling still, I worry that she won't understand what it means to live in skin like mine.

My feelings on the matter are complicated. On the one hand, I obviously don't want her to have to experience racism as I have (which is admittedly mild compared to the experiences of friends of mine who are less *ambiguously* ethnic and more clearly black or brown). On the other hand, I have to admit to feeling a sense of loss, as though her peaches-and-cream complexion somehow makes her less like me or will create some kind of distance between us since our experiences with colorism will undoubtedly be so different. The most disturbing aspect of this, especially given what I teach and study in my professional life, is that I can't seem to stop worrying about what the color of her skin will mean for our relationship.

In other words, my whole life I've been marked as Other. I'm the question mark in a room full of periods. I've been both hurt and fascinated by the many implications of skin color, and now, as a new parent, another aspect of the complexity of colorism is inserting itself into my life: I wonder how the color of my skin will impact my daughter's life. She may never be faced with that ridiculous question—*What are you?*—but what other questions will she have to answer? *Where is your mom from? Are you adopted? Is she your step-mom?*

In this new chapter of my life, I have no answers, only more questions. How will she identify? Will she be closer to her dad because she looks more like him than like me? Will she be able to understand how skin color influences my daily life? And, worst of all, will she even care? I can only hope that she will find her own Amy Tan—some artist whose work reflects her own experiences back at her so she can see that there are others like her. That she is not alone. That her story is worthwhile, and that no matter what others may say, skin color is but one tiny facet of what makes her who she is.

20

Born Filipina, Somewhere in Between

Kim D. Chanbonpin, FILIPINA AMERICAN, 40

In 2008, I was finishing up a two-year teaching fellowship in New Orleans and was looking forward to moving to Chicago for my first tenure-track job. I knew I was going to miss the Crescent City, so I was trying to enjoy as much of it as I could before I left. Fortunately, I have a dear friend who was just as enthralled with the city as I. She and I had every classic New Orleans experience possible—Mardi Gras, St. Patrick's Day, Jazzfest, Tipitina's, Gautreau's, Parkway Tavern—and we did it all together. That March, she and I decided to go to Taylor Park just off Claiborne Avenue to attend Super Sunday. Super Sunday is the largest gathering of Mardi Gras Indians before the masking season ends. She picked me up, and in the car ride over, as we burbled about how excited we were to be attending the event, my dear friend said to me, "Kim, you know we're going to be the only white people there, right?" In that moment, it was as if the needle on the record of the Mardi Gras soundtrack in my mind skidded off the vinyl in slow motion, and what replaced it were the words in the Oscar Brown Jr. song told from Tonto's point of view: "What do you mean, we, White man?"

It wasn't just my friend who couldn't quite figure out how to categorize me; it was everyone—from the cashier at Target to the dean of the law school where I taught to my neighbors in the condo building on Cherokee and Maple where I lived for two years. Folks in New Orleans knew I wasn't black, and they were pretty sure I wasn't white, but what exactly was I? "Oriental," Mexican, or Chinese-Japanese were the most common theories.

I suppose that their confusion and lack of adequate vocabulary has to do with the way we talk about race. Although Latinxs, Asian

Americans, and mixed-race folks are the most rapidly growing groups in the United States, politicians and the media continue to speak about race and racism in terms of black and white. This dichromatic perspective is a result of history. Because of black chattel slavery, Jim Crow laws, and the Civil Rights Movement, the African American experience has been central to the formation of race and racial identity in this country. And slavery and de jure racial discrimination were based on an ideology of white supremacy and a clearly imposed hierarchy—white over black.

Despite the incremental gains heralded by the Civil Rights Movement, the race and color hierarchy persists. That hierarchy is bounded by black on one end (the bottom) and white at the other (the top). Whiteness affords innumerable unearned social and cultural privileges while blackness imposes automatic penalties. The two-tiered hierarchy has recently had to adapt to accommodate the size and growing power of other ethnic and racial groups, but the perpetual beneficiaries of this system of social, cultural, and economic control will always be white or those groups with proximity to whiteness. The new version of the old hierarchy is organized on more nuanced gradations of color, though the sorting of intermediary groups remains unclear and intensely debated.

The question I would pose to Asian Americans is, *What side will we choose?* It may seem odd to frame identity as a matter of volition, as if we had a say about the race into which we are born. But I think in terms of choice because in the race-color hierarchy I've just described, some Asian Americans are positioned to accept or reject the privileges of so-called honorary whiteness. Because of my light skin color, because of the economic advantages I've enjoyed thanks to the laws that encouraged my physician parents to immigrate here from the Philippines, and because of the enduring Model Minority Myth, I, for example, am empowered with substantial agency regarding how I express my racial identity and what political acts I opt to participate in. I have choice. To be clear, within the structure of white supremacy, those choices are limited. Any privilege I might gain by allying myself with whiteness will always be conditioned on that affiliation, and I do not hold the keys controlling my entry to that group. But rejecting any proffered affiliate status means actively refusing to be complicit in a system that subordinates black people to benefit whites.

Living in New Orleans put the white-over-black dichotomy into sharp focus for me. Besides a few short years in Ohio, I grew up in an ethnoburb east of Los Angeles, where Asian Americans and Latinxs shared back yards and churches and the only black or white people I remember seeing on a regular basis were on television. High school wasn't that different, except that one of my closest friends was Apache Indian and, although I went to a Catholic college prep, I had several Muslim classmates. No boys, though; it was an all-girls school. I went to college in the Bay Area and was active in the large and visible Filipino American student organization, and then found myself part of an even larger Asian Pacific Islander community when I moved to Honolulu for law school. It wasn't until my mid-twenties when I returned to the continent to live in the South (Washington, DC) and then the Deep South (New Orleans) that I was finally confronted with the race dynamics so familiar to everyone else.

Although I grew up around people who looked like me, I was always aware of the mainstream's mandate to identify racially. And I suppose I decided early on that if I had to choose, I was going to be black. Alex P. Keaton was cute and all, but he was white and a Republican.

My identity choices were shaped by the television shows and other cultural products that I consumed as an adolescent and young adult. I did not identify with the white, middle-class families of popular 1980s sitcoms—the Keatons of *Family Ties* or the Seavers on *Growing Pains*. I admired strong white female characters such as Murphy Brown (*Murphy Brown*) and Julia Sugarbaker (*Designing Women*), but I didn't want to be anyone on TV until I met Claire Huxtable on *The Cosby Show*. Claire was a lawyer who spoke Spanish and was the queen of her house and didn't take shit from anyone. She was a feminist with progressive politics. She was also black. By watching *The Cosby Show*, I began to learn about African American history and culture through a combination of observation and osmosis. I clung to those images and stories because they made sense to me, and also because there weren't that many other options available to me. Even though the Huxtables brought some diversity to sitcom television in the 1980s, there were no Asian Americans. Like, at all.

Look: I knew I wasn't black, but I also knew that I was not going to be white. In high school, my senior English class read Toni Morrison's *The Bluest Eye*. I remember falling in love with the lyricism of Morrison's prose and feeling my heart break for the protagonist, Pecola Breedlove—the girl who was told she was ugly because of her dark skin. Pecola believed that if she could only have blue eyes, she would be loved. Our teacher, Sister Elise, guided a classroom filled with young Latina and Asian American women through intense discussions about racism and the colonial mentality and pushed us to articulate the reasons why mainstream standards of beauty did not include us.

The first time I remember being conscious about the color difference between me and my peers was in kindergarten. I was six years old and at the time, my family was living in Newark, Ohio, a small community just outside of Columbus. I was the only Asian kid in my all-white class. I came home from school one day and asked my father why my skin was different than that of the other kids in my class. My father and I aren't close, but I will always remember and appreciate the answer he gave me then. He said, "Do you know how much your white classmates would pay to get your beautiful *kayumanggi* (Tagalog for brown) skin?" My father's words to me when I was six were formative. The notion that my gold-toned skin had value over that of my white peers had a deep impact on my developing worldview. My father acknowledged the difference between my skin color and theirs, and told me mine was beautiful. And I believed him.

I am 100 percent Asian American (and I have the results from my National Geographic–branded racial admixture DNA test to prove it), but I grew up in a bicultural household. My parents were both born in the Philippines, but my father is ethnic Chinese. I confess that one driving force behind spending the money on the admixture test was to determine—"scientifically"—whether there was any Spanish blood in my family. My mother is fair-skinned, and in her childhood photos, she favors a brunette Shirley Temple. People always referred to her as "mestiza," someone with mixed Filipino and Spanish racial heritage. I wanted to know whether it was actually true. But no, according to the test, 64 percent of my ancestry is associated with Southeast Asia and Oceania, and the remainder is from Eastern Asia.

National Geographic also sent me two reference populations to help me understand my results—Bougainville-Nasioi (a region in Papua New Guinea) and Filipino. These reference populations are groups in the database that contain genetic markers similar to mine—meaning that I am genetically similar to both populations. After googling "Bougainville-Nasioi," I saw photos of very dark-skinned Pacific Islanders. Their skin tone is as dark as any West African's, and they look a little like the Aeta people, the dark-skinned indigenous residents of northern Luzon in the Philippines.

This was so exciting to me. Despite the fact that I am phenotypically more "Chinese-looking"—I have bone-straight dark brown hair, almond-shaped eyes (one with a monolid), and light skin, with golden undertones—I have always identified culturally as Filipino American. I speak Tagalog, I can cook *pancit*,[1] I "*mano po*"[2] my elders, and will turn around if someone whispers "*hoy, psssssst*" on a crowded street. In addition, growing up alongside Mexican Americans and other Latinxs who traded in the same cultural currency as Filipinos (thanks to our shared history as colonies of Spain) reinforced the system of values and identity that I was constructing for myself as a young adult. By contrast, several years of Chinese school, forced piano lessons, and being overfed on Chinese takeout ruined my appetite for appreciating my father's ancestry.

But the discrepancy between how people see me and how I see myself has resulted in frequent identity mistakes and mismatches. Sometimes it's funny because my secret identity means I can eavesdrop on conversations between Filipino elders on the bus. But a lot of the times it's infuriating. I once walked into a Filipino grocery store with a dark-skinned Filipina friend. I wanted to buy *buko pandan* ice cream, and my friend casually asked the woman at the cash register what *pandan* was. I offered an answer: "It's a plant; you use the leaves to flavor and to color food." As if they didn't hear me, the woman at the cash register replied that she "didn't know" and then asked a customer who was entering the store. That man said he "didn't know" either. Thinking that perhaps they had not heard me the first time, I again offered what I happened to know about *pandan*—this time in a louder, more assertive voice: "They're green leaves you can use to flavor and to color food." Still, no reaction nor recognition of what I had just said from any of the three. When someone who looked like the owner of the store emerged from the storeroom, the woman at the cash register asked her, "Do you know what *pandan* is?" She declared, "It's a green plant; you use the leaves to flavor and to color food"—at which point, the customer, the woman at the cash register, and my friend all exclaimed, "Oh! Why didn't we know that before?"

On another occasion, two close Filipino American friends came to visit me while I was teaching as a visiting professor in Las Vegas. Next to Spanish, Tagalog is the second most spoken foreign language in the state of Nevada. We decided to meet up at a popular local Filipino buffet. The restaurant is always filled with Filipinos and other buffet lovers, and when we entered, I made eye contact with the hostess, had three fingers up, and said, "*Tatlong tao, po*," the Tagalog equivalent for "party of three." The hostess looked right past me to my friends, who had the benefit of having spent the last three days under the Moab, Utah sun, and asked them in Tagalog how large our party was. Neither of them speaks Tagalog.

For me, these are fairly typical experiences. Though perhaps some may view them as petty, I'm often frustrated and hurt when I am not recognized as a member of the community that I claim membership in. I often wonder whether, if I were darker, or had more texture in my hair, or higher cheekbones, my people might see me for who I am. In this way, I suppose that I am not unlike Pecola, yearning to look different than what I am, so that I can be accepted and loved.

But I also suppose that I should remember that Filipinos look like everyone; that is part of our beauty as a people. Folks with Filipino heritage may have green eyes and very light skin or have very dark skin with kinky hair. Our skin tones are as varied as the color spectrum. Many of us fall somewhere in between, with physical characteristics that are generally associated with East and Southeast Asians—almond-shaped eyes, dark brown or black hair, slight builds. My mother is very mestiza looking: she has fair skin, high cheekbones, and large, double-lidded brown eyes. My father is very Chinese-looking, with a round face and thin, straight black hair. One brother takes after my mom, one after my dad. Me? I'm all yellow undertones during winter, and in the summer, I try to cultivate a golden brown.

As I was finishing up this essay, my wife and I went hiking and swimming in the foothills of central Argentina. She's Afro-Cuban with light skin that easily toasts brown in the sun. The other day, I reached out to hold her hand, and when we both looked down at our arms, she smiled and noted approvingly, "*que negrita!*" And then she told me to take a picture of myself to send in to the editor of this book to prove that I was black, after all.

21

Invisible to My Own People

Kamna Shastri, INDIAN AMERICAN, 23

I used to think sleeping was a waste of time when I was a child.
On one of those nights when I wanted to evade sleep for as long as
possible, I remember an eight-year-old me curling up in my parents'
comforter, looking from the three pink freckles perfectly lined across
my forearm to the blank, cream-colored wall beside the bed. Then I
asked my mother the same six words I had asked her time and again.

"Why do I have peach skin?"

I knew the answer to this very well. My mother had never sugar-
coated the truth, but told me from the very start that I had a genetic
condition called albinism. When I asked her what genes were, she
explained that they were like the instruction manual for making
a human being. She delved into as much detail as one could with
a child on the subject of genetics and told me how genes code for
pigment, which ultimately decides the color of one's skin. She said
my genes couldn't make a lot of pigment, which was why I ended
up white and blonde haired while the rest of my family looked
unmistakably Indian.

If my brother or my parents were to tell you they are Indian,
you wouldn't bat an eye. But if I did, chances are that you'd look at
the pale-skinned, blonde-haired woman in front of you and blink
twice, confused, uncertain, in disbelief. That was often the response
I received even as a child, but back then, I unabashedly offered
newfound acquaintances a short life history: "I am Indian, but I
was born with albinism, which is why I look white!" I wasn't afraid
of the discrepancy between my identity and my phenotype—in
fact, I was proud of my heritage and wanted people to know how
important being Indian was to me.

But I knew all the while that along with albinism-related eyesight and skin-sensitivity issues, it would be a challenge to navigate the nuances of belonging.

Difference has been my normal. Growing up in America, I loved dancing to Hindi songs and had to have my fix of Hindi movies every Friday. I ate *dahl*,[1] *rasam*,[2] yogurt, and rice every day. I knew many a Sanskrit *sloka*[3] and had a pile of Amar Chitra Katha[4] books that I'd sift through along with whatever fantasy novel I was currently reading. I took any occasion to get all dolled up in a *paavadai*[5] or fancy *salwaar kameez*,[6] even if the event was a school-wide picture day. I rarely listened to Miley Cyrus or any of the newest teen celebrities because I was too busy singing along to the songs from Shahrukh Khan's newest film and wishing I could dress up like the beautiful Aishwarya Rai in *Hum Dil De Chuke Sanam*. I felt more Indian than anything else.

Making friends wasn't hard, but I did find myself lacking in cultural capital, falling behind in American pop culture references. I wanted someone to giggle with about my Bollywood crush, and peers who would be as fascinated with Indian history as I was. I invested my hopes of belonging in my Indian peers, dreaming of choreographing Indian dance routines and getting dressed up for Diwali parties.

That never happened. At least not the way I wanted.

Every dinner party at a family friend's home left me feeling out of place and slightly odd, pushed away. I was a shy child, and perhaps it was merely this personality trait that created a distance from the other Indian children, but it was easier to blame my albinism when the strange feeling of being left out happened again and again.

When I was seven, we went to Florida for a distant cousin's wedding. As I was dancing during the reception, a woman came up to me and asked, "Are you an American?" I remember hesitating, unsure of what to say before answering with my usual explanation. At nine, I remember going to the temple and being asked by a girl my age, "Why are you here? You're not Indian." During a trip to India at fifteen, I was sitting with my grandmother one afternoon at an ashram we often visited together. A tour guide approached me and asked where I was from and why I was visiting India. "I'm visiting family," I replied, gesturing to my grandmother. He couldn't believe that I could possibly be Indian. I swallowed the lump in my throat and tried my best to explain what albinism was as calmly as I could despite my quivering legs. He didn't believe me and continued to assert that I must be British. The tears came without warning. It was only when I turned away that he apologized; he thought I had been "pulling his leg."

More recently, a friend (who is also Indian) and I took an Uber ride to get a quick morning snack. We shuffled into the back seat and the driver, a turbaned man from Delhi, proceeded to ask my friend which part of India she was from. He did not acknowledge my presence throughout the entire ride. Though I understood why and didn't let the incident linger for too long in my mind, the moment succinctly captured the epitome of being invisible to my own people.

Navigating Color Labels: Am I "White" or "Brown"?

When I look at pictures of myself as a child, I see a strong little girl looking up at me, wide-eyed and curious, open to the world and all it has to give and take. In my memories, that girl is bolder and far more self-assured than I am now—someone who truly didn't care what other people thought and who wasn't afraid to share her pride in her culture, and explain her circumstance as a simple "matter of fact."

During adolescence, and now in my early adult years, I am beginning to bear the full weight of the quieter pain that has come with albinism even as I continue to discover some of its blessings, such as the sensitivity to withhold judgment, and being able to empathize with those who do not have experiences and identities that fit into a singular, societally imposed label. I am realizing just how much albinism—or my perception of and experience with it—has colored the challenges of my life; it has contributed to the distance I feel from my own community, my yearning to be accepted in the face of a certain kind of invisibility, not to mention that it has greatly influenced my trepidation over future relationships, the idea of family, and my hesitance to dip a toe into that lukewarm pool of "dating."

Albinism itself isn't the problem. The issue lies in how I have connected looking white to my failed attempts at being part of a South Asian community. In a mainstream white American context, I struggle with being washed out and blending into a vast white culture, when in fact I am not white.

It would be dishonest to identify as purely American (or even white) because I am not. I am an Indian-American, a South Asian–American; the hyphen is necessary in my identity and symbolizes the myriad of influences in my life. It connects the space between two cultures, two identities, and the strange space between the two terms that twist about my head during many a sleepless night—"person of color" and "white."

How does someone like me fit into a polarized view of race? Am I "white" just because of the phenotypic whiteness I project? Am I a person of color, a "brown" girl, because of my family background and my ethnic and cultural identity? Why can't there be a term acknowledging the fact that I receive white privilege, while at the same time signifying my experiences of being South Asian–American? This is where I start to find my position as a South Asian with albinism intriguing—a life-long social experiment, if you will. It has led me to question the phenomenon of labeling groups on the basis of color, a pattern that has left me feeling disoriented in conversations about race and identity, and left out of the communities where I want to belong.

Light Skin Privilege? Is Lighter *Always* Better?

I have a distinct memory of running down the steps when I was eight, playing pretend, trailing a chiffon scarf behind me as I imagined myself to be a beautiful Hindi film heroine dancing through waving wheat fields under a blue sky. Like many girls who imagine being singers and actresses, I too imagined myself as a Bollywood heroine . . . until the thought snapped, a brittle branch caught in the wind of a reality check.

I would never, *ever* look like them.

There is a narrative within communities of color that lighter skin is privileged over darker skin tones. This preference is problematic and colonialist, especially as it becomes internalized by women, who bear the brunt of these beauty standards. It's common for South Asian matrimonial ads to advertise would-be brides as "fair" and "wheatish" (literally meaning "the color of wheat"), creating a clear hierarchy among South Asian women based on color. The obsession with "fair and lovely," both the skin-bleaching product and the message it stands for, is confusing, demeaning, and inconsistent.

But even the ideal of fair skin has a limit.

The rhetoric of colorism promises "the fairer, the better." In my experience, possessing light skin has not necessarily been better in the realm of beauty and attraction, challenging the assumptions upon which colorism has been built. In fact, the subtle nuances of social interaction have painted albinism as something that makes me unattractive, unable to fit the mold of how an Indian woman should look, raising difficult questions about what counts as being Indian at all.

My personal perception of beauty privileges brown skin and black hair—traits that I can never have. Along with the shyness that made it hard to get along with other South Asians my age in the first place, I was even more hesitant upon observing the physical traits I noticed in the Indian girls around me. Their lovely long black hair and large dark eyes that could be heavily rimmed with black *kajal*[7] made me feel like I didn't, and couldn't, belong. Maybe I imposed this distance upon myself, or maybe it was a vicious cycle—I felt left out, so I distanced myself more, a behavior that may have led others to think I wasn't interested in getting along in the first place.

Those adolescent feelings of distance and standing on the periphery remain nestled inside me even as an adult. Some days, I think of this distancing as purely superficial, as though albinism makes me less attractive, less physically able to blend into the South Asian circles I wish I could be a part of, but doesn't necessarily define me. Other days, I see albinism and the place it has created for me as a barrier where I can only experience my South Asian identity in the context of childhood memory and nostalgia; it is not something that is visible and cannot be shared with others throughout my life.

The color of my skin negates my background. It makes the most crucial parts of my identity, my ethnicity, and my family history invisible to the world. I do not say this with bitterness, but as a truth that will remain throughout my life. Through each phase of my life, this tryst with color will affect me in different ways. That is a fact. But in the current internal dialogue I'm grappling with, I face questions whose answers only I can determine: *Will I let my skin color affect the kind of life I envision for myself? Will I let it keep me from connecting with the communities of which I wish to be a part?* Only time will reveal the answer to these questions, and while I did not get to choose the color of my skin, I am the only one who will choose the colors and shapes with which to paint my future.

22

Nobody Deserves to Feel like a Foreigner in Her Own Culture

Erika Lee, TAIWANESE/CHINESE AMERICAN, 22

For most of my adolescence, I believed the lie that lighter skin signified worthiness and beauty. As someone who grew up as a dark-skinned Asian, I knew I did not fall into that category.

It was the first thing that anybody would ever point out whenever they saw me. I remember very clearly, on a family vacation to Hong Kong, a stranger saw my mom and me together and stopped us. "Hi, little girl, are you Native American?" he asked me, fake smiling. His voice was condescending and high-pitched. When my mother shook her head, he replied, seemingly confused, "Why is your mom so pale and why are you so dark?" He then asked my mom in Cantonese, unaware that I speak fluent Cantonese, if I was adopted. I remember running to the bathroom and sobbing alone in a stall because I couldn't hold in my tears and because I did not want anybody to see them. I was only seven years old, but at that moment, I began to understand that there was more than one way to look Asian.

The homogeneity of East Asian beauty is startling and in a way, unsettling. If you look in any Korean, Japanese, Chinese, or Taiwanese magazine, every girl has the same porcelain white skin, small pink lips, straight eyebrows, dyed straight hair, and big eyes with double eyelids. Their bodies are uniformly petite and slim.

However, if you asked any American millennial to describe beauty standards in the United States, chances are they would be along the lines of tan skin, full or thick lips, a curvy physique but with a nice flat stomach, and carefully crafted eyebrows. White people actually pay to get darker and frequent the beach or tanning beds just to tan; in America, pale skin is often seen as unhealthy and implies that you don't go out much. Whenever some of my friends suggest going to the beach, I imagine the reactions of my grandparents in Taiwan; they would no doubt urge me to stay in the shade lest I get too "dark." Whenever some of my friends talk about wanting a bigger booty, I think about how curvy bodies are viewed negatively in Asia and in Asian media. I realize that, as an Asian American, I will never completely fit the beauty standards of both of the worlds that I am from—Asia or America.

Over the years, my skin has lightened naturally, probably because I hate playing outdoor sports and prefer indoor activities. However, there are still parts of my body that are darker than others, and I tan extremely easily, especially in the summer. But guess what? I take it with a grain of salt. How can I hate myself when God has made me the way that I am with my best interests in mind? The color of my skin doesn't matter to me anymore, but I can't help but wonder—if it has taken me so many years of self-loathing and self-doubt to come to this conclusion, how many other girls in the world currently hate themselves because they don't meet a certain cultural beauty ideal?

I think of my younger self, the one who thought that drinking milk or bathing in lemons would make herself feel less worthless and more beautiful, who cried in the bathroom, and I would never want any other young teen girl to hate herself because she is bombarded with standards of beauty that she can't live up to.

It's too late to go back and change where it began, but it's not too late to change the way it will end. What's the solution besides the advice that everyone gives, like "love the skin you're in" and "love who you are"? The solution is not only practicing self-love but also increased diversity in media and increased acceptance within our own communities. There are very few celebrities in Asian films and television with dark skin unless they are cast as the villain or in some demeaning role.

Being beautiful and being dark-skinned are not mutually exclusive, and we can all work toward shattering this belief by viewing and treating every person of every hue equally and calling out other people who promote colorism. Nobody deserves to feel like a foreigner in her own culture, and neither do I.

23

Tired

Cindy Luu, VIETNAMESE AMERICAN, 22

"Này Công Dân ơi! Quốc gia đến ngày giải phóng. Đồng lòng cùng đi hy sinh tiếc gì thân sống . . ." I practiced the national anthem of the Republic of Việt Nam under my breath. My high school Vietnamese cultural club's first show was in two days, and we were running our first full dress rehearsal. I was in the dressing room, where the counter was littered with makeup bags, hair styling tools, hairspray, accessories, and opened bags of snacks; the air had been buzzing with the excited nerves and laughter of twenty-five other girls. As much as we had groaned and complained over the previous ten weeks, we had formed a camaraderie from all the hard work we had put into the show.

"Cindy, can you button me up?" Nancy asked from my left, already dressed in her *áo dài* gown, a form-fitted silk robe with a high neckline and long sleeves and matching silk pants. She lifted her right arm over her head to expose the line of buttons and hooks that ran down her side.

"Sure." I bent down at the waist to grasp at the side buttons, trying my best not to pinch her. For such a conservative outfit, I always found it odd that they were impossible to put on without help.

"What do you guys think?" Leanne asked us, holding up two hangers. "My mom let me borrow from her collection, but I can't decide which one to wear. Pink or yellow?"

"I'm borrowing my mom's, too." Nancy's comment made me notice the light green version of her dress that I was buttoning. "Hmm, I like the pink. It's more fun!" she added.

I nodded in absent-minded agreement as I straightened my posture. I offered Leanne a small smile before taking a step back from Nancy. "All done."

"Great, thanks!" Nancy took a few steps forward, leaning over the counter to get closer to the mirror. "Let me know when you need help with your buttons—you'd better hurry, we're supposed to be out there in ten minutes."

As I fingered the zipper of my garment bag for a moment before opening it, unease bubbled in the pit of my stomach. It simmered and grew as I pulled the gown over my head, spreading to the parts of me where the itchy fabric chafed my skin. I stared at myself in the large mirror that lined the wall, glancing back and forth between my reflection and the other girls in the room.

Everyone's gowns were colorful, from light pastels to vibrantly rich colors. Theirs were silky, youthful, figure-hugging, and seemed to compliment them. From the chatter I overheard, it seemed as though everyone had options to choose from, having borrowed gowns from family.

I frowned at my reflection, at the gown I had to purchase for the show because, unlike everyone else, *I* couldn't just borrow one from my mother or aunts because they wouldn't fit me. Even with the wide range of colors and patterns on the racks at the Vietnamese dress shop, I quickly learned that the options weren't meant for me. After the saleswoman took my measurements, she presented me with the only two dresses that would fit me, with the reassurance that the heavier fabric was sophisticated and the dark color would complement my brown complexion. Apparently Vietnamese women came in one size and color, and I was just six inches too tall, three cup sizes too busty, and too dark.

My right arm jerked when I felt something touch my elbow. I turned to my right slightly, catching a glimpse of the top of Nancy's head before being jerked forward again. I watched her return the favor from the mirror. As she grasped the front and back panels of my gown from my right side, tugging them to meet to make it easier to button, I frowned and felt my face grow warm.

Nancy was a first-generation Vietnamese American teenager like me. We both had brown eyes and long raven hair, were the same age, did well in school, and were friendly when in the same social groups. But with all our similarities, we had more differences and, in terms of appearance, she had more in common with the other girls than I did. It was something that was so blatantly obvious that I almost wanted to laugh for not noticing the truth until this moment.

Out on stage, the girls, who were standing in the front rows of the choral risers wearing pretty and colorful gowns once worn by their mothers, had choices and *belonged*. They belonged in the Vietnamese community with their ideally average physicalities of Vietnamese women: petite, thin, and pale. And they belonged in American high school dating terrain as the embodiment of the exoticized, petite, and demure Asian woman. And then there was me, standing in the second-to-last row in the back and wearing the only gown that fit me—one that was black and sequined and obviously designed for a woman much older than sixteen—I'd never felt more out of place. I knew that I never wanted to feel that way again.

≈

"You look ridiculous," my mother said as I took a seat across from her at the kitchen table. My shrug was muffled by the giant hoodie I borrowed from my brother, covering my old t-shirt, running shorts, and fuzzy socks. "And thin—maybe *too* thin."

"I've lost some weight," I admitted with my mouth full. I surrendered my plate, patiently indulging her with the opportunity to serve me more food as mothers do, though the topic of conversation had quickly changed before I even picked up my fork again.

"How's school, Cindy?" my father asked, redirecting the table's attention back to me. The spotlight shone intensely as I had expected, but with more aggressive prodding and scrutiny than usual because I was only a semester away from graduating college. I answered their questions politely, giving vague answers with a practiced confidence that seemed to appease them.

"You look paler," my uncle commented as he passed my brother the bottle of soy sauce. "Prettier."

"Uh, thanks . . ." I waited another beat, for another topic change, before getting up with the excuse of being tired and quickly dumping my plate in the kitchen sink.

I climbed the stairs slowly, the lively conversations of the dinner table fading into a low rumble to make room for my fatigue and exhaustion. Grazing past framed pictures of family that were hung along the wall, I paused midstep when the last one caught my eye. It was a posed family photo—everyone surrounding my youngest cousin, Simon, who was wearing a party hat and beaming behind a cake. I could pick out my mother and her sisters, their matching noses and petite stature giving them away. I remembered my mother once told me that she had the darkest skin among her siblings because, as she was told, her mother had consumed a cup of coffee while pregnant with her. But as I squinted at their faces, I couldn't see the difference. They all looked the same to me: the embodiment of ideal Vietnamese femininity with their thin, petite frames and pale skin reinforced by a shared skin-whitening regimen. No matter what I did—dieting, exercising, listening to my mother's nagging to work on my midsection or to bind my breasts to stop them from growing, and wearing makeup a shade too light—I couldn't change enough.

My steps grew heavier as I reached the top of the staircase. The hardwood floor creaked once outside my bedroom before I fell into bed. I buried my nose further into the worn fabric of my floral comforter. With closed eyes, I breathed in the familiar smell of fresh laundry and home. My body sagged further and further into the mattress as each exhale released bits of tension. I could've fallen asleep right there, my muscles aching and begging to hibernate for the rest of the winter holidays.

But I couldn't sleep. I hadn't been able to sleep without the help of alcohol or Benadryl or just sheer exhaustion for the past seven months. There were so many things to do. Homework to complete, papers to write, meetings for my internships, and two part-time jobs. Birthdays, parties, social obligations. And I just couldn't stop. And no one questioned my precarious juggling act of twelve-hour days. I passed all my classes with As and finished my internships with glowing recommendations. My professors told me I had a bright future. My peers were just as impressed with my work as they were with my alcohol tolerance. But I only just realized how much weight I'd really lost when I looked back on recent pictures with friends during my flight home. I always had a drink in hand and a glazed-over smile, my once-fitted clothes hanging loosely on my body. The sharpness of my chin and my jaw were more prominent. The paleness of my skin was more lackluster than glowing, especially with the dark circles underneath my eyes.

As I lay on this bed in my sparse childhood bedroom, I remembered the resigned rejection my sixteen-year-old self felt as she stood on a stage and wore a gown that hasn't left her closet since. I wish I could tell her that all the hard work and effort pushed her to be where I am now, grasping at a confidence that is defined by others. I wish I could tell her that losing ten pounds and receiving "compliments" about my paleness made me happier.

Was I finally pale enough for others to stop mistaking me as belonging to other ethnicities? Was I finally pretty enough to belong as a Vietnamese woman?

The only thing that I could tell her was that I am *tired.*

Part VI

SKIN—
REDEFINED

According to Lori L. Tharps, professor and author of the book *Same Family, Different Colors*, "The whole world is waking up to [the colorism] issue."[1] In Asia and across the Asian diaspora, especially among South and Southeast Asians, increased attention to colorism in recent years has led to critical dialogue and growing backlash against its toxicity and racist and sexist messaging. In 2013, Bollywood actress and director Nandita Das became a leading activist for the "Dark Is Beautiful" campaign, calling out India's obsession with light skin in a series of public service announcements aimed at Indian women.[2] Repeated requests by directors and camera persons to lighten her dark skin drove her to champion the issue, and her high-profile support has fueled its visibility and growing popularity.[3] One such ad reads, "In a country where 90% of people are dark, it is sad that we grow up with such an inferiority complex about it. Stay UNfair, Stay Beautiful!"

In the same year, Pakistan saw its first anti-colorism campaign, created by social activist Fatima Lodhi, designed to counter the fair-and-lovely mantra of South Asia. She admits that when she launched the campaign, titled "Dark Is Divine," it was a new concept for many, noting that "people were shocked [by the campaign] and they didn't actually get the concept. They said how can this [dark] complexion be beautiful? How can this complexion be divine?"[4] Lodhi's aim is clear: "We're trying to redefine the unrealistic standards of beauty propagated by the media"—even by South Asian celebrities who endorse fairness creams for personal profit.[5] The campaign began in Pakistan, but is markedly global. It first reached neighboring South Asian nations such as India, Nepal, Sri Lanka, and Bangladesh through "awareness drives," though within two years of its inception, it extended to twenty-five nations, including those outside of South Asia such as Mexico, Turkey, and Canada.[6]

Though these campaigns are very young, both have a heavy online and social media presence, allowing for greater connectivity and rapid spread of their anti-colorist message. Others, too, have exploited social media to challenge colorism, including actress and YouTube star Asia Jackson. Jackson, who is multiracial (black and Filipina) and American born, created the online viral sensation #MagandangMorenx, which literally translates to "beautiful brown skin" in Tagalog, and encourages Filipinxs of all genders to love their brown skin. Since its launch in 2016, thousands of Filipinxs worldwide have posted their dark-skinned selfies under the popular hashtag. Dark-skinned South Asians are similarly showcasing their brown beauty online with the hashtag #UnfairAndLovely, a campaign created by three students from the University of Texas. Launched in 2016, the movement was inspired by Pax Jones, a black student at the same university, who created a photographic series showcasing the beauty of dark skin, beginning with Jones's South Asian American classmates.[7] The photos went viral on social media, and thousands of dark-skinned women around the world began posting photos of themselves alongside the hashtag, which was directly inspired by the whitening cream Fair & Lovely, popular in South Asia and among South Asian American communities. Though early attention was given to dark skin among South Asian women, Jones has broadened the campaign's inclusivity to include all people of color who experience colorism.[8]

Collectively, these activist campaigns confront and interrogate the social stigma surrounding dark skin, though the battle is an uphill one. It is no easy task to challenge racist and sexist social messaging across societies that for centuries, perhaps even millennia, have told women that their brown skin is ugly. These campaigns, though progressive and positive, must continually compete with colorist messages that saturate many societies and condition its people—messages found on television, in film, on billboards, in magazines, and even within families. Moreover, while anti-colorism campaigns are growing among South and Southeast Asian cultures where dark skin is common, no known parallel campaigns currently exist in East Asia, where colorism is similarly pronounced. In countries like China, Japan, and Korea, the "light-skin-is-superior-to-dark" mantra remains unchallenged, though perhaps the aforementioned campaigns on social media will eventually change this.

In this final collection of essays, women share their personal journeys towards self-acceptance and their embrace of their skin shade. They describe colorism in their lives (as in Part I), and, most importantly, they challenge the "light-skin-is-beautiful" message, often in direct defiance of mothers, grandmothers, friends, and society. Joanne Rondilla, Filipina American, describes growing up feeling "fat and dark," though she writes of her path to healing as an adult. Daniela Pila, Filipina American, writes of her own struggles growing up in the Philippines and her "reprogramming" since moving to the United States. She writes of "winning the daily battles" against the inner demons of her childhood, allowing her to recognize and embrace her beauty. Lillian Lu, Chinese American, and Rowena Mangohig, Filipina American, both write of their defiance of mothers and grandmothers who press them to preserve and protect their light skin, each embracing their West Coast tans and themselves. Rowena writes of her realization as an adult that "the lightness of [her] skin doesn't mean shit." And Julia DeCook, multiracial Korean and white, describes the Korean standard for light skin (as taught to her in many ways, including by her Korean mother and grandmother) and her embrace of her "mixed raceness" and "darkened skin."

For some women, the process of acceptance is decades long and, for at least two contributors, a labor of love for the next generation—their daughters. Mindful of their own struggles with colorism, they express their hopes that their daughters will come to recognize their own value and beauty, and they labor to halt the cycle that is often seen in Asian families as colorist beliefs are passed from one generation to the next. Unlike some of the other essays in this book that reveal the pressures that often stem from women in the family, such as mothers and grandmothers, these mothers aim to parent in ways intended to minimize the effects of colorism on their daughters. Kathy Tran-Peters, Vietnamese American, writes a powerful essay to her future unborn daughter about her personal struggles growing up in America, and her hopes that her child will "embrace" what it has taken her years to embrace: her skin. And finally, Betty Ming Liu, Chinese American, writes of her decades-long journey to self-acceptance and self-love, and the lessons she is trying to impart to her multiracial daughter, who, like herself, has struggled with her skin color. Each essay in this final section illustrates the power of self-love and the journey to self-acceptance. Dark skin, often vilified and stigmatized across Asia and among Asian American communities, is redefined and re-claimed as beautiful. Theirs are stories of evolution and transformation, and while not all women in this book are at the same point of acceptance, these stories are powerful and reveal what is possible.

24

The Very Best of You

Joanne L. Rondilla, FILIPINA AMERICAN, 41

At a young age, I learned that my skin color matters. Now that I am an adult and a scholar of colorism, the combination of age and education has not made my skin color less significant. I am reminded of this on the first day of class each semester when students are surprised that the person standing in front of the room passing out the syllabus is the actual instructor (and not his fill-in assistant). As curious strangers express disappointment when I answer their "Where are you from?" question, I forget that my bland "California" response never matches their exotic expectations.

Strangers aside, my own colorism story starts with my parents. Though they're from neighboring provinces in the Philippines, Mom grew up middle-class in a business-owning family. She had relatives who were local politicians and who worked in various positions of authority. Though her life was not easy, she definitely did not grow up poor. In contrast, my *lola* (grandmother) on my father's side was a widow. As the eldest, Pop had to help raise his two younger siblings by helping *lola* earn money to feed the family. My memories of Pop are filled with him telling stories of how difficult it was for him to grow up poor in the Philippines. The difference in my parents' lives was, in many ways, illustrated in their skin color.

To this day, my mother is as light as porcelain. When we're in the Philippines, her skin color gives her access to high-class treatment when we walk through the mall. When we visit the provinces (countryside), her skin color attracts random stares from strangers. Pop wasn't much darker than Mom, though both social class and skin color would be defining differences between them. As an adult, Pop was college educated and worked as a mechanical engineer for the US Navy in Guam (a US territory, which many considered as good as the mainland United States). For the sake of their courtship and eventual marriage, these credentials would work in his favor.

During visits to the Philippines, it is easy to see everyday life as color coded. These codes are part of a complex historical and colonial system that continues to create assumptions about one's class standing and overall humanity. Dark-skinned people are coded as poor, while the lighter-skinned are coded as rich. Almost always, realities do not matter when so many Filipinos seem to rely heavily on appearances to determine a person's story. Color codes are especially apparent when one watches Philippine television. Years ago, Mom was obsessed with a television show called *Bakekang*. It was a story of a dark-skinned, flat-nosed woman who has two daughters: one ugly and one beautiful. The ugly one is dark-skinned and flat-nosed like her mother, and the beautiful one is light-skinned with a slim nose. I want to believe that ultimately, Mom's reason for watching this show is a compelling story line and not the trials and tribulations of having an ugly daughter. However, the basis of the story was troubling to me, and I had no interest in watching. It raised personal pain for me—why would I want to watch a show that reminded me of my own upbringing as the ugly daughter?! In Philippine television, beautiful people are light and rich. Ugly people are dark and poor (the redeeming ones are comical at best). US media is no different. Though many people can acknowledge that this is problematic, no one seems to concretely do anything about it.

Spike Lee's 1988 film, *School Daze*, illustrates these tensions among black college students when during a school rally, a group of dark-skinned women with natural hair chant the following to the Gamma Ray sorority sisters: "Your eyes are blue, but you ain't white. Your hair is fake because you pressed it last night." In response, the sorority sisters chant, "Who is that jigaboo?! And why don't you take it to a local zoo? Cause you spent the other day at the local zoo. It had a big nappy beast and it looked like you . . ." The sorority sisters are seen as assimilationists who want to be white; the darker-skinned women are described as subhuman through the term "jigaboo" and references to a "beast" at the "local zoo." The film points to in-group tensions that reflect correlations between skin color and humanity, and differences are enforced in intimate spaces such as within specific social groups, friends, and family.

Colorism—a looks-based discriminatory institution existing within the same racial and/or ethnic group—is distinct from racism. Where racism is the discrimination between people of different races (e.g., discrimination of black people by whites; discrimination of Asians by whites, etc.), I see colorism as the start-ing point of such bigotry. Within the same national borders, shared communities, and families, we learn to discriminate against each other based on, initially, physical features. In my family, I learned the idea that dark skin, flat noses, kinky hair, and fat bodies are un-desirable. These are markers of the unsightly. When I step out into the world, these markers hold the same meaning when I interact with non-Filipinos. Thus, colorism informs racism, and vice versa. I see them as "cousins," related though not identical. While colorism is manifested on the body, its consequences go beyond the mere physical. The negative ideas associated with undesirable bodies are attached to larger, unfair assumptions about a person's humanity. These include presumptions about class and civility—that low-class, "savage" people have these physical traits. These are assertions imposed within and across ethnic and racial communities.

There are a few incidents of colorism that led me to believe that what I looked like made me the family outcast. The first instance happened when I was seven years old. My family and I spent the summer in the Philippines. We stayed with rich relatives in an exclusive housing area called Alabang. I knew they were rich because they had servants, which is a marker of high social status in the Philippines. Each morning, my siblings, other visiting cousins, and I would wake up to the sweet smell of hot Ovaltine and *pan de sal* (bread rolls) waiting for us at one corner of our assigned bedrooms. Once we were done, we would leave the dishes on the table for the staff to pick up and clean. This was very different from my own house, where no one waited on us. My rich cousins also took ballet and equestrian classes. On certain nights, our families would gather in the living room to watch our cousins dance and sing. The approving looks my mother gave them were unfamiliar to me. I had no such talent for the classic arts and had never been the recipient of high-culture doting.

Our relatives also had access to a country club, where we were able to indulge in some of their swanky benefits, such as swimming lessons (a gift to me from my wealthy aunt and uncle that was related to their belief that I needed to lose weight). After I spent my summer under the sun, my normally caramel-colored skin quickly became a dark chocolate color. I did not mind the change because I was used to seeing my skin transform color depending on the season. Up until that point, I cannot recall my skin color being a topic of negative discussion. Yet, this particular summer, my family and I visited a tourist park where we could see indigenous Filipinos in loincloths demonstrate exoticized indigenous activities like spear fighting. When we took pictures with the performers, my wealthy aunt made me hold hands with one of the little boys. She snickered and declared that we needed to hold hands because our dark skin "matched." My child self was confused, then humiliated. Despite the daily swimming lessons not being my choice, I was subjected to constant ridicule for getting darker. The nose pinching (to sharpen my flat nose), first from my mom, then my aunt, also made me uncomfortable and self-conscious. For the first time in my life, I felt the weight of my skin color and my ugliness. I didn't want to hold the boy's hand, but I didn't let go of it either. Perhaps that was because I didn't want to disobey an elder. Perhaps my seven-year-old self didn't want him to feel the same humiliation I felt. Perhaps I held on because I didn't want to feel the double embarrassment of him letting go of me. Although we were Filipinos of the same skin color, there was suddenly a clear distinction between "us" (the boy and I) and "them" (my wealthy aunt and her family).

This incident had a profound effect on me and how I understood my body. At the end of the trip, my mother's side of the family (all seven siblings and their respective families) gathered in Alabang to bid us good-bye. A major part of the good-bye process included taking photos. Again, my dark skin became an issue. I was told to smile with my teeth so that the camera could capture a glimpse of me. Otherwise, I'd be a "dark blob." Years later, looking at the photos, I see that I'm not actually much darker than anyone else, but I was perceived as "the dark cousin," which warranted ridicule by the rest of the family. What my personal story and the media demonstrate is that in the Philippines, one is *supposed* to treat dark-skinned people a certain way—even if they're family—because dark skin is not worthy of humanity.

When I recall the summer with my cousins now, they're shocked at my bitter feelings. As far as they're concerned, I was a happy-go-lucky kid. Since I'm smiling in the photos, they assumed that I enjoyed holding the boy's hand, and that I had a good time like the rest of the family. My response is this: *Faking happiness is part of the protocol of existence.* This is especially important when you're the dark one. Like the little boy whose hand I held onto so tightly, I was accustomed to performing. Happiness, especially when fabricated, indicates that you can take the taunting. In truth, the perception of happiness does not decrease the hurt. When we returned to Guam, I noticed that the comments about not staying out in the sun occurred even more frequently, along with the nose pinching (this included the use of clothespins). Comments about being fat also became a common narrative in my life. Years of these messages would turn me numb to how problematic this all was. As a defense mechanism, I turned to school. If I couldn't be pretty, I sure as hell could be smart (and when needed, I could also fake this because I'm smart like that!). Intelligence eased the discomfort of being fat and dark because it meant I had talent. Smart women are also self-sustaining, economically independent—something I would apparently need since I was repeatedly told no man would marry me because of the whole "fat-and-dark" thing.

By the time I was in graduate school, I was armed with critical race theory and a baseline knowledge of colonialism and imperialism and an understanding of controlling images. The challenge was contextualizing this theory and history with everyday life—even my own. When I was a teaching assistant, our class watched a film about Filipina domestic workers in Europe. During the class discussion, one of my students expressed dissatisfaction with the documentary. When I asked why, she said that the documentary misrepresented Filipina domestic workers as highly educated. She was from Singapore and her family had Filipina domestics, so she claimed to know first-hand that these "maids" are not well educated as the documentary illustrated. While I could, for a moment, listen to her point, what was infuriating was that she wouldn't let it go. She went on and on about how the domestic workers that she knows are not as smart, articulate, and educated as the ones in the film. Trying to remain calm and patient, I could feel the wrath of the three Filipino students in the class. Their seething stares demanded an immediate and angry reaction from me to their peer. Unfortunately, I let the three students down. While I did not confirm the student's comments about Filipina domestics, I did not challenge her either. I reverted to the insecurities of my youth. I related to these women in the film. We looked like each other. Here was my student: light-skinned, wealthy, and privileged enough to not be responsible, thoughtful, or kind with her words. There was me: the teaching assistant living paycheck to paycheck, fat and dark, with a debilitating case of imposter syndrome.

As a Filipina, I am seen in a particular way, personally and professionally. Legacies of war and colonization in the Philippines inform dominant views, and fellow Asians, Asian Americans, and non-Asians have directly (and indirectly) inherited these perceptions. Filipinas are known globally as domestic workers and sex workers. As with my privileged student, these controlling images, coupled with skin-color hierarchies within Asian American communities, enable negative perceptions. Regardless of my extensive education, I'm still seen as dark, fat, and incapable of intellectualism. The expectation is that I remain hidden, for only thin, light, beautiful people can shine in the spotlight. People like me are relegated to the background. For most of my life, I believed in these expectations because they were reinforced in popular media, at home, and at my job, and it would take a long time before I would reach a healing place.

One day, I came across an interview with Doris Roberts, an actress from the TV show *Everybody Loves Raymond*. She explained that the horrific beauty standards in Hollywood are related to the way the industry teaches young women to deny themselves what they can truly accomplish. She said when you try to become something you're not, you prevent yourself from becoming what you were meant to be. When you starve your body, you starve yourself from being the person you *should* be. And that is a complete shame not only to yourself, but to the world. She said women should choose to share the very best of themselves with the world, and harsh beauty standards deny us this. Her words continue to have an incredibly profound effect on me. So much of my life has been inundated with messages of everything wrong with my body. Everything I accomplished had been diminished because I was the dark and fat cousin/professor/person in the room. Yet words from a white actress forced me to dig deep and break out of these confines while reminding me that we can *all* share in resistance.

There is no perfect formula for healing. But I would like to tell the seven-year-old me to keep holding on to that boy's hand. In a world that deems us unworthy, I want our younger selves to know that faith in yourself and approaching life fearlessly matter more than your skin color. To the Filipino students who witnessed my silence, I am sorry. While I cannot go back to that day, I continue to do better in the classroom. I teach critically and unapologetically, and work with students through the difficult conversations regarding racial prejudice, colorism, and societal violence against our bodies. My wish for those who are on the road to healing is this: refrain from starving yourself and the world of your true value. In these times, the world needs the very best of you, and you and we deserve more.

25

Reprogramming

Daniela Pila, FILIPINA AMERICAN, 28

"You are so beautiful," my boyfriend told me as he gazed adoringly at my face. I visibly cringed. The words sounded so foreign to me.

"Uhh, I'm not sure what to say," I awkwardly replied.

"Well, I guess you'll have to get used to it," he quipped.

Growing up in the Philippines, I realized that I was the antithesis of classic Filipina beauty. My *morena* (brown) skin and nonmestizo[1] features—my short, flat nose, my small, rounded eyes, my round, chubby face—were unattractive. My hair is a mix of wavy-curly and not the ideal straight texture. I hated putting on sunscreen when we were at the beach or playing tennis, so my brown skin was constantly tanned. It did not help that I also loved to eat and that my body showed it. My childhood is filled with memories of my grade school classmates telling me that I was "*pangit*" (ugly), that I was a "*baboy*" (pig), and that I was "*taba*" (fat).

Family parties reinforced the negative attention to my body. Every time I saw my well-meaning relatives, they would ask, "How did you gain so much weight?"; "How did you get so dark?"; and "Why is your nose so short?" After getting my usual barrage of questions, I would listen to their conversations as they assessed the present children's beauty on the basis of their skin color, the color of their hair, and the length of their noses.

"Maria is such a pretty girl. I hope she keeps that light skin out of the sun."

"David's nose is so perfect. He's so lucky his grandmother is from Spain!"

I could not escape this reinforcement at home. *Lola* (my grandmother) was the main caregiver to my siblings and I since my parents both worked full-time jobs. Unprovoked, she would point out how fat I was getting and how big my ass and my breasts were. During mealtimes she would bark, "Sige lang ka'g kaon! [You're eating so much!]," even though it was she who determined the portion sizes of our meals. To avoid her, I would hide in the bedroom I shared with my two siblings and only leave to eat and to use the restroom.

As a result, I hated my body immensely. My self-esteem was nonexistent, and I had no friends in- or outside of school. Some of my classmates thought I was entertaining due to my constant barrage of questions to my teachers in the classroom—telltale signs of a future academic. Outside of the classroom, however, I barely existed. I was extremely lonely, and I resorted to eccentric ways to gain friends. I used my weekly allowance to try to buy friendships, to no avail. I still remember Papa's incredulous face when, for my fifth grade birthday, we squeezed twenty fifth graders into our five-passenger sedan to treat them at every Filipino child's favorite fast food restaurant, Jollibee (Philippine driving laws are more relaxed than those in the United States). I grew more and more conscious of my status as an "outsider" due to my appearance. I started to notice that the kids who were deemed the most attractive had the lightest skin and were usually half-non-Filipino. (Half-Caucasian and half-Japanese were okay, but not half-Indian. God forbid.) Even if those same kids were cruel to others, their appearance, above all else, determined their top place in the school hierarchy.

While they were at the top of the food chain, I was barely at the bottom of the barrel.

The media also influenced my perception about myself. *Lola* usually took a nap in the afternoon. During this time, our two maids were allowed to use the TV in the living room and watch *teleseryas* (Philippine TV dramas) as long as their work was completed. Since I got home from school at the same time, I would watch the series with them. Over the ridiculous overacting and the nonsensical plots, the maids would discuss the actors' appearances: "Tan-awa na si Judy Ann [Santos]. Kagwapa gyud niya oi! [Look at Judy Ann Santos. She's so beautiful!]." The actress was light-skinned, with long, straight black hair in a low ponytail, and looked like she weighed less than a hundred pounds. Regarding another actress: "Itum na kaayo si Nora [Aunor]! Nidako na pud siya! [Nora Aunor is too dark! She also got fatter!]." I did not understand why they were so fixated on the actors' appearance, rather than the plot of the show.

Realizing my affinity for the arts, my parents enrolled me in classes in Lu Chin Bon Performing Arts Center. Despite the forty-minute one-way commute from our house, I had finally found my escape. I immediately fell in love with performing and readily took acting, dancing, and singing classes. Through our practices, rehearsals, and performances, I slowly gained confidence in myself. The intense physical activity built muscle where there was formerly none. Thanks to puberty, I was the second tallest girl in my high school at five feet four inches; the tallest girl was five feet seven inches. I was standing out in school again, but the difference was that I had my performing classes to look forward to.

By the time I was in high school, I was no longer called "*pangit*," "*baboy*," or "*taba*" to my face, though the pressure to be light-skinned and thin continued—especially as a young Filipina adult. One day, I tired of all the negative attention and bought papaya soap.[2] I spent an hour in the bathroom trying to scrub my brown skin white, filled with self-loathing as tears streamed down my face. Even at 130 pounds, I continued to think that I was too fat. In an effort to lose more weight, I stopped eating real food and only ate fruit. The pain from my bowel movements was worth it: It stopped people from making verbal attacks on my body. I got what I wanted, but I was miserable and constantly hungry. After I blacked out one day due to hunger, I reluctantly started eating food again.

Moving to the United States saved my life. Mama received a US work visa, and in 2003, Papa, my two younger siblings, and I moved to West Covina, California. My world was turned upside down. My argumentative personality—a problem in Filipino collectivistic culture—was perceived as a positive trait in the American classroom. Within the first month of attending my California high school, I had received compliments for my tanned skin. "How did you get it to be that color?" my white classmates asked excitedly. "Um, I was born like this?" I replied with confusion. Amid the sea of black and brown of my multiracial school, I no longer stood out in school. No one pointed out my weight gains or losses, commented on my dark skin, or questioned why I didn't straighten my hair. For the first time in my life, I felt normal. People saw me for who I truly was—beyond the color of my skin. I made friends in my school that I am still close to even today. And though I gained twenty pounds in my first four years of living in the United States, I had never been happier or more content.

My life took yet another unexpected turn in my junior year of college when I met my boyfriend. We were extremely different people—I, a 1.5-generation Filipina immigrant,[3] he, a fourth-generation Jewish American—but our first date lasted for six hours. It was my first serious relationship . . . and with a white man at that.

Every time he told me I was beautiful, I felt like an imposter. I didn't know how to react to the adulation that he constantly showered me with. "Why do you look confused when I tell you that you're beautiful?" he asked me more than once. Even though I had been living in the United States for seven years at that point, the Filipino standards of beauty were still deeply embedded within me. I would look in the mirror and see what I perceived as the worst parts of myself—my dark brown skin, my small nose, my curly-wavy hair. It was hard to feel worthy enough to be someone's partner.

My boyfriend could not believe that he was my first boyfriend: "Did no boys really ever ask you out?!?" The idea of someone being romantically interested in me was as foreign to me as was the idea that I was beautiful. I worried incessantly that he would look at me one day and realize that I had somehow tricked him. Then, he would break up with me and I would once again be alone.

Every time he said I was beautiful, I instead thought the opposite: "No. I am actually dark-skinned, fat, and disgusting."

Reprogramming my inner dialogue is a constant work in progress. After years of being with my then-boyfriend, now-husband, I have slowly grown to like the way I look. When I see myself in the mirror, I no longer see all my flaws and imperfections. I like how my body is curvy and how it fills in dresses. I admire the feel of my skin and how my short hair falls on the back of my neck. My short nose allows me to kiss my husband straight on without having to tilt my head. I have yet to win the war against the inner demons of my childhood, but I am winning the daily battles.

"I'll never get tired of telling you how beautiful you are," my husband remarked one day. I am finally starting to believe him.

26

Cartographies of Myself

Lillian Lu, CHINESE AMERICAN, 23

This summer, while conducting graduate research on orientalism, I took a shopping trip to UNIQLO, a Japanese clothing brand, and bought a dress. The dress, white with deep blue flowers printed all over, recalled the Chinese blue willow porcelain patterns so coveted by the English that it launched China mania throughout the eighteenth and nineteenth centuries. I was aware of the irony while buying it, and each time I wear it, I think of it, only half-jokingly, as a reclamation of commodified Chinese porcelain, known for its durability and smooth pearliness.

Interestingly, it was porcelain that older Chinese Americans used to describe my pale skin as a toddler. It was meant as a compliment, a mark of beauty, an auspicious sign of future femininity. The dress, which I sometimes hesitate to wear because of all the weight its design seems to carry, has also become for me a physical reminder of this history, my grappling with the commodification of light skin within Asian American communities. My transition into adulthood has been a many-forked journey—one of those a road to accepting and understanding the image of the woman in my mirror, beyond a simplistic binary of dark and light.

I often wear the blue willow dress here in Southern California. Until last year, I'd lived on the East Coast, most recently in New England, and I'd never been much of an outdoorswoman until a few months ago, when I was stirred into needed physical activity by the sedentary habits of graduate school. I look upon visiting home with eagerness, but also with a knowing trepidation, for there, there are people who can trace the history of my skin tone, from that porcelain whiteness to the California tan I am now. When I last visited for Christmas, my grandmother told me, with a clicking of her tongue and fingers as she adjusted my collar, that I had gotten darker, that I didn't look like myself.

Myself.

She meant well. She is my grandmother on my mother's side, the side of my family that hailed from Guangzhou in southern China, found themselves in Vietnam in between wars, and fled by boat. The Cantonese, her people as well as mine, are a people stereotyped, even in China, as darker, less urban, less cultured, and shorter. Their dialect, containing more tones than the four that distinguish Mandarin words, is tougher for the native English and even Mandarin speaker to learn, and it is they who were brought to the Americas in the 1600s as unfree miners, and later came to the States as underpaid laborers on plantations, in fisheries, and on the railroads.

Yes, she meant well. She wanted me to have an easier life than she had had, and for Asian women, that generally means a life of having light skin. She didn't know her comment struck a chord in me: how throughout my adolescence, I had several times been called "not Chinese," or a "bad Asian." My high school had been filled with Mandarin-speaking peers, so I frequently had to explain that while my father was from Qingdao and spoke the common dialect, half my childhood had been steeped in the six-toned lilts of Cantonese. I have often felt myself straddling my Chinese and American identities, and within the former, my southern and northern Chinese identities. There are many lines and borders to navigate across this cartography of myself.

To my Chinese peers, my Cantonese half somehow contaminated me, making me racially impure, the looming images of darker skin tones signaling to them that I was somehow less academically ambitious, someone descended from so-called coolie laborers. My Cantonese half summons a history of a Chinese people who were not accepted as Americans and not even given the right to citizenship until the 1950s; they were migrants exploited for their labor, rather than welcomed as immigrants to the United States. It is a twisted piece of US history that, for some, feels comforting to ignore in exchange for the warm embrace of the "model minority" stereotype. And even in the context of China, colorism runs rampant: Those who live in southern China, of course, live in warmer climates, which, as in the West, has long carried a host of deterministic associations—warmer climates mean agricultural work, which means darker skin, which means an assumed difference in ability, education, and intellect. The same classmate who, on my first day of school in a new town, sidled up to me and laid his arm next to mine, saying, "Look! We're the same color!" was the one who later told me I wasn't *really* Chinese when he found out I was half-Cantonese. That I defied one expectation led to a cascade of slippery categories and twisted constellations that drew curious connections among skin tone, racial belonging, ethnicity, and even definitions of beauty.

Though I spent my childhood porcelain-passing, I no longer am. The whiteness of the dress's bodice blinds in the Californian sunlight, softened by my yellow-brown skin. To me, my tan means those weekends I spent hiking, breathing in the aroma of plants that only grow at that elevation. It means the days riding my bike near the shore, looking out into the distance after a day of fixating my eyes on my readings. It means remembering nature around me, and being in it. It means that I have traversed the country to make a life for myself here. It means that I have lived to see and do all of that, and that I can grow more into myself, into new versions of that self, just as my skin remakes itself every few months. In Southern California, the seasons do not mark the passage of time, so my skin does.

The story of my maternal family is one more colorful than anything textbooks or stereotypes have told. Their cartographies go beyond borders, too. My grandmother's tan tells the story of her life in Vietnam—how she was seen as an outsider there, and in China too, and how she picked vegetables in the hills and packed her bags and her family of six onto a boat to escape persecution, all to come to the States. My mom has a similar tan, which tells of her days as a child selling bean sprouts that she herself grew in order to earn money, the weeks when she and her family lived on a beach on their way to Hong Kong because the boat had sprung a leak, the months exposed to the elements, to so many languages, until she finally landed on English.

Last week, she video-called me from New Jersey, telling me that she had her first age spot on her cheeks. She pointed to it: It was dark, a smudge the size of a thumbprint, as if she'd wiped her face absentmindedly while writing. She has been talking more, she tells me, to recuperate memories she thought she had lost. One day, she hopes to write. She was becoming more herself, too.

I thought it fitting that she and I both have October birthdays—October being the month when the leaves on the East Coast change color, when the West Coast sun becomes gentler.

"We are older now," she said to me, to which I replied, "And you look beautiful."

The "and" was the bridge and the key.

27

The Sun Is Calling My Name

Rowena Mangohig, FILIPINA AMERICAN, 46

"Stay out of the sun or you'll get dark."

This was something I heard frequently from my mother, and she didn't say it because she was worried about the sun increasing my chance of getting skin cancer. She said it because she was convinced that the lighter my skin, the prettier I would be. As a result, it seems I've always understood that skin color was important in determining my level of beauty; however, there was little I could do to avoid dark skin while growing up in the sun-drenched southern half of the United States. My parents immigrated to the United States from the Philippines when I was only a few months old. They made do with very little, so they were naturally inclined to use the free resources available to them, meaning that we spent a lot of time on the docks fishing, crabbing, shrimping, gathering clams from the beaches, wading waist deep for scallops, and harvesting guavas, coconuts, and papayas from neighbors' trees. My time spent in the sun was generally without fear of the "consequences," and I did very little to keep the sun from touching my skin. What did it matter back then? I was a kid and I had my priorities, and taking care of my skin at the risk of restricting my outdoor play time was not one of them.

I have a picture of my three sisters and myself ranging in ages from one to eight years old during this decadent, carefree time of my life when we were living in Key West, Florida. Sitting at the top center of the photo is me, the oldest of the bunch, with flushed brown skin because the picture was taken just after my run home from school with friends under the bright Florida sun. Hot and sweaty, I was in complete contrast to my younger sister at the bottom corner. She was a chubby preschooler and, despite her self-cut bangs, was the real beauty of the photo because her skin was the lightest of us all. She had big, round eyes, not small or "chinky," as the grown-ups would say, and based on that picture, she could have perhaps belonged to a different family. She was certainly special. When my parents would introduce us to their Filipino friends, even they knew how special she was, and they would often comment that of the four of us, she was the one who could be Miss America.

I never begrudged my sister for being the "fairest one of all." She just happened to be lucky, taking after my mother, while the rest of us shared the coloring of my darker-skinned father. It wasn't until junior high that I started doing things to either lighten my skin or else keep myself from getting darker. I think the change came when I actually became interested in what other people thought of me—especially the boys. In those days, I decided that the sun was not my friend after all, and I began to insist on long sleeves even in the hottest weather. I avoided the beach, but if forced to go, I was the one sitting under the shade of a picnic shelter, fully clothed and wearing a wide-brimmed hat, while everyone else played in the surf or leisurely lounged in the sand. When I heard that lemon juice could whiten skin, I was ecstatic. We were living in Southern California by then, and everyone had lemon trees growing in their back yards. Pretty soon, with access to lemons and this new-found knowledge, I'd be Miss-America-beautiful just like my little sister. Okay, so Miss America wasn't really what I was striving for since I wasn't actually into pageants and parading myself around for people to ogle—but I could finally be a *princess*. This was a big deal because, according to my childhood friends, there was no such thing as a brown princess. The lack of diversity in movies, television shows, and books certainly reinforced this idea. So here it was, my chance to be the princess-who-never-was thanks to a little lemon juice! It didn't take long to dash those dreams into the dirt because all the lemon juice did was turn my face into a scaly mess.

I bet the *mixed* kids never had this problem, I thought. I was so jealous of those half-white/half-Filipino children because I thought they were truly beautiful. I thought that their lives must be so much better than mine—filled with flowers and fairies and woodland animals that would eat right out of their hands. They always seemed smarter, happier, friendlier. They were popular. They were surrounded by admirers. They were richer. Their lives were filled with love and golden opportunities. They had privileges that didn't exist for those of us with darker skin. For some of these kids, not only were they lighter skinned, but some could even "pass" for white. Or, at the very least, they could be ambiguous and keep people guessing. I'd never be able to keep them guessing— although people often guessed wrong since they often confused Asian groups and pegged me as Cambodian rather than Filipino. Perhaps exotic was the best I could hope for.

On my first visit to the Philippines, I was eighteen and for the first time introduced to skin-whitening lotion. *Why had I never heard of this?!* Why would my mother continually say, "Stay out of the sun or you'll get dark," when all I needed was to put on this lotion? Based on the variety of whitening products on store shelves and the prevalence of these products in TV commercials and printed ads, I saw that light skin was valuable and something coveted by the many consumers in this country—so valuable in fact that it could even determine whether or not you got a job. I discovered this during an outing with my cousins in Manila. While they were showing us around the city, I noticed a "Help Wanted" sign for table help in a restaurant window. As at any business establishment, I assumed that they were looking for a hard worker, someone with a certain amount of experience waiting tables, someone who was a team player and willing to go the extra mile for their customers. At least, that's what I would imagine they would want, but since we were in the Philippines, there was an additional requirement: "Must have light skin." I couldn't help but feel incensed and sad for the locals who would not qualify regardless of their skills because they didn't have the "correct" skin tone. I suppose a person who wanted that job could potentially use skin-whitening lotion to help increase his or her chances—though if these creams actually worked, surely all of the Philippines would be populated by light-skinned people. Despite my sense of injustice, I gave a skin-whitening lotion a try. I don't really remember my impression of it. For whatever reason, it wasn't one to keep as part of my beauty regimen. Perhaps it didn't work as quickly as I had hoped.

So I remained dark-skinned and regular, still unable to achieve the status of "light-skinned and beautiful." Then I moved to the Pacific Northwest, away from the sunshine of my youth. I was older and looking for a change. I'd been living in Washington State for a couple of years before finally venturing back down to Southern California to visit the family, and one thing that I remember was that my Miss-America-sister complimented my skin. Not that it was flawless—I'd been plagued with pimples as a teenager and even occasionally as an adult. My skin tends to blemish at the slightest little offense, despite my best efforts. No, what she was referring to was the lightness of my skin, which had seen very little sunshine for the past couple of years thanks to the infamous gray skies of my new home. At the time I was flattered, especially since I hadn't realized that my skin had changed so significantly. I knew I was lighter, but I didn't think the change was enough to warrant a compliment from Miss America. Had I finally achieved what I'd been searching for all these years? Could I say that I was beautiful now that my skin was a shade lighter? Her comment directly appealed to my vanity, and I became convinced that the sunless skies were where I should be. I'd continue to visit family in SoCal only in the cooler months, I thought to myself, and always be covered to protect my newfound light skin from darkening.

Of course, time has a tendency to change the way we view things, and for me, this change came after an exceptionally long, wet spring. I'd gone through the rain and darkness of fall and winter, so by the time spring rolled around, I'd had enough. I was suffering from Seasonal Affective Disorder. I needed sunshine. When spring finally gave way to a slow-starting summer and I was eventually able to go outside, take walks, work in the garden, and revel in the sun, I called my mother and recounted all the wonderful outdoor activities I'd been able to enjoy that week. I'd been feeling good. It was such a relief from the previous lows of the past few weeks. Despite my enthusiasm and euphoria at the moment, my mother took it upon herself to remind me of the most important thing: "Don't stay in the sun too long. You'll get dark."

I felt a blanket was pulled over me, throwing me once again into the darkness. I'd been walking around with my head in a fog for months, and now that the sun was out, I wanted to reap the benefits of this vital resource. Years ago, I was so happy to finally have an autumn with oranges, yellows, and reds, an occasional snow in winter, spring tulips, and, yes, the rain on cold, gray days. It was so different from everything I had ever known. So new and exciting. I had taken the sun for granted when I was younger, thinking it was only there to make me sweaty, dark, and ugly. Only now do I realize its true importance. Not only does the sun provide us with light, help grow our foods, and warm our bodies; it also nourishes our souls. So why is it so important to my mother that I stay away from it? It is difficult to impress upon this woman the importance of sunshine. I can't blame her for not understanding, but I can be a little incensed that she feels it her duty to remind me of the perils of getting too dark. These days, my skin color determines more than my beauty; it determines my sanity. I know I need the sun and appreciate it much more than I ever did. I won't hide from it, as my skin needs to drink up its healing powers—safely, of course, with plenty of SPF. My mom still tells me the same thing each time I call, and each time I visit, she notices a few more freckles and spots on my face, which I'm sure have more to do with aging than exposure to the sun, but I don't argue with her.

At this point in my life I have no qualms about being once again the color of that flushed, brown-skinned girl in that photograph with my sisters taken so many years ago. I've learned that the lightness of my skin doesn't mean shit. It doesn't mean I'm ugly when my skin is dark, or beautiful when my skin is lighter. I've learned that it doesn't matter whether or not someone can guess my ethnicity on the basis of my skin color. I've learned that I don't want to strive to look ambiguous or exotic. I've learned that even a brown girl can be a princess. After many years of gloominess and miserable weather, this princess is finally ready for the sun to touch her skin regardless of the "consequences." The sun is calling my name, and this time I'll answer without long pants, long sleeves, and a wide-brimmed hat.

28

Abominable *Honhyeol*

Julia R. DeCook, MULTIRACIAL KOREAN/WHITE AMERICAN, 25

I grew up in Korea, but went to college in South Dakota. When I returned home to Korea for winter break after my first semester, one of the first things on my mother's to-do list was for us to go and visit a bath house. There she paid an *ajumma* (older/married woman) to scrub my body clean of all of the dead skin that had accumulated in the six months that I had been away in the States. Getting rid of *ddeh* (which is what the dead skin is called in Korean) is a cleansing process, a tradition, and a time-honored ritual.

After this particular cleansing, my mother remarked that I was glowing and looked "clean" again, and that my skin had become "so white." In the elevator on the way out, a man—a stranger—remarked, audibly, with a gasp, when he saw me, "My, she is so pale!" and he turned to my mother and said, "You must be so proud to have such a beautiful daughter." My mother loves hearing these compliments and thanked him profusely; I stared at the floor. To him, my mother, and those around me, my beauty exists in my alabaster skin, which I had so meticulously curated like fragile porcelain, making sure to never go out into the sun without protection, actively avoiding the sun if at all possible, using "brightening" (whitening) skin products, and having my skin scrubbed until it was red to achieve the perfect . . . paleness.

I am half-Korean and half-white, and I have spent nearly all of my life in Korea. As a result, I have always been careful to maintain my light skin. Light skin has always been my idea of what is beautiful, because I have been praised for my skin color since I was a child. As a baby, I had pale light skin, light hair, and light eyes. As I grew older, my "Korean" genes started showing more—my hair became darker, my eyes darker, and I started doing the normal things that children do: swimming and playing outside in the summertime, which naturally darkened my skin. I have not been that tan since I was eleven, which is when the pressure to be pale became more salient. Growing up in Korea will do that. I was constantly surrounded by family members and exposed to celebrities who were obsessed with cultivating perfect, blemish-free, wrinkle-free, light skin.

Unlike in the United States, tanning in Korea is an alien concept. In fact, the concept of "tan" equating to "beautiful" is so foreign that I remember seeing a documentary on Korean TV about a woman who . . . gasp! . . . tanned. Although she tanned to excess, the very idea that there was a documentary about her that aired on television points to how strange the concept of someone *intentionally* tanning is to Korean people. Even if my own family and those around me never explicitly told me I needed to be pale to be beautiful, it was whispered to me from every advertisement, movie, television show, and every time my grandmother, mother, or aunts warned me that I had become "too dark." My American father would often lament how pale I was, and would remark often that I looked "ghostly," with my long, dark hair and ivory skin. To him, it was beautiful when my skin, under the hot sun, became a golden color.

Korea (and much of Asia) places light skin on a pedestal as a standard of beauty. However, within the walls and barbed wire of the American military bases where I attended school and interacted with other Americans, being tan was the cultural standard of beauty, even if we were thousands of miles away from the United States. What I have learned after living in the United States is that American standards of beauty value tan skin, but not *dark* skin. No doubt, whiteness, paleness, lightness is still a standard of beauty, even in the United States— though in Asia and many Asian American communities, the preference for white skin is more pronounced and explicit. These views of what constitutes beautiful skin present an internal battle within myself, and other questions of beauty based on other aspects of my appearance haunt me, even today. I have a raised bridge in my nose, but I have small, almond-shaped eyes. I have the eyelid fold and the long eyelashes, but the high cheekbones. I have the dark hair, but it is curly and wavy. My grandmother would often tell me that I was blended well, like I was some kind of designer dog, a golden doodle. It always made my heart drop into my stomach because of what those words meant—that I was "blended well" and turned out "pretty," unlike some other *honhyeol* (mixed-race) children. I have been told repeatedly throughout my life that I am pretty because of my mixed blood, for my features that are neither East nor West, and, most of all, for my pale skin.

My blended background, along with my affinity for some aspects of American culture that I was exposed to on the military bases and in school, was reason enough for many Koreans to deny me my "Koreanness." In Korea, racial purity is the standard, and pale skin is a part of this pureness. For me, being pale was my one way of molding my body and myself into what I believed would make me seem "more Korean." Whenever I saw tan lines appear, I felt shame and contempt that I had become darker and lost what I believed was my only connection to being accepted as Korean. This fear was amplified in comments made by Korean family and friends— "You can tell they're not *really* Korean by how dark they are"— comments that, looking back, were absolutely absurd, though they had snaked their way into my subconscious as methods to showcase my level of Koreanness as superior to theirs.

I am only now beginning to balance out my Korean and American ideas of beauty after nearly a decade of living in the United States. Today, I am the darkest I have been since I was a child. When I recently had to buy a new shade of foundation from sitting in the sun for too long, I avoided doing so as long as possible. Why? Perhaps the reason was that I have not yet learned to wholly accept the new tanned skin that I am in. Being tan still sometimes feels alien to me, though being tan is also a symbol of how much I am challenging the cultural standards of beauty that have been drilled into my brain from birth. Even so, I have not yet quieted the battle that I have deep within me screaming that "I need to be pale! I need to be pale! I need to be pale to be beautiful!

I need to be pale to be Korean!" I immediately think of what my family would say if they saw how dark I have become—they would tell me that I look like someone from Southeast Asia, that I look Mexican, that I look like a farmer—and inevitably they would chortle at their cleverness in equating my dark skin with something they view as "lesser." My mother would remind me that pale skin is beautiful because pale skin is something afforded to the upper class, while dark skin belongs to peasants who labor in the sun.

My inner voice tells me to embrace my skin, but nonetheless I encounter voices, both in Korea and in the United States, blasted from every screen and image, that tell me that only truly white, light skin and white features, belonging to white or white-passing women, are beautiful. I have tried to learn how to stop caring what "they" see as beautiful. Perhaps it is the cultural "abominations" of beauty that are the most beautiful because of the mere fact that they question our very standards, disrupt our inner voices, and challenge socialized self-hatred. Although small and incredibly minute, my own rejection of American and Korean beauty standards is embracing both my mixed-race-ness and my darkened skin.

I am the abominable *honhyeol*. I am neither here nor there. And the color of my skin will no longer define me.

29

Dear Future Child

Kathy Tran-Peters, VIETNAMESE AMERICAN, 24

Dear Future Child,

You may not understand what your mother has gone through because of the color of her skin, the shape of her eyes, the color of her hair, or the shape of her nose. Maybe someday, you will look in the mirror and hate the parts of your face and your body that I have given you. You may despise this side of you because the schoolchildren call you "chink" as they did when I was younger; you may feel unsafe walking downtown as men harass you and call you "oriental" or "exotic"; you may experience stereotypes such as being seen as only an A student, a bad driver, sexually obedient, or submissive and quiet—all of this simply because of the physical parts of you that you may see as "different." You may shun this side of you because of what you experience, the discrimination that you may face, and the hurt that it may cause. Just please remember that your mom has faced the same experiences whole-bodily and whole-heartedly.

Please remember your mom on those days when you wish you were more white, had rounder eyes, had lighter hair, or did not have such a flat and big nose. For she had wished this for herself many times. Please remember your mom when you dismiss this side of you and wish you looked more like your dad. Please remember your mom when you look at Asian women and think you are prettier because your dad has given you lighter skin than theirs, lighter hair than their pitch-black color, and double eyelids. Please realize the privilege that your dad has afforded you in possibly passing as white and not having to deal with the stereotypes and hurt these Asian women experience on a regular basis.

Please acknowledge your connection to your mom, Vietnamese culture, and the traumatic history of our ancestry that we may or may not share through our melanin. When you look at your Vietnamese features, you may experience the generational trauma of European colonialism and the Vietnam War. Your melanin may be your connection to your grandparents' experiences of fleeing the ravages of war. Your almond-shaped eyes may help you see into what your grandparents had to endure when they immigrated to America, a new and foreign place that did not accept them because they did not resemble your dad.

When you wish your hair to be lighter, please recognize that your mom's first major experience with race was in the aftermath of 9/11, when your grandmother first dyed my eight-year-old virgin hair because she worried that my darker hair would make me a target for violence. Your grandmother's fears were palpable as Islamophobia and racism found fuel. If you decide to reject the features I have given you, please remember that I could not hide my physical appearance. I could not conceal my skin, my eyes, my nose. My mother especially powered this need as she consistently reminded me that I needed to be whiter—not only to be safe from violence but to be successful and more attractive. Because of all this, I tried whitening creams. I hid from the sun. I taped my eyelids to create a double eyelid. And I squeezed the sides of my nose every night in hopes of a longer and thinner nose by morning.

When you reach junior high and high school, please remember that your mom was just like you and only wanted to fit in with her peers and be liked by her crushes; but, because she looked "different," she became isolated and found refuge in being alone. Please imagine your high school mother sitting in the back corner of your classes. I am the quiet Asian girl with no confidence. I knew the answers, but was afraid that I would say a wrong answer and not live up to the Asian stereotypes that my classmates inscribed upon me.

In today's age of Instagram and other social media, you might post photos of yourself and get many followers and likes, but please know that your mom did not do so because she felt inadequate, self-conscious, and ugly in her own skin. Please recognize the days when you feel worthless and may not want to live or function anymore. Please understand that you are not alone as I also suffered from mental illness, just like many of my deep-melanin peers. I had to practice self-care every day and in everything I did.

It was not until college that your mom began to embrace being Vietnamese. It was then that I gained the courage to resist white supremacy as I found refuge in ethnic student groups. I no longer felt alone once I met others who shared similar experiences and struggles with American ways versus traditional Vietnamese teachings. But, please also remember my efforts in being an ally for the Black Lives Matter Movement, resisting white supremacy, and finding my identity. It was difficult and the battle fatigue real, especially in the age of Donald Trump. Please understand that through all of this, dating and then eventually marrying your dad was very challenging for me. I did not trust white people, especially white men. I was often accused of wanting the white dick because it afforded me a piece of the privilege given to those who are white. I did not trust your dad, especially in moments when he did not think white privilege existed. I did not always feel safe around your dad—especially when he told me that "everything is going to be okay and there is nothing to worry about," when he did not acknowledge the rise of the alt-right movement and neo-nazis, as well as the harmful racist, sexist, ableist, classist, and homophobic policies arising out of the Trump administration.

Though your mom loves your dad very much, please remember that race has impacted her life in the past, in the present, and now with you, my future child. Being biracial has a whole host of issues that you will deal with, but please remember your mom and her struggles. Know that your mom continues to resist tirelessly, emotionally, and with her whole self in order to bring you into a world that values *all* of you.

As I grow into myself, I am learning to accept who I am, including my skin, my eyes, my nose, my hair. What I once hated about myself—as society taught me to do—I now embrace. I looked "different," and wanted to be beautiful and valued. After years of struggle, I know I am beautiful. My hope for you is that you, too, will learn to embrace who you are and see the beauty that I already see in you.

With much love,
Mommy Tran-Peters

30

Teeth

Betty Ming Liu, CHINESE AMERICAN, 62

She was a little Chinese girl with a bowl cut. The chin-length hair and straight bangs looked like a shiny, black helmet. But old family photos reveal her true armor. It was that tight, fake smile that she learned from her mother.

"A lady never shows her teeth," warned her mom, in hopes of making her little girl strong and resilient.

It would take that kid decades to finally drop the mask and show her teeth. This is the story of my journey.

≈

In the 1950s, my Chinese immigrant parents settled in an all-white New Jersey town. When I started kindergarten at age five, I was the only student of color in an all-white elementary school. Curious kids asked what I saw through "slanty" eyes. They held up milky or freckled arms next to mine, comparing skin tones. They called me names.

"Flat-nose Chinese."

"Ching-Chong."

Through it all, I kept my mouth shut. I didn't show my teeth.

One Sunday, my younger sister and I came out of the house in our church finery. I felt pretty in my dress with the puffy princess skirt—until a group of teenage boys drove by. *"Chinnnnnk!"* they yelled. What did the strange word mean?

I looked up at my parents. Daddy had turned a furious purple. Mommy's lipstick mouth flattened into a hard, red line. "Ignore them," she said quietly.

But it was too late.

I felt ashamed and confused. Here I was, in my best outfit. Yet, I was still ugly. An outsider. Foreign. Different.

As the laughing boys zoomed past in their car, we stood stoic, jaws clenched.

I didn't show my teeth.

Soon after that, we moved across the Hudson River to join relatives in Manhattan's Chinatown. "Our people," my father grinned. Clearly, he finally felt safe. But at age nine, I was thrown into culture shock. We'd gone from total whiteness to Chinese New Yorkers everywhere.

This is when my life got *really* ugly.

After school, the family women fussed over me and my sister. They fed us fresh custard tarts and warm roast pork buns. While we snacked, they eyeballed us up and down. They praised my sister for being pale and slim. Even though they adored me, too, I was sturdy, four-eyed, pimply, and relatively swarthy. My looks led to endless chastising.

"You so dark!"

"Look how big your wrists!"

"How much you weigh now?"

Instead of reacting, I kept eating. Chewing with my mouth closed, of course.

They never saw my teeth.

Sometimes, I'd look away and stare at the calendar on their kitchen wall. Every month featured another gorgeous Hong Kong starlet. I got the message. "Attractive" meant ivory complexion, oval face, double eyelids, and some sort of nose bridge. Unlike me, these hotties showed off pearly teeth. Why couldn't I do that, too?

At twenty-one, I finally discovered my teeth. A cute guy at work asked me out. He was black. In those days, interracial love was so taboo that Chinatown parents disowned daughters who dated white guys. Getting involved with a black man was unthinkable.

My mother assured our horrified relatives that this boyfriend was "not that dark" because he was actually Native American.

Then, she thanked God that two years earlier, a fatal heart attack has already taken my dad. "If he was still alive, you would've killed him," she told me.

I shrugged. Who cares what "my people" thought? I was too busy losing my virginity, falling in love, and enjoying a sudden, unexpected change in status. I went from "too dark" among Asians to "light-skinned" in black culture. What a boost to my broken self-esteem. Finally, it seemed, I could be beautiful.

We were a black-Asian couple in the '80s, long before anyone used the word "Blasian." While we had good friends of all colors, our marriage also led to crap from haters on every side—whites, blacks, Asians. I was also among the first wave of Asian American journalists breaking into the white media, and facing career discrimination battles of my own. With so much going on, I had to step up and speak up.

I started baring my teeth.

Then in 1995, my husband and I were blessed with a beautiful baby girl. Our brown daughter had curly, frizzy hair, full lips, and expressive, espresso eyes. Her arrival transformed me. As her mommy, I was ready to fight anyone and anything to keep her safe. This is when my teeth came out for good.

But there was one problem: I wanted her to be a happy, female human—a three-word description beyond my personal experience. I wondered: Who would be her people? How would she know that she is strong and beautiful?

As I obsessed, time kept moving. Soon, a version of history repeated itself. When I was five, my parents marched me off to a white school, armed with helmet hair, never showing my teeth. Now, my husband and I were arguing about living in an upscale, vanilla suburb. I worried—what if our daughter was The Only One in kindergarten? If classmates played with her puffy hair or pulled her braids, would she fake-smile? Would she never show her teeth?

One argument led to another. Just before our daughter turned five, we split up.

I moved to a town closer to New York City that was still mostly white. We stood out as Asian-mom-with-the-mixed-kid. And yes, kids noticed she was "different." They said things. They touched her hair. My heart broke.

For the first time, I genuinely understood my own mother's fear. She felt my survival depended on hiding my teeth. Don't say anything. Deny difficult feelings. But unlike her, I wanted to mother without smothering. So to save my child, I had to reinvent myself—and save me first.

Once our daughter was in school and spending weekends with her dad, I took salsa lessons, dated, and started working as a part-time professor. Today, I teach communication skills and writing. Eventually, I learned to oil paint, which healed my heart. Handling rich, saturated colors even seemed familiar. After all, I was already an expert on color, wasn't I?

Wherever I turned, I have been judged by the color of my skin. How light? How dark? No wonder I judged myself. And unfortunately, my baby girl was just like me. The two of us would walk into any store, restaurant, or play space, instantly self-aware. Without even thinking about it, we compared ourselves to others in nuances of complexion, hair texture, and facial features.

But painting changed me into a colorist. I took a color theory art class, where we mixed the primary pigments of red, blue, and yellow into subtle shades, hues, and tints. The results were unpredictable and exciting. I realized that this is how our complexions should be celebrated, too.

When it comes to color, anything can happen. Some days, I'll stare at the mud mess on my canvas and want to give up. Then, I'll take a few breaths and carry on. The same goes for dealing with color on the human canvas.

I can't stop colorism; it's been here forever. But inhaling and exhaling keeps me in the moment—free of ancestors, the past, the future. Today, at sixty-two, I talk, laugh, and smile—all while showing my teeth. When I learned to show my teeth, I discovered I was beautiful.

These are the new lessons I've tried to pass on to my daughter. She's in her twenties now. My late, brave mom is still part of our spiritual circle. She loved us. We honor her struggle as a woman, as a mother and grandmother, and as an immigrant. But we have gone on to recognize our worth in a world that devalues dark skin.

And my daughter is beautiful, because she knows how to show her teeth.

NOTES

INTRODUCTION

1　The advertisement can be viewed online with English subtitles here: "'Whiteness Makes You Win': Thai Ad Promotes Skin-Whitening Pills—Video," *Guardian*, January 8, 2016, available at https://www.bing.com.

2　Angela R. Dixon and Edward E. Telles, "Skin Color and Colorism: Global Research, Concepts, and Measurement"; Evelyn Nakano Glenn, "Yearning for Lightness: Transnational Circuits in the Marketing and Consumption of Skin Lighteners"; Evelyn Nakano Glenn, "Consuming Lightness: Segmented Markets and Global Capital in the Skin-Whitening Trade."

3　For examples, see Shehzad Nadeem's discussion of skin-whitening advertisements in "Fair and Anxious: On Mimicry and Skin-Lightening in India."

4　Annie Paul, "Beyond the Pale? Skinderella Stories and Colourism in India."

5　Pierre Van den Berge and Peter Frost, "Skin Color Preference, Sexual Dimorphism, and Sexual Selection: A Case of Gene Culture Co-Evolution."

6　Margaret Hunter, *Race, Gender, and the Politics of Skin Tone*, p. 1.

7　Alice Walker, "If the Present Looks like the Past, What Does the Future Look Like?"

8　Darrick Hamilton, Arthur H. Goldsmith, and William Darity Jr., "Shedding 'Light' on Marriage: The Influence of Skin Shade on Marriage for Black Females," p. 131.

9　Margaret Hunter, "'If You're Light You're Alright': Light Skin Color as Social Capital for Women of Color," p. 176.

10　See Arthur Goldsmith, Darrick Hamilton, and William Darity Jr., "Shades of Discrimination: Skin Tone and Wages"; Arthur Goldsmith, Darrick Hamilton, and William Darity Jr., "From Dark to Light: Skin Color and Wages among African Americans"; Matthew S. Harrison and Kecia M. Thomas, "The Hidden Prejudice in Selection: A Research Investigation on Skin Color Bias"; Joni Hersch, "Skin Tone Effects among African Americans"; Mark E. Hill, "Color Differences in the Socioeconomic Status of African American Men"; Mark E. Hill, "Skin Color and the Perception of Attractiveness among African Americans: Does Gender Make a Difference?"; Michael Hughes and Bradley Hertel, "The Significance of Skin Color Remains: A Study of Life Chances, Mate Selection, and Ethnic Consciousness among Black Americans"; Margaret Hunter, "Colorstruck: Skin-Color Stratification in the Lives of African American Women"; Margaret Hunter, *Race, Gender, and the Politics of Skin Tone*; Verna M. Keith and Cedric Herring, "Skin-Tone Stratification in the

Black Community"; Ellis P. Monk Jr., "Skin-Tone Stratification among Black Americans, 2001–2003"; Ellis P. Monk Jr., "The Cost of Color: Skin Color, Discrimination, and Health among African Americans"; Richard Seltzer and Robert C. Smith, "Color Difference in the Afro-American Community and the Differences They Make."

11 Cedric Herring, Verna M. Keith, and Hayward Derrick Horton (eds.), *Skin Deep: How Race and Complexion Matter in the "Color Blind" Era*; Margaret Hunter, *Race, Gender, and the Politics of Skin Tone*; Keith B. Maddox, "Perspectives on Racial Phenotypicality Bias."

12 St. Clair Drake and Horace R. Cayton, *Black Metropolis: A Study of Negro Life in a Northern City*; Margaret Hunter, "Colorstruck: Skin-Color Stratification in the Lives of African American Women"; Margaret Hunter, *Race, Gender, and the Politics of Skin Tone*; Nikki Khanna, *Biracial in America: Forming and Performing Racial Identity*; Kathy Russell, Midge Wilson, and Ronald E. Hall, *The Color Complex: The Politics of Skin Color among African Americans*.

13 Joanne L. Rondilla and Paul Spickard, *Is Lighter Better? Skin Tone Discrimination among Asian Americans*.

14 G. Reginald Daniel, "Passers and Pluralists: Subverting the Racial Divide"; Nikki Khanna, *Biracial in America: Forming and Performing Racial Identity*; Kathy Russell, Midge Wilson, and Ronald E. Hall, *The Color Complex: The Politics of Skin Color among African Americans*; Lori L. Tharps, *Same Family, Different Colors: Confronting Colorism in America's Diverse Families*.

15 G. Reginald Daniel, *More Than Black? Multiracial Identity and the New Racial Order*; Angela R. Dixon and Edward E. Telles, "Skin Color and Colorism: Global Research, Concepts, and Measurement," p. 407; Nikki Khanna, *Biracial in America: Forming and Performing Racial Identity*.

16 Ronald E. Hall, "The Bleaching Syndrome: African Americans' Response to Cultural Domination vis-à-vis Skin Color."

17 Jeff Zeleny, "Reid Apologizes for Remarks on Obama's Color and 'Dialect.'"

18 See also Vesla M. Weaver, "The Electoral Consequences of Skin Color: The 'Hidden' Side of Race in Politics."

19 Mark E. Hill, "Skin Color and the Perception of Attractiveness among African Americans: Does Gender Make a Difference?"

20 Darrick Hamilton, Arthur H. Goldsmith, and William Darity Jr., "Shedding 'Light' on Marriage: The Influence of Skin Shade on Marriage for Black Females"; Margaret Hunter, "The Persistent Problem of Colorism: Skin Tone, Status, and Inequality."

21 Mark E. Hill, "Skin Color and the Perception of Attractiveness among African Americans: Does Gender Make a Difference?" p. 88.

22 Naomi Wolf, *The Beauty Myth: How Images of Beauty Are Used against Women*, p. 12.

23 Margaret Hunter, "The Persistent Problem of Colorism: Skin Tone, Status, and Inequality," p. 247.

24 Alanna Vagianos, "Zendaya on Colorism: 'I am Hollywood's Acceptable Version of a Black Girl.'"

25 Blackness has historically been defined in the United States as having any degree of black ancestry. According to F. James Davis in *Who Is Black? One Nation's Definition*, the one-drop rule, only used in the United States, defined anyone as black who had any black ancestor anywhere in his or her family tree; thus many multiracial Americans with black ancestry are often raced as black even today. Actresses Halle Berry, Thandie Newton, and Paula Patton all have multiracial ancestry (including white ancestry), yet the larger society often categorizes them as black. For example, Halle Berry, a child of a white mother and black father, accepted her Academy Award for Best Actress in 2002 as the first black woman to win the award.

26 For a discussion on colorism in Hollywood, see Tiffany Onyejiaka, "Hollywood's Colorism Problem Can't Be Ignored Any Longer"; and for more on the link between dark skin and masculinity, see Ronald E. Hall, "Dark Skin and the Cultural Ideal of Masculinity."

27 Catherine Knight Steele, "Pride and Prejudice: Pervasiveness of Colorism and the Animated Series *Proud Family*," p. 62.

28 Jessica Bennett, "Exclusive: Mathew Knowles Says Internalized Colorism Led Him to Tina Knowles Lawson."

29 Nikki Khanna, *Biracial in America: Forming and Performing Racial Identity*; Kerry Ann Rockquemore, "Negotiating the Color Line: The Gendered Process of Racial Identity Construction among Black/White Biracials."

30 The "x" in Latinx (and, later, Filipinx) is used in lieu of "o" and "a" (as in "Latino" or "Latina"), in order to denote gender inclusivity.

31 For examples, see Hector Y. Adames, Nayeli Chavez-Duenas, and Kurt C. Organista, "Skin Color Matters in Latino/a Communities: Identifying, Understanding, and Addressing Mestizaje Racial Ideologies in Clinical Practice"; Carlos H. Arce, Edward Murguia, and W. Parker Frisbie, "Phenotype and Life Chances among Chicanos"; R. Costas Jr., M. R. Garcia-Palmieri, P. Sorli, and E. Hertzmark, "Coronary Heart Disease Risk Factors in Men with Light and Dark Skin in Puerto Rico"; Rodolfo Espino and Michael M. Franz, "Latino Phenotypic Discrimination Revisited: The Impact of Skin Color on Occupational Status"; Sandra D. Garza, "Decolonizing Intimacies: Women of Mexican Descent and Colorism"; Lance Hannon, "Hispanic Respondent Intelligence Level and Skin Tone: Interviewer Perceptions from the American National Election Study"; Margaret Hunter, Walter R. Allen, and Edward E. Telles, "The Significance of Skin Color among African Americans and Mexican Americans"; Edward Murguia and Edward E. Telles, "Phenotype and Schooling among Mexican Americans"; Raquel Reichard, "11 Examples of Light-Skin Privilege in Latinx Communities"; Edward E. Telles and Edward Murguia, "Phenotypic Discrimination and Income Differences among Mexican Americans."

32 See Raquel Reichard, "11 Examples of Light-Skin Privilege in Latinx Communities."

33 Janice Williams, "From Black to White: Why Sammy Sosa and Others Are Bleaching Their Skin."

34 According to federal guidelines, Latinx is conceptualized as an ethnic group, not a racial group, and many Latinxs have African ancestry. See US Census categories: Office of Management and Budget (OMB), "Race and Ethnic Standards for Federal Statistics and Administrative Reporting," Centers for Disease Control and Prevention (CDC), May 12, 1977, available at: https://wonder. cdc.gov.

35 Lance Hannon, "White Colorism."

36 Raquel Reichard, "11 Examples of Light-Skin Privilege in Latinx Communities."

37 Trina Jones, "The Significance of Skin Color in Asian and Asian-American Communities: Initial Reflections," p. 1106.

38 Evelyn Nakano Glenn, "Consuming Lightness: Segmented Markets and Global Capital in the Skin-Whitening Trade," p. 179.

39 Seimu Yamashita, "Colorism and Discrimination in Japan's Marriage Scene"; Evelyn Yeung, "White and Beautiful: An Examination of Skin-Whitening Practices and Female Empowerment in China."

40 Seimu Yamashita, "Colorism and Discrimination in Japan's Marriage Scene."

41 Eric P. H. Li, Hyun Jeong Min, and Russell W. Belk, "Skin Lightening and Beauty in Four Asian Cultures," p. 445.

42 Seimu Yamashita, "Colorism and Discrimination in Japan's Marriage Scene."

43 Seimu Yamashita, "Colorism and Discrimination in Japan's Marriage Scene."

44 Rebecca Chiyoko King-O'Riain, *Pure Beauty: Judging Race in Japanese American Beauty Pageants.*

45 Rebecca Chiyoko King-O'Riain, *Pure Beauty: Judging Race in Japanese American Beauty Pageants.*

46 Joanne L. Rondilla and Paul Spickard, *Is Lighter Better? Skin Tone Discrimination among Asian Americans,* p. 53.

47 "Skin Whitening Big Business in Asia."

48 Joanne L. Rondilla and Paul Spickard, *Is Lighter Better? Skin Tone Discrimination among Asian Americans,* p. 4.

49 Evelyn Yeung, "White and Beautiful: An Examination of Skin-Whitening Practices and Female Empowerment in China."

50 Marianne Bray, "Skin Deep: Dying to Be White."

51 Hsin Chen, Careen Yarnal, Garry Chick, and Nina Jablonsky, "Egg White or Sun-Kissed: A Cross-Cultural Exploration of Skin Color and Women's Leisure Behavior," p. 261.

52 Marianne Bray, "Skin Deep: Dying to Be White"; Lori L. Tharps, *Same Family, Different Colors: Confronting Colorism in America's Diverse Families*; Evelyn Yeung, "White and Beautiful: An Examination of Skin-Whitening Practices and Female Empowerment in China."

53 Evelyn Yeung, "White and Beautiful: An Examination of Skin-Whitening Practices and Female Empowerment in China," p. 7.

54 Serenitie Wang and Sherisse Pham, "A Startup That Helps You Look Slimmer and Paler Is Worth Nearly $5 Billion."

55 Bill Chappell, "On Chinese Beaches, the Face-Kini Is in Fashion"; Lori L. Tharps, *Same Family, Different Colors: Confronting Colorism in America's Diverse Families.*

56 Gary Xu and Susan Feiner, "Meinu Jingji/China's Beauty Economy: Buying Looks, Shifting Value, and Changing Place," p. 315.

57 Gary Xu and Susan Feiner, "Meinu Jingji/China's Beauty Economy: Buying Looks, Shifting Value, and Changing Place," p. 317.

58 Ye Tiantian, "Why Do People Prefer Whiter Skin?"

59 Marianne Bray, "Skin Deep: Dying to Be White."

60 Evelyn Yeung, "White and Beautiful: An Examination of Skin-Whitening Practices and Female Empowerment in China," p. 9.

61 Rae Chen, "I'm a Light-Skinned Chinese Woman, and I Experience Pretty Privilege."

62 Pal Ahluwalia, "Fanon's Nausea: The Hegemony of the White Nation," p. 334.

63 Joanne Rondilla, "Filipinos and the Color Complex: Ideal Asian Beauty."

64 Joanne Rondilla, "Filipinos and the Color Complex: Ideal Asian Beauty," p. 78.

65 Maya Oppenheim, "Emma Watson Responds to Criticism over 'Skin-Whitening' Advert."

66 Joanne L. Rondilla and Paul Spickard, *Is Lighter Better? Skin Tone Discrimination among Asian Americans.*

67 Joanne L. Rondilla and Paul Spickard, *Is Lighter Better? Skin Tone Discrimination among Asian Americans,* p. 55.

68 Kevin Nadal, "My Trip to the Philippines, Part 2: The Power of Colorism and Colonial Mentality."

69 Sonora Jha and Mara Beth Adelman, "Looking for Love in All the White Places: A Study of Skin-Color Preferences on Indian Matrimonial and Mate-Seeking Websites."

70 Jyotsna Vaid, "Fair Enough? Color and the Commodification of Self in Indian Matrimonials."

71 Eric P. H. Li, Hyun Jeong Min, and Russell L. Belk, "Skin Lightening and Beauty in Four Asian Cultures."

72 Neha Mishra, "India and Colorism: The Finer Nuances."

73 Jyotsna Vaid, "Fair Enough? Color and the Commodification of Self in Indian Matrimonials," p. 148.

74 Lori L. Tharps, *Same Family, Different Colors: Confronting Colorism in America's Diverse Families,* p. 101.

75 Evelyn Nakano Glenn, "Consuming Lightness: Segmented Markets and Global Capital in the Skin-Whitening Trade," p. 176.

76 Kanishka Singh, "Post-1947, the Mixed Fortunes of the Mixed-Race Anglo-Indians."

77 Lori L. Tharps, *Same Family, Different Colors: Confronting Colorism in America's Diverse Families,* p. 102.

78 Neha Mishra, "India and Colorism: The Finer Nuances," p. 734; Annie Paul, "Beyond the Pale? Skinderella Stories and Colourism in India."

79 Neha Mishra, "India and Colorism: The Finer Nuances."

80 Anna North, "Vaseline Crowdsources Racism with New Skin-Whitening App."

81 Shobita Dhar, "In Search of Fair Babies, Indians Chase Caucasian Donors for IVF."

82 Shobita Dhar, "In Search of Fair Babies, Indians Chase Caucasian Donors for IVF."

83 Deepi Harish, "Why Are India's Beauty Standards So Messed Up?"

84 T. Jerome Utley and William Darity Jr., "India's Color Complex: One Day's Worth of Matrimonials"; see also Jyotsna Vaid, "Fair Enough? Color and the Commodification of Self in Indian Matrimonials."

85 Evelyn Nakano Glenn, "Yearning for Lightness: Transnational Circuits in the Marketing and Consumption of Skin Lighteners," p. 282; see also Jyotsna Vaid, "Fair Enough? Color and the Commodification of Self in Indian Matrimonials."

86 See also T. Jerome Utley and William Darity Jr., "India's Color Complex: One Day's Worth of Matrimonials."

87 Fatima Lodhi, "'No One Will Marry You': My Journey as a Dark-Skinned Woman in Pakistan."

88 Maria Sartaj, "In Pakistan, a Disease Called Dark Skin."

89 Megan Willett, "No, Asian Eyelid Surgery Is Not about Looking More 'White.'"

90 Project E Beauty, "Project E Beauty Magic Beautiful Double Eyelid Exerciser Eyes Beautiful Style Glasses Double-Fold Eyelids Trainer," Amazon, available at https://www.amazon.com.

91 Patricia Marx, "About Face: Why Is South Korea the World's Plastic Surgery Capital?"

92 Anthony Youn, "Asia's Ideal Beauty: Looking Caucasian."

93 Euny Hong, "I Got Eyelid Surgery, but Not to Look White."

94 Maureen O'Connor, "Is Race Plastic? My Trip into the 'Ethnic Plastic Surgery' Minefield."

95 Maureen O'Connor, "Is Race Plastic? My Trip into the 'Ethnic Plastic Surgery' Minefield."

96 Euny Hong, "I Got Eyelid Surgery, but Not to Look White."

97 Joanne L. Rondilla and Paul Spickard, *Is Lighter Better? Skin Tone Discrimination among Asian Americans*, p. 111.

98 Joanne L. Rondilla and Paul Spickard, *Is Lighter Better? Skin Tone Discrimination among Asian Americans*, p. 111.

99 Allison Takeda, "Julie Chen Reveals She Got Plastic Surgery to Look Less Chinese: See the Before and After Pictures."

100 Hsin Chen, Careen Yarnal, Garry Chick, and Nina Jablonsky, "Egg White or Sun-Kissed: A Cross-Cultural Exploration of Skin Color and Women's Leisure Behavior."

101 Joanne L. Rondilla and Paul Spickard, *Is Lighter Better? Skin Tone Discrimination among Asian Americans*, p. 58.

102 Trina Jones, "The Significance of Skin Color in Asian and Asian-American Communities: Initial Reflections," p. 111.

103 Olivia Cole, "Why I'm Not Here for #WhiteGirlsRock."

104 Maisha Johnson, "10 Ways the Beauty Industry Tells You Being Beautiful Means Being White."

105 For more Eurocentrism in American media, see the discussion of "white-oriented material" in fashion and beauty magazines by Lisa Duke, "Black in a Blonde World: Race and Girls' Interpretations of the Feminine Ideal in Teen Magazines."

106 Hsin Chen, Careen Yarnal, Gerry Chick, and Nina Jablonsky, "Egg White or Sun-Kissed: A Cross-Cultural Exploration of Skin Color and Women's Leisure Behavior."

107 Sriya Shrestha, "Threatening Consumption: Managing US Imperial Anxieties in Representation of Skin Lightening in India."

108 Sabina Verghese, "Sun Tans and Dark Skin: Unpacking White Privilege."

109 "Q & A: Chris Rock."

110 Sriya Shrestha, "Threatening Consumption: Managing US Imperial Anxieties in Representation of Skin Lightening in India," p. 111.

111 As cited in Meeta Rani Jha, *The Global Beauty Industry: Colorism, Racism, and the National Body*, p. 88.

112 Mia Tuan, *Forever Foreigners or Honorary Whites: The Asian Ethnic Experience Today*.

113 Rae Chen, "I'm a Light-Skinned Chinese Woman, and I Experience Pretty Privilege."

114 Andrea Cheng, "Why So Many Asian-American Women Are Bleaching Their Hair Blond," p. 4.

115 Lori L. Tharps, *Same Family, Different Colors: Confronting Colorism in America's Diverse Families*, p. 111.

116 "About," United States Census Bureau, January 23, 2018, available at https://www.census.gov.

117 Joanne L. Rondilla and Paul Spickard, *Is Lighter Better? Skin Tone Discrimination among Asian Americans*, p. 49.

PART I. COLORISM DEFINED

1 JeffriAnne Wilder, "Revisiting 'Color Names and Color Notions': A Contemporary Examination of the Language and Attitudes of Skin Color among Young Black Women," p. 202.

2 Ross Szabo, "What Does an American Look Like? Racial Diversity in the Peace Corps."

CHAPTER 1. WHEATISH

1 Literally meaning "the color of wheat"; light-skinned.

2 "*Haldi*" is the Hindi world for turmeric. It is commonly used in Indian cooking and skin care due to its health benefits. "*Beta*" is a term of endearment that

literally means "son" in Hindi, though it also informally translates to "child"; thus, it is often used by parents to address their sons or daughters.

CHAPTER 4. YOU'RE SO WHITE, YOU'RE SO PRETTY

1 Khmer is an ethnic group and native to Cambodia—a modernized name of Kambuja or Kampuchea. Cambodian is a modern name, referring to either a native or a citizen of Cambodia.

CHAPTER 5. YOU HAVE SUCH A NICE TAN!

1 Evelyn Nakano Glenn, "Yearning for Lightness: Transnational Circuits in the Marketing and Consumption of Skin Lightener"; Roger Lee Mendoza, "The Skin Whitening Industry in the Philippines."

2 Launched in the early 2000s, the "Real Beauty" campaign was Dove's attempt to transform the conversation about female beauty, challenge traditional notions of beauty, and highlight different forms (including body size and color) of beauty (see "Dove Campaigns," Dove, https://www.dove.com).

PART II. PRIVILEGE

1 See the sources cited in the introduction.

2 Kim Rahn and Kim Tae-Jong, "Southeast Asians Feel Discriminated against in Korea." *Korea Times*, January 18, 2011. Retrieved on November 12, 2018, at http://www.koreatimes.co.kr.

3 E. J. R. David, "The Marginalization of Brown Asians."

4 "Confronting Racism against Asian-Americans," *New York Times*, October 18, 2016, available at https://www.nytimes.com.

5 E. J. R. David, "An Open Letter to the 'New York Times' Who Told Brown Asians They Don't Matter."

6 Hannah Ellis-Petersen and Lily Kuo, "Where Are the Brown People? *Crazy Rich Asians* Draws Tepid Response in Singapore."

7 Jose G. Santos, "10 Years after Sikh Murder over 9/11, Community Continues to Blend In and Stand Out."

CHAPTER 12. MAGNETIC REPULSION

1 I feel strongly that in my writing, the "B" in "Black" should be capitalized. For me, and for many other American Black people who lack knowledge about their African ethnic roots, capitalizing the "B" in Black signifies my stance that for me Blackness is my ethnic identity and culture, not only my race. I use it as a proper noun like "American," "Asian," "Ghanaian," and "Chippewa."

PART III. ASPIRATIONAL WHITENESS

1 Annabel Fenwick Elliot, "'Do You Wanna Be White?' Korean Skincare Brand Sparks Backlash by Posing Controversial Question on a Billboard in New York."

2 Andrea Cheng, "Why So Many Asian-American Women Are Bleaching Their Hair Blond."

3 Joanne L. Rondilla and Paul Spickard, *Is Lighter Better? Skin Tone Discrimination among Asian Americans*, p. 52.

4 Eliza Romero, "Asian Brands Need to Do Better: Stop Using White Models."

5 Elaine Y. J. Lee, "Why Do So Many Asian Brands Hire White Models?"

6 Elaine Y. J. Lee, "Why Do So Many Asian Brands Hire White Models?"

7 Lee Ellis and Ping He, "Race and Advertising: Ethnocentrism or 'Real' Differences in Physical Attractiveness? Indirect Evidence from China, Malaysia, and the United States."

8 Katherine Toland Frith, Hong Cheng, and Ping Shaw, "Race and Beauty: A Comparison of Asian and Western Models in Women's Magazine Advertisements"; Katherine Toland Frith, Ping Shaw, and Hong Cheng, "The Construction of Beauty: A Cross-Cultural Analysis of Women's Magazine Advertising."

9 Jaehee Jung and Yoon-Jung Lee, "Cross-Cultural Examination of Women's Fashion and Beauty Magazine Advertisements in the United States and South Korea."

10 According to Elaine Y. J. Lee in "Why Do So Many Asian Brands Hire White Models?" black models are sometimes used in Asian marketing "if their inspiration is hip-hop or streetwear."

11 Jaehee Jung and Yoon-Jung Lee, "Cross-Cultural Examination of Women's Fashion and Beauty Magazine Advertisements in the United States and South Korea."

12 Eliza Romero, "Asian Brands Need to Do Better: Stop Using White Models."

13 Amy B. Wang, "*Vogue India* Faces Backlash for Putting Kendall Jenner on 10th Anniversary Cover."

14 John Kenneth White and Sandra L. Hanson, "The Making and Persistence of the American Dream," p. 1.

15 Ellis Cose, "What's White Anyway?"

16 Many groups have stood before US courts asking to be racially reclassified as white—including Afghans, Arabs, Syrians, Armenians, Mexicans, Hawaiians, and Native Americans. In addition to the cases described above involving Indians and the Japanese, other Asian groups have also asked to be classified as white, including Chinese, Burmese, Koreans, and Filipinos. See Ian Haney Lopez, *White by Law: The Legal Construction of Race*. For a summary of these cases, see "Racial Prerequisite Cases—Chronological Order," University of Dayton, December 22, 2009, available at https://academic.udayton.edu.

17 Noy Thrupkaew, "The Myth of the Model Minority."

18 Frantz Fanon, *Black Skin, White Masks*.

19 Joanne Rondilla, "Filipinos and the Color Complex: Ideal Asian Beauty," p. 63.

20 Joanne Rondilla, "Filipinos and the Color Complex: Ideal Asian Beauty, p. 64.

21 Joanne L. Rondilla and Paul Spickard, *Is Lighter Better? Skin Tone Discrimination among Asian Americans*.

CHAPTER 13. DIGITAL WHITENESS

1 A person or place of Indian, Pakistani, or Bangladeshi origin.

PART IV. ANTI-BLACKNESS

1 Maya Wesby, "Japan's Problem with Race."

2 Martin Fackler, "Biracial Beauty Queen Challenges Japan's Self-Image."

3 Maya Prabhu, "African Victims of Racism in India Share Their Stories."

4 Maya Prabhu, "African Victims of Racism in India Share Their Stories."

5 Max Fisher, "A Fascinating Map of the World's Most and Least Racially Tolerant Countries."

6 Robert Mackey, "Beating of African Students by Mob in India Prompts Soul-Searching on Race."

7 Arun Dev, "Tanzanian Girl Stripped, Beaten in Bengaluru: 'Deeply Pained' Says Sushma Swaraj."

8 Ishaan Tharoor, "China and India Have a Huge Problem with Racism towards Black People."

9 Nimisha Jaiswal, "Being Black in India Can Be Deadly."

10 Lucy Pasha-Robinson, "China Bans Hip-Hop Culture and Tattoos from All Media Sources."

11 Casey Quackenbush and Aria Hangyu Chen, "'Tasteless, Vulgar, and Obscene': China Just Banned Hip-Hop Culture and Tattoos from Television."

12 Aris Folley, "Racist Chinese Laundry Commercial Sparks Outrage."

13 A. Moore, "8 of the Worst Countries for Black People to Travel."

14 Ryan General, "Taiwanese School Sparks Outrage for Saying It's Not Hiring 'Black or Dark-Skinned' Teachers."

15 Nicole Cooper, "Black in Taiwan: My Experience."

16 Dave Hazzan, "Korea's Black Racism Epidemic."

17 Dave Hazzan, "Korea's Black Racism Epidemic."

18 Benny Luo, "Meet the Most Famous Black Man in Korea."

19 Jezzika Chung, "How Asian Immigrants Learn Anti-Blackness from White Culture, and How to Stop It."

20 Lori L. Tharps, *Same Family, Different Colors: Confronting Colorism in America's Diverse Families*, p. 107.

21 Lexi Browning and Lindsey Bever, "'Ape in Heels': W.Va. Mayor Resigns amid Controversy over Racist Comments about Michelle Obama."

22 Chris Fuchs, "Behind the 'Model Minority' Myth: Why the 'Studious Asian' Stereotype Hurts."

23 Chris Fuchs, "Behind the 'Model Minority' Myth: Why the 'Studious Asian' Stereotype Hurts."

24 Tyrus Townsend, "The Anti-Blackness of the Asian Community."

25 Lori L. Tharps, *Same Family, Different Colors: Confronting Colorism in America's Diverse Families*, p. 122.

26 Catalina Camia, "Bobby Jindal of Portrait: 'I'm Not White?'"

27 Lori L. Tharps, *Same Family, Different Colors: Confronting Colorism in America's Diverse Families*.

CHAPTER 16. CREATION STORIES

1 Deferred Action for Childhood Arrivals (DACA) is a program designed to provide children brought undocumented by their parents into the United States with protection from deportation as well as eligibility for a work permit.

CHAPTER 17. WHAT IT MEANS TO BE BROWN

1 Toni Morrison, "On the Back of Blacks."

CHAPTER 18. THE PERPETUAL OUTSIDER

1 Some Native Hawaiian scholars and activists have argued that the term "*hapa*" has been culturally appropriated to mean "part Asian," as the term has historically meant "part Hawaiian."

2 Cham Americans are an ethnic Southeast Asian minority group who hail primarily from Cambodia and Vietnam as a result of the Khmer Rouge genocide and the Vietnam War, respectively. Cham people are also indigenous as they are descendants of the Kingdom of Champa, which is occupied by present-day Vietnam. The 1999 General Statistics Office of Vietnam indicate that there are 132,000 Cham people who reside in Vietnam. Although Cham ethnicity may not always be recognized in census counts, Cham language and the Islamic religion indicated significant importance in identifying ethnic Cham people. According to the 2008 Cambodia General Population Census, approximately 204,000 Cambodian residents claim "Chaam" as their "mother tongue," and approximately 257,000 Cambodian residents follow the Islamic religion. In the 2010 United States Census, 891 Cham language speakers were reported.

3 Dustin Tahmahkera, "Custer's Last Sitcom."

4 Dustin Tahmahkera, "Custer's Last Sitcom."

PART V. BELONGING AND IDENTITY

1 Nikki Khanna, *Biracial in America: Forming and Performing Racial Identity*, p. 78.

2 NewsOne Staff, "Do You Consider Soledad O'Brien a Black Woman?"

3 Margaret Hunter, "The Lighter the Berry? Race, Color, and Gender in the Lives of African American and Asian American Women," as cited in Margaret Hunter, "Light, Bright, and Almost White: The Advantages and Disadvantages of Light Skin," p. 35.

4 Lori L. Tharps, *Same Family, Different Colors: Confronting Colorism in America's Diverse Families*, p. 121.

5 Anjulu Sastry, "People of Color with Albinism Ask: Where Do I Belong?"

6 Anjulu Sastry, "People of Color with Albinism Ask: Where Do I Belong?"

CHAPTER 20. BORN FILIPINA, SOMEWHERE IN BETWEEN

1 *Pancit* is one of the most popular dishes in the Philippines. "*Pancit*" refers to any of the large variety of noodle dishes that are frequently garnished with lemons, hard-boiled eggs, and green onions.

2 To show respect, a younger person will greet older people by taking the older person's right hand in both of hers and pressing them to her forehead.

CHAPTER 21. INVISIBLE TO MY OWN PEOPLE
1 A curried lentil dish commonly eaten with rice or flatbread.
2 A south Indian specialty; a spicy, tangy broth eaten with rice.
3 Hindu prayers.
4 Comic books depicting Indian mythological tales and folklore.
5 A south Indian dress worn by young girls, consisting of a skirt and blouse, usually in bright colors with intricate borders.
6 Another form of dress consisting of a long tunic, trousers, and matching stole.
7 An Indian term for eyeliner, specifically a thick, creamy natural black pigment.

PART VI. SKIN—REDEFINED
1 Lori L. Tharps, *Same Family, Different Colors: Confronting Colorism in America's Diverse Families*, p. 128.
2 Saif Khalid, "Fighting India's Ugly Fancy for Fair Skin"; Simra Mariam, "Daring to Be Dark: Fighting against Colorism in South Asia."
3 Saif Khalid, "Fighting India's Ugly Fancy for Fair Skin."
4 Syed Hamad Ali, "Activist Fights Bias against Dark Skin."
5 Sonia Waraich, "Forget Fair and Lovely, Dark Is Divine: Pakistan's First Anti-Colorism Campaign."
6 Sonia Waraich, "Forget Fair and Lovely, Dark Is Divine: Pakistan's First Anti-Colorism Campaign."
7 Geeta Pandey, "#Unfairandlovely: A New Social Media Campaign Celebrates Dark Skin."
8 Sarah Jasmine Montgomery, "The Founder of 'Unfair and Lovely' Is Here to Reclaim Their Movement."

CHAPTER 25. REPROGRAMMING
1 In the Philippines, "mestizo" refers to people of mixed Filipino and any foreign ancestry, typically white Americans. Today, the word is shortened as "Tisoy," a combination of "Pinoy" (Filipino) and "mestizo."
2 Most toiletry products in the Philippines have skin-lightening properties, but papaya soap is popular because of its affordability and accessibility. Today, middle-class Filipinas use glutathione injections to lighten their skin, despite the lack of clinical studies for long-term use.
3 The term "1.5 generation immigrants" refers to people who have spent half of their formative years in their home country and half in their receiving country. I grew up in both cultures, so I always use "1.5 generation" to define myself.

BIBLIOGRAPHY

Abraham, Tamara. 2010. "Bollywood Bond Girl Furious over *Elle* Magazine Cover 'Skin-Whitening' Scandal." *Daily Mail*, December 31. Retrieved on April 25, 2018, at http://www.dailymail.co.uk.

Adames, Hector Y., Nayeli Y. Chavez-Duenas, and Kurt C. Organista. 2016. "Skin Color Matters in Latino/a Communities: Identifying, Understanding, and Addressing Mestizaje Racial Ideologies in Clinical Practice." *Professional Psychology: Research & Practice* 47(1): 46–55.

Ahluwalia, Pal. 2003. "Fanon's Nausea: The Hegemony of the White Nation." *Social Identities* 9(3): 341–56.

Ali, Syed Hamad. 2015. "Activist Fights Bias against Dark Skin." *Gulf News, July 22.* Retrieved on November 12, 2018, at https://gulfnews.com.

Arce, Carlos H., Edward Murguia, and W. Parker Frisbie. 1987. "Phenotype and Life Chances among Chicanos." *Hispanic Journal of Behavioral Sciences* 9(1): 19–32.

Bennett, Jessica. 2018. "Exclusive: Mathew Knowles Says Internalized Colorism Led Him to Tina Knowles Lawson." *Ebony*, February 2. Retrieved on November 8, 2018, at https://www.ebony.com.

Bray, Marianne. 2002. "Skin Deep: Dying to Be White." *CNN*, May 13. Retrieved on April 26, 2018, at http://edition.cnn.com.

Browning, Lexi, and Lindsey Bever. 2016. "'Ape in Heels': W.Va. Mayor Resigns amid Controversy over Racist Comments about Michelle Obama." *Washington Post*, November 14. Retrieved on June 4, 2018, at https://www.washingtonpost.com.

Camia, Catalina. 2015. "Bobby Jindal of Portrait: 'I'm Not White?'" *USA Today*, February 9. Retrieved on November 12, 2018, at https://www.usatoday.com.

Chappell, Bill. 2012. "On Chinese Beaches, the Face-Kini Is in Fashion." NPR's *The Two-Way*, August 20. Retrieved on June 7, 2018, at https://www.npr.org.

Chen, Hsin, Careen Yarnal, Garry Chick, and Nina Jablonsky. 2018. "Egg White or Sun-Kissed: A Cross-Cultural Exploration of Skin Color and Women's Leisure Behavior." *Sex Roles* 78: 255–71.

Chen, Rae. 2017. "I'm a Light-Skinned Chinese Woman, and I Experience Pretty Privilege." *Teen Vogue, October 10*. Retrieved on April 26, 2018, at https://www.teenvogue.com.

Cheng, Andrea. 2018. "Why So Many Asian-American Women Are Bleaching Their Hair Blond." *New York Times*, April 9. Retrieved on April 25, 2018, at https://www.nytimes.com.

Chung, Jezzika. 2017. "How Asian Immigrants Learn Anti-Blackness from White Culture, and How to Stop It." *Huffington Post, September 7*. Retrieved on May 28, 2018, at https://www.huffingtonpost.com.

Cole, Olivia. 2013. "Why I'm Not Here for #WhiteGirlsRock." *Huffington Post, November 4.* Retrieved on May 10, 2018, at https://www.huffingtonpost.com.

Cooper, Nicole. 2018. "Black in Taiwan: My Experience." *Medium, January 10.* Retrieved on November 9, 2018, at https://medium.com.

Cose, Ellis. 2000. "What's White, Anyway?" *Newsweek, September 17.* Retrieved on May 29, 2018, at http://www.newsweek.com.

Costas Jr., R., M. R. Garcia-Palmieri, P. Sorli, and E. Hertzmark. 1981. "Coronary Heart Disease Risk Factors in Men with Light and Dark Skin in Puerto Rico." *American Journal of Public Health* 71(6): 614–19.

Daniel, G. Reginald. 1992. "Passers and Pluralists: Subverting the Racial Divide." Pp. 91–107 in *Racially Mixed People in America,* edited by Maria P. P. Root. Newbury Park, CA: Sage.

———. 2002. *More Than Black? Multiracial Identity and the New Racial Order.* Philadelphia: Temple University Press.

David, E. J. R. 2016a. "The Marginalization of Brown Asians." *Seattle Globalist,* October 25. Retrieved on November 12, 2018, at http://www.seattleglobalist.com.

———. 2016b. "An Open Letter to the 'New York Times' Who Told Brown Asians They Don't Matter." *Huffington Post, October 16.* Retrieved on November 12, 2018, at https://www.huffingtonpost.com.

Davis, F. James. 1991. *Who Is Black? One Nation's Definition.* University Park: Pennsylvania State University Press.

Dev, Arun. 2016. "Tanzanian Girl Stripped, Beaten in Bengaluru; 'Deeply Pained' Says Sushma Swaraj." *Times of India, February 4.* Retrieved on November 9, 2018, at https://timesofindia.indiatimes.com.

Dhar, Shobita. 2013. "In Search of Fair Babies, Indians Chase Caucasian Donors for IVF." *Times Crest—Times of India, July 20.* Retrieved on June 11, 2019, at http://www.timescrest.com.

Dixon, Angela R., and Edward E. Telles. 2017. "Skin Color and Colorism: Global Research, Concepts, and Measurement." *Annual Review of Sociology* 43: 405–24.

Drake, St. Clair, and Horace R. Cayton. 1993. *Black Metropolis: A Study of Negro Life in a Northern City.* Chicago: University of Chicago Press.

Duke, Lisa. 2000. "Black in a Blonde World: Race and Girls' Interpretations of the Feminine Ideal in Teen Magazines." *Journalism and Mass Communication Quarterly* 77(2): 367–92.

Elliott, Annabel Fenwick. 2014. "'Do You Wanna Be White?' Korean Skincare Brand Sparks Backlash by Posing Controversial Question on a Billboard in New York." *Daily Mail, July 8.* Retrieved on November 12, 2018, at https://www.dailymail.co.uk.

Ellis, Lee, and Ping He. 2011. "Race and Advertising: Ethnocentrism or 'Real' Differences in Physical Attractiveness? Indirect Evidence from China, Malaysia, and the United States." *Mankind Quarterly* 51(4): 471–89.

Ellis-Petersen, Hannah, and Lily Kuo. 2018. "Where Are the Brown People? *Crazy Rich Asians* Draws Tepid Response in Singapore." *Guardian,* August 21. Retrieved on November 12, 2018, at https://www.theguardian.com.

Espino, Rodolfo, and Michael M. Franz. 2002. "Latino Phenotypic Discrimination Revisited: The Impact of Skin Color on Occupational Status." *Social Science Quarterly* 83(2): 612–23.

Fackler, Martin. 2015. "Biracial Beauty Queen Challenges Japan's Self-Image." *New York Times*, May 30. Retrieved on May 28, 2018, at https://www.nytimes.com.

Fanon, Frantz. 2018. *Black Skin, White Masks*. New York: Grove Press (originally published in 1952; this edition is translated from French into English).

Fisher, Max. 2013. "A Fascinating Map of the World's Most and Least Racially Tolerant Countries." *Washington Post*, May 15. Retrieved on November 9, 2018, at https://www.washingtonpost.com.

Folley, Aris. 2016. "Racist Chinese Laundry Commercial Sparks Outrage." *NBC News, May 27*. Retrieved on May 28, 2018, at https://www.nbcnews.com.

Frith, Katherine Toland, Hong Cheng, and Ping Shaw. 2004. "Race and Beauty: A Comparison of Asian and Western Models in Women's Magazine Advertisements." *Sex Roles* 50: 53–61.

Frith, Katherine Toland, Ping Shaw, and Hong Cheng. 2005. "The Construction of Beauty: A Cross-Cultural Analysis of Women's Magazine Advertising." *Journal of Communication* 55: 56–70.

Fuchs, Chris. 2017. "Behind the 'Model Minority' Myth: Why the 'Studious Asian' Stereotype Hurts." *NBC News, August 22*. Retrieved on May 28, 2018, at https://www.nbcnews.com.

Gabler, Ellen, and Sam Roe. 2010. "FDA to Investigate Skin Creams for Mercury." *Chicago Tribune, May 21*. Accessed on November 12, 2018, at https://www.chicagotribune.com.

Garza, Sandra D. 2014. "Decolonizing Intimacies: Women of Mexican Descent and Colorism." *Aztlan* 39(2): 35–63.

General, Ryan. 2018. "Taiwanese School Sparks Outrage for Saying It's Not Hiring 'Black or Dark-Skinned' Teachers." *Nextshark: The Voice of Global Asians, June 12*. Retrieved on November 9, 2018, at https://nextshark.com.

Glenn, Evelyn Nakano. 2008. "Yearning for Lightness: Transnational Circuits in the Marketing and Consumption of Skin Lighteners." *Gender & Society* 22(3): 281–302.

———, ed. 2009. "Consuming Lightness: Segmented Markets and Global Capital in the Skin-Whitening Trade." Pp. 166–87 in *Shades of Difference: Why Skin Color Matters*, edited by Evelyn Nakano Glenn. Stanford, CA: Stanford University Press.

Goldsmith, Arthur H., Darrick Hamilton, and William Darity Jr. 2006. "Shades of Discrimination: Skin Tone and Wages." *American Economic Review* 96(2): 242–45.

———. 2007. "From Dark to Light: Skin Color and Wages among African Americans." *Journal of Human Resources* 42: 701–38.

Hall, Ronald E. 1995. "The Bleaching Syndrome: African Americans' Response to Cultural Domination vis-à-vis Skin Color." *Journal of Black Studies* 26(2): 172–84.

———. 1995/1996. "Dark Skin and the Cultural Ideal of Masculinity." *Journal of African American Men* 1(3): 37–62.

Hamilton, Darrick, Arthur H. Goldsmith, and William Darity Jr. 2009. "Shedding 'Light' on Marriage: The Influence of Skin Shade on Marriage for Black Females." *Journal of Economic Behavior & Organization* 72: 30–50.

Hannon, Lance. 2014. "Hispanic Respondent Intelligence Level and Skin Tone: Interviewer Perceptions from the American National Election Study." *Hispanic Journal of Behavioral Sciences* 36(3): 265–83.

——. 2015. "White Colorism." *Social Currents* 2(1): 13–21.

Harish, Deepi. 2016. "Why Are India's Beauty Standards So Messed Up?" *Huffington Post: Canada Edition, October 14*. Retrieved on June 7, 2018, at https://www.huffingtonpost.ca.

Harrison, Matthew S., and Kecia M. Thomas. 2009. "The Hidden Prejudice in Selection: A Research Investigation on Skin Color Bias." *Journal of Applied Social Psychology* 39(1): 134–68.

Hazzan, Dave. 2014. "Korea's Black Racism Epidemic." *Groove Magazine, February edition*. Retrieved on May 28, 2018, at http://groovekorea.com.

Herring, Cedric, Verna M. Keith, and Hayward Derrick Horton, eds. 2003. *Skin Deep: How Race and Complexion Matter in the "Color Blind" Era*. Chicago: Institute for Research on Race and Public Policy, University of Illinois at Chicago.

Hersch, Joni. 2006. "Skin Tone Effects among African Americans: Perceptions and Reality." *American Economic Review* 96(2): 251–55.

Hess, Amanda. 2016. "Asian-American Actors Are Fighting for Visibility: They Will Not Be Ignored." *New York Times*, May 29. Retrieved on April 25, 2018, at https://www.nytimes.com.

Hill, Mark E. 2000. "Color Differences in the Socioeconomic Status of African American Men." *Social Forces* 78(4): 1437–60.

——. 2002. "Skin Color and the Perception of Attractiveness among African Americans: Does Gender Make a Difference?" *Social Psychology Quarterly* 65: 77–91.

Hong, Euny. 2013. "I Got Eyelid Surgery, but Not to Look White." *Wall Street Journal, September 18*. Retrieved on April 28, 2018, at https://www.wsj.com.

Hughes, Michael, and Bradly Hertel. 1990. "The Significance of Color Remains: A Study of Life Chances, Mate Selection, and Ethnic Consciousness among Black Americans." *Social Forces* 68: 1105–20.

Hunter, Margaret. 1998. "Colorstruck: Skin Color Stratification in the Lives of African American Women." *Sociological Inquiry* 68(4): 517–35.

——. 1999. "The *Lighter* the Berry? Race, Color, and Gender in the Lives of African American and Mexican American Women." Unpublished dissertation at UCLA: UMI.

——. 2002. "'If You're Light You're Alright': Light Skin Color as Social Capital for Women of Color." *Gender & Society* 16(2): 175–93.

——. 2004. "Light, Bright, and Almost White: The Advantages and Disadvantages of Light Skin." Pp. 22–44 in *Skin/Deep: How Race and Complexion Matter in the "Color-Blind" Era,* edited by Cedric Herring, Verna M. Keith, and Hayward Derrick Horton. Chicago: University of Illinois Press.

——. 2005. *Race, Gender, and the Politics of Skin Tone*. New York: Routledge.

——. 2007. "The Persistent Problem of Colorism: Skin Tone, Status, and Inequality." *Sociology Compass* 1(1): 237–54.

Hunter, Margaret, Walter R. Allen, and Edward E. Telles. 2001. "The Significance of Skin Color among African Americans and Mexican Americans." *African American Perspective* 7(1): 173–84.

Jablonsky, Nina. 2012. *Living Color: The Biological and Social Meaning of Skin Color*. Berkeley: University of California Press.

Jackson, Will. 2014. "Beneath the Skin: The Reality of Being Black in Cambodia." *Phnom Penh Post, February 28.* Retrieved on November 15, 2018, at https://www.phnom-penhpost.co.

Jaiswal, Nimisha. 2016. "Being Black in India Can Be Deadly." PRI, February 25. Retrieved on November 9, 2018, at https://www.pri.org.

Jha, Meeta Rani. 2016. *The Global Beauty Industry: Colorism, Racism, and the National Body.* New York: Routledge.

Jha, Sonora, and Mara Beth Adleman. 2009. "Looking for Love in All the White Places: A Study of Skin-Color Preferences on Indian Matrimonial and Mate-Seeking Websites." *Studies in South Asian Film and Media* 1(1): 65–83.

Johnson, Maisha Z. 2016. "10 Ways the Beauty Industry Tells You Being Beautiful Means Being White." *Everyday Feminism,* January 3. Retrieved on January 23, 2017, at http://everydayfeminism.com.

Jones, Trina. 2013. "The Significance of Skin Color in Asian and Asian-American Communities: Initial Reflections." *UC Irvine Law Review* 3: 1105–23.

Jung, Jaehee, and Yoon-Jung Lee. 2009. "Cross-Cultural Examination of Women's Fashion and Beauty Magazine Advertisements in the United States and South Korea." *Clothing & Textiles Research Journal* 27(4): 274–86.

Keith, Verna M., and Cedric Herring. 1991. "Skin-Tone Stratification in the Black Community." *American Journal of Sociology* 97(3): 760–78.

Khalid, Saif. 2013. "Fighting India's Ugly Fancy for Fair Skin." *Al Jazeera,* October 2. Retrieved on June 2, 2018, at https://www.aljazeera.com.

Khanna, Nikki. 2011. *Biracial in America: Forming and Performing Racial Identity.* Lanham, MD: Lexington Books.

Khanna, Nikki, and Cherise A. Harris. 2015. "Discovering Race in a 'Post-Racial' World: Teaching Race through Primetime Television." *Teaching Sociology* 43(1): 39–45.

King-O'Riain, Rebecca Chiyoko. 2006. *Pure Beauty: Judging Race in Japanese American Beauty Pageants.* Minneapolis: University of Minnesota Press.

Lawler, Kelly. 2016. "Whitewashing Controversy Still Haunts 'Doctor Strange.'" *USA Today,* November 7. Retrieved on April 25, 2018, at https://www.usatoday.com.

Lee, Elaine Y. J. 2016. "Why Do So Many Asian Brands Hire White Models?" *Highsnobiety,* May 2. Retrieved on May 26, 2018, at https://www.highsnobiety.com.

Li, Eric P. H., Hyun Jeong Min, and Russell W. Belk. 2008. "Skin Lightening and Beauty in Four Asian Cultures." *Advances in Consumer Research* 35: 444–49.

Lodhi, Fatima. 2015. "'No One Will Marry You': My Journey as a Dark-Skinned Woman in Pakistan." *Citizen: India's 1st Independent Online Daily, December 8.* Retrieved on January 20, 2017, at http://www.thecitizen.in.

Lopez, Ian Haney. 1996. *White by Law: The Legal Construction of Race.* New York: NYU Press.

Luo, Benny. 2017. "Meet the Most Famous Black Man in Korea." *Nextshark: The Voice of Global Asians, May 30.* Retrieved on November 9, 2018, at https://nextshark.com.

Mackey, Robert. 2014. "Beating of African Students by Mob in India Prompts Soul-Searching on Race." *New York Times,* October 1. Retrieved on November 9, 2018, at https://www.nytimes.com.

Maddox, Keith B. 2004. "Perspectives on Racial Phenotypicality Bias." *Personality and Social Psychology Review* 8: 383–401.

Mariam, Simra. 2017. "Daring to Be Dark: Fighting against Colorism in South Asian Cultures." *Huffington Post, May 17*. Retrieved on June 3, 2018, at https://www.huffingtonpost.com.

Marx, Patricia. 2015. "About Face: Why Is South Korea the World's Plastic Surgery Capital?" *New Yorker*, March 23. Retrieved on January 20, 2017, from http://www.newyorker.com.

McIntosh, Peggy. 1989. "White Privilege: Unpacking the Invisible Knapsack." *Peace and Freedom Magazine*, July/August: 10–12.

Mendoza, Roger Lee. 2014. "The Skin-Whitening Industry in the Philippines." *Journal of Public Health Policy* 35(2): 219–38.

Mishra, Neha. 2015. "India and Colorism: The Finer Nuances." *Washington University Global Studies Law Review* 14(4): 725–50.

Monk, Ellis P., Jr. 2014. "Skin Tone Stratification among Black Americans, 2001–2003." *Social Forces* 92(4): 1313–37.

———. 2015. "The Cost of Color: Skin Color, Discrimination, and Health among African-Americans." *American Journal of Sociology* 121(2): 396–444.

Montgomery, Sarah Jasmine. 2018. "The Founder of 'Unfair and Lovely' Is Here to Reclaim Their Movement." *Daily Dot, March 26*. Retrieved on November 19, 2018, at https://www.dailydot.com.

Moore, A. 2014. "8 of the Worst Countries for Black People to Travel." *Atlanta Black Star*, January 8. Retrieved on May 28, 2018, at http://atlantablackstar.com.

Morrison, Toni. 1970. *The Bluest Eye*. New York: Vintage Books.

———. 1993. "On the Backs of Blacks." *Time, December 2*. Retrieved on November 15, 2018, at http://content.time.com.

Murguia, Edward, and Edward E. Telles. 1996. "Phenotype and Schooling among Mexican Americans." *Sociology of Education* 69(4): 276–89.

Nadal, Kevin. 2017. "My Trip to the Philippines, Part 2: The Power of Colorism and Colonial Mentality." *Huffington Post, July 28*. Retrieved on April 26, 2018, at https://www.huffingtonpost.com.

Nadeem, Shehzad. 2014. "Fair and Anxious: On Mimicry and Skin-Lightening in India." *Social Identities* 20(2–3): 224–38.

NewsOne Staff. 2010. "Do You Consider Soledad O'Brien a Black Woman?" *NewsOne, November 5*. Retrieved on November 9, 2018, at https://newsone.com.

North, Anna. 2010. "Vaseline Crowdsources Racism with New Skin-Whitening App." *Jezebel, July 13*. Retrieved on January 23, 2017, at http://jezebel.com.

O'Conner, Maureen. 2014. "Is Race Plastic? My Trip into the 'Ethnic Plastic Surgery' Minefield." *Huffington Post*, July 30. Retrieved on April 26, 2018, at https://www.huffingtonpost.com.

Onyejiaka, Tiffany. 2017. "Hollywood's Colorism Problem Can't Be Ignored Any Longer." *Teen Vogue, August 22*. Retrieved on April 25, 2018, at https://www.teenvogue.com.

Oppenheim, Maya. 2016. "Emma Watson Responds to Criticism over 'Skin-Whitening' Advert." *Independent, March 30*. Retrieved on November 9, 2018, at https://www.independent.co.uk.

Pandey, Geeta. 2016. "#Unfairandlovely: A New Social Media Campaign Celebrates Dark Skin." *BBC News, March 12*. Retrieved on June 3, 2018, at http://www.bbc.com.

Pasha-Robinson, Lucy. 2018. "China Bans Hip-Hop Culture and Tattoos from All Media Sources." *Independent, January 23*. Retrieved on November 9, 2018, at https://www.independent.co.uk.

Paul, Annie. 2016. "Beyond the Pale? Skinderella Stories and Colourism in India." *Centre for Tourism and Policy Research* 14: 133–45.

Prabhu, Maya. 2017. "African Victims of Racism in India Share Their Stories." Al Jazeera, May 3. Retrieved on May 28, 2018, at https://www.aljazeera.com.

"Q & A: Chris Rock." 2014. *CBS News. Sunday Morning, November 30*. Retrieved on November 9, 2018, at https://www.cbsnews.com.

Quackenbush, Casey, and Aria Hangyu Chen. 2018. "'Tasteless, Vulgar, and Obscene': China Just Banned Hip-Hop Culture and Tattoos from Television." *Time, January 22*. Retrieved on May 28, 2018, at http://time.com.

Rajesh, Monisha. 2013. "India's Unfair Obsession with Lighter Skin." *Guardian*, August 14. Retrieved on April 25, 2018, at https://www.theguardian.com.

Ravichandran, Nalini. 2013. "Skin-Whitening Creams Can Cause Long-Term Damage, Doctors Warn." *DailyMail, August 4*. Retrieved on April 25, 2018, at http://www.dailymail.co.uk.

Reichard, Raquel. 2016. "11 Examples of Light-Skin Privilege in Latinx Communities." *Everyday Feminism*, March 25. Retrieved on May 10, 2018, at https://everydayfeminism.com.

Rockquemore, Kerry Ann. 2002. "Negotiating the Color Line: The Gendered Process of Racial Identity Construction among Black/White Biracials." *Gender & Society* 16(4): 485–503.

Romero, Eliza. 2017. "Asian Brands Need to Do Better: Stop Using White Models." *Nextshark: The Voice of Global Asians, May 30*. Retrieved on May 26, 2018, at https://nextshark.com.

Rondilla, Joanne L. 2009. "Filipinos and the Color Complex: Ideal Asian Beauty." Pp. 63–80 in *Shades of Difference: Why Skin Color Matters*, edited by Evelyn Nakano Glenn. Stanford, CA: Stanford University Press.

Rondilla, Joanne L., and Paul Spickard. 2007. *Is Lighter Better? Skin Tone Discrimination among Asian Americans*. Lanham, MD: Rowman & Littlefield.

Russell, Kathy, Midge Wilson, and Ronald E. Hall. 1992. *The Color Complex: The Politics of Skin Color among African Americans*. New York: Anchor Books.

Santos, Jose G. 2012. "10 Years after Sikh Murder over 9/11, Community Continues to Blend In and Stand Out." CNN, August 5. Retrieved on November 12, 2018, at http://religion.blogs.cnn.com.

Sartaj, Maria. 2015. "In Pakistan, a Disease Called Dark Skin." *Dawn, September 30*. Retrieved on April 26, 2018, at https://www.dawn.com.

Sastry, Anjulu. 2015. "People of Color with Albinism Ask: Where Do I Belong?" NPR. *Code Switch*, December 7. Retrieved on November 9, 2018, at https://www.npr.org.

Seltzer, Richard, and Robert C. Smith. 1991. "Color Differences in the Afro-American Community and the Differences They Make." *Journal of Black Studies* 21(3): 279–86.

Shrestha, Sriya. 2013. "Threatening Consumption: Managing US Imperial Anxieties in Representations of Skin Lightening in India." *Social Identities* 19(1): 104–19.

Singh, Kanishka. 2017. "Post-1947, the Mixed Fortunes of the Mixed-Race Anglo-Indians." *Indian Express, August 3.* Retrieved on June 4, 2018, at http://indianexpress.com.

"Skin Whitening Big Business in Asia." 2009. PRI's *The World,* March 30. Retrieved on November 9, 2018, at https://www.pri.org.

Steele, Catherine Knight. 2016. "Pride and Prejudice: Pervasiveness of Colorism and the Animated Series *Proud Family.*" *Howard Journal of Communications* 27(1): 53–67.

Szabo, Ross. 2012. "What Does an American Look Like? Racial Diversity in the Peace Corps." *Huffington Post, January 4.* Retrieved on May 22, 2018, at https://www.huffingtonpost.com.

Tahmahkera, Dustin. 2008. "Custer's Last Sitcom." *American Indian Quarterly* 32(3): 340.

Takasaki, Kara. 2017. "What Disney's Andi Mack Reveals about Asian Americans." *Racism Review,* April 18. Retrieved on April 25, 2018, at http://www.racismreview.com/blog/2017/04/18/andi-mack-asian-americans.

Takeda, Allison. 2013. "Julie Chen Reveals She Got Plastic Surgery to Look Less Chinese: See the Before and After Pictures." *US Magazine, September 12.* Retrieved on January 23, 2017, at http://www.usmagazine.com.

Tandon, Suneera. 2017. "Beauty Companies Are Obsessed with Turning Indian Men White." *Quartz India, April 24.* Retrieved on April 26, 2018, at https://qz.com.

Telles, Edward E., and Edward Murguia. 1990. "Phenotypic Discrimination and Income Differences among Mexican Americans." *Social Science Quarterly* 71(4): 682–96.

Tharoor, Ishaan. 2016. "China and India Have a Huge Problem with Racism towards Black People." *Washington Post,* May 27. Retrieved on November 9, 2018, at https://www.washingtonpost.com.

Tharps, Lori L. 2016. *Same Family, Different Colors: Confronting Colorism in America's Diverse Families.* Boston: Beacon Press.

Thrupkaew, Noy. 2002. "The Myth of the Model Minority." *American Prospect, March 25.* Retrieved on May 25, 2018, at http://prospect.org.

Tiantian, Ye. 2015. "Why Do People Prefer Whiter Skin?" *JAPANsociology,* May 18. Retrieved on April 26, 2019 at https://japansociology.com.

Townsend, Tyrus. 2017. "The Anti-Blackness of the Asian Community." *Jet, February 27.* Retrieved on November 9, 2018, at https://www.jetmag.com.

Tuan, Mia. 1998. *Forever Foreigners or Honorary Whites: The Asian Ethnic Experience Today.* New Brunswick, NJ: Rutgers University Press.

Utley, T. Jerome, Jr., and William Darity Jr. 2016. "India's Color Complex: One Day's Worth of Matrimonials." *Review of Black Political Economy* 43: 129–38.

Vagianos, Alanna. 2018. "Zendaya on Colorism: 'I Am Hollywood's Acceptable Version of a Black Girl.'" *Huffington Post, April 23.* Retrieved on April 25, 2018, at https://www.huffingtonpost.com.

Vaid, Jyotsna. 2009. "Fair Enough? Color and the Commodification of Self in Indian Matrimonials." Pp. 148–65 in *Shades of Difference: Why Skin Color Matters,* edited by Evelyn Nakano Glenn. Stanford, CA: Stanford University Press.

Van den Berge, Pierre, and Peter Frost. 1986. "Skin Color Preference, Sexual Dimorphism, and Sexual Selection: A Case of Gene Culture Co-Evolution." *Ethnic and Racial Studies* 9: 87–113.

Verghese, Sabina. 2018. "Sun Tans and Dark Skin: Unpacking White Privilege." *Brown Girl Magazine, September 20*. Retrieved on November 9, 2018, at https://www.browngirlmagazine.com.

Walker, Alice. 1983. "If the Present Looks Like the Past, What Does the Future Look Like?" in *In Search of Our Mothers' Gardens*. San Diego, CA: Harvest Books.

Wang, Amy B. 2017. "*Vogue India* Faces Backlash for Putting Kendall Jenner on 10th Anniversary Cover." *Washington Post*, May 6. Retrieved on May 26, 2018, at https://www.washingtonpost.com.

Wang, Serenitie, and Sherisse Pham. 2016. "A Startup That Helps You Look Slimmer and Paler Is Worth Nearly $5 Billion." CNN, December 14. Retrieved on January 20, 2017, at http://money.cnn.com.

Waraich, Sonia. 2015. "Forget Fair and Lovely, Dark Is Divine: Pakistan's First Anti-Colorism Campaign." *India West, June 30*. Retrieved on June 3, 2018, at http://www.indiawest.com.

Warren, Cortney S. 2014. "The Race to Be Beautiful." *Psychology Today, August 4*. Retrieved on January 23, 2017, at https://www.psychologytoday.com/blog/naked-truth/201408/the-race-be-beautiful.

Weaver, Vesla M. 2012. "The Electoral Consequences of Skin Color: The 'Hidden' Side of Race in Politics." *Political Behavior* 34(1): 159–92.

Wesby, Maya. 2015. "Japan's Problem with Race." *Newsweek, August 19*. Retrieved on May 28, 2018, at http://www.newsweek.com.

White, John Kenneth, and Sandra L. Hanson. 2011. "The Making and Persistence of the American Dream." Pp. 1–16 in *The American Dream in the 21st Century,* edited by Sandra L. Hanson and John Kenneth White. Philadelphia: Temple University Press.

Wilder, JeffriAnne. 2010. "Revisiting 'Color Names and Color Notions': A Contemporary Examination of the Language and Attitudes of Skin Color among Young Black Women." *Journal of Black Studies* 41(1): 184–206.

Willett, Megan. 2014. "No, Asian Eyelid Surgery Is Not about Looking More 'White.'" *Business Insider, July 31*. Retrieved on April 26, 2018, at http://www.businessinsider.com.

Williams, Janice. 2017. "From Black to White: Why Sammy Sosa and Others Are Bleaching Their Skin." *Newsweek, July 13*. Accessed on April 29, 2018, at http://www.newsweek.com.

Wolf, Naomi. 2002. *The Beauty Myth: How Images of Beauty Are Used against Women.* New York: Perennial.

Xu, Gary, and Susan Feiner. 2007. "Meinu Jingji/China's Beauty Economy: Buying Looks, Shifting Value, and Changing Place." *Feminist Economics* 13(3–4): 307–23.

Yamashita, Seimu. 2014. "Colorism and Discrimination in Japan's Marriage Scene." *JAPANsociology*, January 30. Retrieved on April 25, 2018, at https://japansociology.com.

Yee, Lawrence. 2016. "CAPE 25th Anniversary Gala: Asians in Hollywood Celebrate Milestone, Push for Greater Inclusion." *Variety, October 23*. Retrieved on April 25, 2018, at http://variety.com.

Yeung, Evelyn. 2015. "White and Beautiful: An Examination of Skin-Whitening Practices and Female Empowerment in China." *On Our Terms: The Undergraduate Journal of the Athena Center for Leadership Studies at Barnard College* 3(1): 35–47.

Youn, Anthony. 2013. "Asia's Ideal Beauty: Looking Caucasian." CNN, June 25. Retrieved on January 23, 2017, at http://www.cnn.com.

Zaru, Deena. 2018. "News Flash! The Oscars Are Still So White; Just Take a Look at the Most Excluded Group." CNN, March 2. Retrieved on April 25, 2018, at https://www.cnn.com.

Zeleny, Jeff. 2010. "Reid Apologizes for Remarks on Obama's Color and 'Dialect.'" *New York Times*, January 10. Retrieved on April 28, 2018, at https://www.nytimes.com.

Nikki Khanna is Associate Professor of Sociology at the University of Vermont, where she regularly teaches courses on race relations for the Department of Sociology and the Critical Race and Ethnic Studies Program. She has a PhD in Sociology from Emory University in Atlanta. Her area of study is Race and Ethnicity, and her work examines racial and multiracial identity, transnational and transracial adoption, and the politics of skin color. She is the author of *Biracial in America: Forming and Performing Identity.*

Her research has been featured in *Time, The Root,* and *Slate,* and has also appeared on National Public Radio. She frequently provides commentary on stories related to racial identity and current race relations in the United States, which can be found in outlets such as *USA Today,* BBC Newsnight (UK), CBC Radio (Canada), and the Associated Press. Some of this commentary has been reprinted in the *New York Times, US News & World Report,* the *Washington Post,* ABC News.com, the *Seattle Times,* the *Washington Sun Herald, Salon,* the *New Zealand Herald,* the *Japan Times,* and more.

She was raised in Atlanta, Georgia, and still proudly identifies as a "southern girl," though she now resides just outside of hippy Burlington, Vermont, with her husband, Michael, and daughter, Olivia. While she was writing and editing this book, her family was also fortunate to host Meng Jou (Coco) Chen, an exchange student from Taiwan, who also provided great discussions on the topic of skin color during her stay. When not teaching and writing, she enjoys reading fiction and history, traveling to new places, learning about other cultures, trying new foods (especially if she does not have to cook them herself), and practicing her broken French with French-Canadians just across the border. Perhaps now that this book is finished, she can go back to doing some of these things! For more on her professional work, please visit www.nikkikhanna.com.

Tanzila "Taz" Ahmed is an activist, storyteller, and politico based in Los Angeles. Taz was honored in 2016 as White House Champion of Change for AAPI Art and Storytelling. She is cohost of the *#GoodMuslimBadMuslim* podcast, which has been featured in *Oprah Magazine*, *Wired*, and *Buzzfeed*, as well as live shows recorded at South by Southwest and the White House. An avid essayist, she had a monthly column called *Radical Love* and has written for *Sepia Mutiny*, *Truthout*, the *Aerogram*, the *Nation*, *Left Turn Magazine*, and more. She is published in the anthologies *Love, Inshallah* (2012), *Good Girls Marry Doctors* (2016), *Six Words Fresh off the Boat* (2017), *Modern Loss* (2018), and a poetry collection, *Coiled Serpent* (2016). She also makes disruptive art annually with *#MuslimVDayCards*.

Rosalie Chan is a software engineer and freelance writer based in the Bay Area. Her work has appeared in *Time*, *Vice*, *Teen Vogue*, *Racked*, and more. Besides writing, she enjoys reading, running, badminton, hiking, and photography.

Kim D. Chanbonpin is Professor of Law and Director of the Lawyering Skills Program at the John Marshall Law School in Chicago. Her scholarly writing considers redress and reparations law, policy, and social movements, and draws on anti-subordination and narrative principles rooted in LatCrit and Critical Race Theory scholarship. She grew up in Southern California's San Gabriel Valley and is a proud alumna of Ramona Convent Secondary School, where she studied Spanish under Sister Joan Frances Ortega.

Julia R. DeCook is a doctoral student at Michigan State University in Information and Media Studies. She grew up in South Korea and spent most of her life in Daegu, with brief stints in Guam and Washington, DC, due to her father's occupation with the US Army. She studies online communities and their role in identity formation and construction of social reality, informed by her own personal struggle negotiating mixed-race identity. She is an avid television watcher, a social media lurker, a cat enthusiast, and would have been a food critic in another life.

Noelle Marie Falcis received her BA in English with an emphasis in Creative Writing at the University of California, Irvine, and her MFA at Antioch University LA. Her fiction explores her heritage and both the deserts and cities in which she grew up. She uses fiction to better understand the diasporic, postcolonized life and how it has affected her as a Filipina American. She teaches English and Dance in Los Angeles. Her work has been published in *VIDA: Women in Literary Arts, Kartika Review, Drunk Monkeys,* and *Hawaii Pacific Review,* among others, and she is currently a Voices of Our Nation Arts Foundation (VONA) fellow.

Rhea Goveas is a Senior at the University of Vermont majoring in Sociology and Global Studies. Her parents emigrated from India to America in the 1980s. Rhea and her younger brother were both born and raised in New Jersey. As a child, Rhea always wanted to get as far away from New Jersey as possible. She loves writing, cooking, horseback riding, reading, and travel. She speaks five languages and hopes to do research on women's economic development abroad.

Noor Hasan is a Pakistani American writer from Skokie, Illinois. Noor is an avid reader, poet, and musician who hopes to enter legal academia. She is a JD student at the University of California–Berkeley School of Law, where she is a Staff Editor on the *Berkeley Business Law Journal,* Symposium Editor of the *Asian American Law Journal,* and Academic Empowerment Chair for the

Coalition for Diversity at Berkeley Law. Noor is also a Diversity and Inclusion Corporate Strategist and alumna of the Allstate Insurance Leadership Development Program. She earned a BA from Northwestern University in English and Legal Studies, with a minor in Asian American Studies. In 2016, she was recognized as one of Chicago's 35 under 35. She has presented her research on social justice frameworks for corporate diversity strategy at numerous national business conferences, including the Forum on Workplace Inclusion and the Diversity Awareness Partnership Summit.

Sairah Ḥuṣain studied Economics and South Asian Studies, seeking to academically understand the historical and sociological underpinnings of poverty in the region. Finding shortcomings in this approach, she has moved toward examining the poverty of individual mindsets, including her own, that collectively contribute to structural colorism. When she is not reflecting on these topics, Sairah works at her local library in southeastern Michigan. She also explores different methods of peeling pomegranates.

Miho Iwata is Assistant Professor of Sociology at Towson University. Her passion for social justice guides her research interests, and she studies social inequalities in the United States and Japan. She is a native of Japan, and she often visits her family and stays with them at the house where her beloved grandmother raised her. She has been a US resident for seventeen years.

Anne Mai Yee Jansen is Assistant Professor of English at the University of North Carolina at Asheville, where she also runs the US Ethnic Studies minor and bikes across the quad with reckless abandon. She subsists on a steady diet of yoga, books, and hot chocolate, and does what she can to keep the local coffee shops in business so she can have a place to do her writing. She lives in a little bungalow with her human and feline families and is currently working on a book exploring the politics of contemporary genre fiction by authors of color in the United States.

Erika Lee is a Junior at the University of Southern California, majoring in Print and Digital Journalism. She is the lifestyle editor for her school paper, the *Daily Trojan,* and regularly writes about Asian American identity and feminism in her weekly column, "Asian Amerikan Heroine." She grew up in Southern California in Diamond Bar, just east of Los Angeles, where more than half of the population self-identifies as Asian.

Betty Ming Liu is the recovering daughter of control-freak Chinese immigrant parents. She is also a life coach, writing coach, communications and creative writing professor, painter, blogger, and pet lady.

Lillian Lu is currently a PhD student in English at UCLA. Her research interests include nineteenth-century British literature, Orientalism, and the Gothic. She is a proud daughter of two Chinese Americans with two very different immigration stories.

Cindy Luu is a first-generation Vietnamese American writer. Her perspective on life is heavily influenced by her upbringing in the diverse San Francisco Bay Area. Her journey to understanding herself and her position as a woman of color parallels her growth as a writer; her undergraduate studies at Emerson College challenged both her understanding of her experiences and her skills as a storyteller. She is currently working at San Jose State University, and continues to write with the hope that her voice can speak to the experiences of others.

Catherine Ma emigrated from Hong Kong and became a naturalized citizen of the United States at the age of eight. She received her PhD in Social-Personality Psychology and is currently an Assistant Professor of Psychology. Her current research interests include breastfeeding ideology, maternal experiences, and the lived experiences of immigrants. When she is not teaching her undergraduate students, she enjoys spending time with her husband of twenty-eight years and their three children.

Rhea Manglani is a Senior at Bryn Mawr College in Pennsylvania, majoring in History. She is Indian American and Sindhi—her family originated from the Sindh Province in what is today modern-day Pakistan. She was raised with her older sister in Southern California. She hopes to one day work in politics to fight on behalf of marginalized communities.

Rowena Mangohig is a Children's Librarian with the King County Library System in Washington State, where she has lived for the past twelve years. When she is not in a tutu singing songs and telling stories to children, she is outside working on her garden, foraging for mushrooms, or harvesting razor clams on the coast. Her current passions are dancing in her living room and pretending she can play the ukulele and guitar.

Sambath Meas's family fled a war-torn Cambodia when she was six years old. She grew up in the mean streets of Uptown Chicago, Illinois, and has worked in the legal industry for eighteen years while pursuing her writing career. She is three classes and a thesis away from obtaining her master's degree in Creative Writing, if she ever finds the time from her busy work schedule to go back to Northwestern University. Currently, she is writing science fiction and fantasy young adult novels. Interestingly, she can only write during her train commutes. She has published two books: one is a memoir about her father's trials and tribulations during the Khmer Rouge era, and the second one is a murder mystery set in French colonial Cambodia.

Julia Mizutani is a law student at Georgetown University Law Center in Washington, DC, where she studies Civil Rights and Environmental Law. She is most interested in working with communities of color that are disproportionately impacted by environmental hazards. In her spare time, she organizes and attends protests, reads sci-fi, goes hiking, drinks coffee, and works pro bono on issues around homelessness and housing.

Marimas Hosan Mostiller is an American Studies PhD student at the University of Hawai'i at Mānoa. A first-generation college student, Marimas holds a BS in Psychology from the University of La Verne, an MEd in Postsecondary Administration and Student Affairs from the University of Southern California, and an MA in Ethnic Studies from San Francisco State University. Marimas is a second-generation Cham American, a descendant of the Kingdom of Champa, which is present-day Vietnam. Her parents came to the United States as refugees of the Khmer Rouge genocide in Cambodia. Marimas's experience growing up in a Muslim household in a working-class, immigrant community among other marginalized people of color prompted her interests in higher education, ethnic studies, and social justice issues.

Sonal Nalkur is a Visiting Assistant Professor in the Department of Sociology at Emory University. Her research interests focus on cultural sociology and the sociology of organizations. Most recently, her writing explores the power of the sociological perspective in deepening personal narratives. She has lived in the United States on and off for about twenty years.

Ethel Nicdao is Associate Professor and Chair in the Department of Sociology at California State University, San Bernardino. Trained as a medical sociologist, she applies a community-based participatory research approach to examine health disparities among minority populations. She lives in Northern California with her wife and their two cattle dogs and enjoys escaping into the mountains for her nature fix and eating her favorite Filipino dishes at her mother's house!

Brittany Ota-Malloy is a doctoral student in the Department of Educational Leadership and Policy Analysis at the University of Wisconsin–Madison. Her research interests include the study of multiracial college students, their experiences, and their contributions. She is also interested in the experiences of black women in college and student activism in higher education. Brittany is also a Student Assistance Specialist at the UW–Madison Dean of Students Office, where she directly impacts students' campus experiences. In each of her academic and professional experiences, Brittany actively combats the educational practices and policies that serve as gatekeepers for the socioeconomically and culturally underserved students she serves.

Daniela Pila is a PhD candidate in Sociology at the State University of New York–Albany. She is currently working on her dissertation, which explores how legal status affects ethnic identity formation in Filipino immigrant young adults in the greater New York metropolitan area. When not working on dismantling institutional discrimination, Daniela enjoys photography, traveling, learning languages, and spending time with her husband and their furchild, Luna.

Agatha Roa is an MFA candidate at the University of North Carolina at Wilmington, where she is the recipient of the Kert Fellowship in Creative Writing. She is an alumnus of the Voices of Our Nations Foundation (VONA) and Hedgebrook VORTEXT, has blogged at the *New York Times'* artsbeat.com and urbangardensweb.com, and has published in various anthologies. She has a BA in Communications and Culture from the City University of New York.

Joanne L. Rondilla is an Assistant Professor in Sociology and Interdisciplinary Studies at San Jose State University. Originally from Dededo, Guam, she holds degrees from UC–Berkeley (MA, PhD) and UC–Santa Barbara (BA). Her research interests include colorism, race, gender, beauty, media representations, pop culture, and colonialism. She runs the website skinmemoirs.com.

Kamna Shastri is a freelance writer and media maker based in Seattle. She is always thinking about current framings of race, ethnicity, and identity—themes that come up in her journalistic and creative work. She has written for local publications and is currently working on a podcast that explores how people think about and experience their South Asian American identities in the Pacific Northwest. She has a BA in Sociology and Environmental Studies, disciplines that continue to inspire her current work and future goals. She loves sunny summer afternoons, made all the better when accompanied by a cup of tea.

Wendy Thompson Taiwo is a writer and Assistant Professor of Ethnic Studies at Metropolitan State University, where she specializes in black cultural studies, race and wealth, mixed racial identity, and migration and diaspora communities. Her writing and photography have appeared in *carte blanche, Nokoko, Meridians: feminism, race, transnationalism,* and several anthologies, including *War Baby/ Love Child: Mixed Race Asian American Art.*

Bhoomi K. Thakore is Assistant Professor in the Department of Sociology at the University of Central Florida. She is author of *South Asians on the U.S. Screen: Just like Everyone Else?* (2016) and coeditor of *Race and Contention in 21st–Century U.S. Media* (2016). She is the only child of Gujarati immigrants who came to the United States from India in 1970. Her parents worked on the East Coast before settling in the Chicago area and later purchasing motels and other small business ventures. She is married and has one daughter, Risha.

Kathy Tran-Peters is a graduate student in History and Comparative Gender and Sexuality at the University of Utah. She lives in Bountiful, Utah, with her husband, Tony, and two Labrador retrievers, Goose and Bruce. "Dear Future Child" is a culmination of all the hardships and struggles her ancestors endured in the face of colonialism, her parents' adversity in immigrating to the United States, and her continued battle fatigue as a feminist of color living in a predominantly white and conservative state. "Dear Future Child" is also a growing reflection on her future as a mother in a world where fear is real and the stakes are high.

INDEX

advertising: aspirational whiteness and, 105–6, *106–107*; Caucasian models and, 15, 105, *106*; Chinese laundry detergent, 127; for English teachers in Taiwan, 127–28; racism and, 1–2, 3–4; skin-whitening industry and, 1–2, 3–4; Snowz and, 1–2; South Asian themes for, 3–4; white mannequins and, 105, *107*

African Americans, colorism and, 4, 64; actors and, 6; black authenticity and, 7; black women stereotypes and, 139; gendered colorism, 6–7; identity, belonging and, 149–50, 153; Jim Crow era and, 5, 108, 130, 163; light-skin privilege and, 5; marriage and, 6; media and, 7; one-drop rule and, 90, 223n25; slavery and, 5, 97, 130, 140–41, 163; women and, 6. *See also* anti-blackness; Ota-Malloy, Brittany

Africans, 116, 128; in India, 126

Ahluwalia, Pal, 14

Ahmed, Tanzila, 41; Barbie dolls and, 68, 70–71; downward financial mobility of, 69; family gifts and, 67–68; father of, 69; friend of, 70–71; in graduate school, 74–75; on love, 74; middle sister of, 67–68; mother of, 66, 68–69; school children and, 70; skin color awareness and, 70

albinism, 30; identity, belonging and, 152; privilege and, 152–53; Shashri and, 152, 169–71

Aloha, 85–86

American Dream, 108, 109

anti-blackness, 97, 100; African descent and, 126; Asian immigrants and, 129, 138; in China, 126–27; geography and, 125–26; Husain on, 132, 133–36; in India, 126; in Korea, 128–29; Miyamoto and, 125; model minority stereotype and, 130–31; Mostiller on, 132, 143–47; stereotypes of, 30, 40, 125–26, 128, 130, 132, 145, 146; in Taiwan, 127–28; Taiwo on, 132, 137–42

apps, whitening: in China, 12; Facebook and, 18; in Japan, 10

Asian American literature, 155–56

Asian Americans. *See specific topics*

Asian definition, 32

Asians, colorism and: apps and, 12; China and, 12, 13; class and, 10–11, 14, 103; cosmetic surgery and, 20–22; Eurocentric ideals and, 10, 13–14, 15, 20; gender and, 18; immigrants and, 23; India and, 16–17; Japan and, 10–11, 12; Jones, T., on, 9–10; marrying practices and, 16; in Pakistan, 19–20; in Philippines, 14–15, 16; in Taiwan, 11–12. *See also specific topics*

aspirational whiteness: advertising and, 105–6, *106, 107*; blonde hair and, 103–4; colonization and, 104–5, 107–8; digital representation and, 110; economic disparities and, 109–10; Elisha Coy ad and, 103; Falcis on, 119–23; globalization and, 107; Hasan and, 111–13; Roa and, 107, 114–18; skin-whitening industry and, 110; status and, 107; Supreme Court cases and, 108–9

Bakekang, 188

Barbie dolls, 68, 70–71

Barr, Roseanne, 130

beautiful women in America, 24, 25

heteronormative culture, 33

hierarchy, race-color, 78–79; Chanbonpin on, 163; Falcis on, 122; Jones, T., on, 24

Hill, Mark E., 6

Hindu, Hinduism, 1, 16, 17, 19, 43, 57, 73, 109, 232n3

Hong, Euny, 21–22

Hunter, Margaret, 4, 6, 151

Husain, Sairah: on colonialism, 134, 135; creation story and, 133, 134–35, 136; ICE and, 135–36; on oppression, 135; on self-hate, 132, 134; tanning for, 134

ICE. See Immigration and Customs Enforcement

identity and belonging: African Americans and, 149–50, 153; albinism and, 152; Asian Americans and, 151, 153, 154; Chanbonpin and, 152, 162–68; choice and, 163–64; Filipinx culture and, 152; Indian American community and, 72–73, 75, 149, 169–70; Jansen on, 151, 155–61; Lee, Erika, and, 175–76; Luu and, 153–54, 177–81; Mexican Americans and, 151, 153; Mizutani on, 90; multiracial, 150, 151; O'Brien and, 150; Shashri and, 152, 169–74

"I'm a Light-Skinned Chinese Woman, and I Experience Pretty Privilege" (Chen, R.), 77

Immigration and Customs Enforcement (ICE), 135–36

India, 227n2; anti-blackness in, 126; Bollywood and, 16, 170, 172–73, 183; caste system in, 16–17; colonialism in, 16, 17; "Dark Is Beautiful" campaign in, 183; eye color in, 20; Fair & Lovely in, 83; IVF in, 18; marriage in, 18–19; Nalkur and, 95–96; racism in, 126; Shashri, 170–71; skin-whitening industry in, 17–18, 24–25; violence against Africans in, 126; Vogue India, 105–6

India Abroad, 18–19

Indian American community, 1–2; albinism and, 152; Eurocentric traits and,

24; identity, belonging and, 72–73, 75, 149, 169–70; Shashri and, 169–70; tanning and, 23; Thakore and, 72–73, 75. See also Goveas, Rhea

interracial sex, 137–39

in-vitro fertilization (IVF), 18

Islamophobia, 78, 86, 213

IVF. See in-vitro fertilization

Jackson, Asia, 184

Jackson, Jesse, 150

Jackson, Will, 144–45

Jansen, Anne Mai Yee, 151; appearance of, 157; cousins of, 156; daughter of, 160–61; otherness and, 160; racism and, 157, 159, 160; school for, 156; Tan and, 155–56, 161; travel of, 157–58, 159; US ethnic studies and, 158–59

Japan, 28, 103; apps in, 10; class and, 10–11; colorism and, 10–11, 12; gendered colorism in, 48; hafu and, 78, 89, 125; makeup in, 49; Miho in, 38–39, 48–49, 50–51; Miss Universe Japan (2015), 125; proverb in, 48; Vogue Japan, 105–6

Jenner, Kendall, 105

Jim Crow, 108, 130, 163; skin-whitening industry and, 5

Jindal, Bobby, 131; self-hate and, 132

Johansson, Scarlett, 86

Jones, Pax, 184

Jones, Trina: on colorism in Asia, 9–10; on race-color hierarchy, 24

joo (black guy), 144

Kaw, Eugena, 26

Kerr, Miranda, 105

Khanna, Nikki: Biracial in America by, 149

Khmer, 55, 57, 145, 228n1

King-O'Riain, Rebecca, 11

Korea, 105; anti-blackness in, 128–29; body scrubbing in, 208; DeCook in, 185, 208–9; Filipino discrimination in, 78; Hazzan in, 128; Okyere in, 128–29; racial purity in, 210

Lancôme, 15, *15*

Latinx community, colorism and, 7, 64; as ethnic group, 224n34; marriage and, 8; Mexican Americans and, 151, 153, 166

Lee, C. N., 104

Lee, Elaine Y. J., 105

Lee, Erika, 153, 154; on beauty stereotypes by country, 175–76; in China, 175; self-hate and, 176

Lee, Spike, 188–89

LGBTQ individuals, 33; Nicdao, and, 65–66

Li, Eric, 10

Liu, Betty Ming, 186; in Chinatown, 217; daughter of, 218–20; interracial relationship of, 217–18; mother of, 216–18, 220; painting for, 219; racial slurs and, 216–17; school of, 216, 218

Lodhi, Fatima, 19, 183

L'Oreal, 25

Lu, Lillian, 185; Cantonese and, 200–201; maternal family of, 199–200, 201–2; tanning and, 199–200, 201–2; UNIQLO dress of, 199

Luu, Cindy, 153–54; in college, 179, 181; family of, 179–80; Nancy and, 177, 178–79; physical appearance of, 178–79, 181; Vietnamese cultural club show and, 177–78

Ma, Catherine, 37; body shaming and, 53; on eyes, 53, 54; lookisms and, 52, 53; on racism, 53–54; self-hatred and, 54

Madame Butterfly, 85

Malaysia, 105; skin-whitening in, *11*

male gaze, 33

Manglani, Rhea: privilege and, 77–78, 82–83; skin-whitening and, 82–83

Mangohig, Rowena, 185; multiracial kids and, 204–5; Philippines and, 203, 205; Seasonal Affective Disorder and, 206–7; sisters of, 203–4; skin-whitening and, 204, 205–6; tanning and, 203, 206, 207

marriage: ads for, 18–19, 173; African Americans and, 6; Cambodia and, 60;

heteronormative culture and, 33; in India, 18–19; Latinx community and, 8; male gaze and, 33; Pakistan and, 19–20; in Philippines, 16; Shashri on ads for, 173

Mathew, Paco, 40

McIntosh, Peggy, 78

Meas, Sambath, 37–38, 60; bullying of, 59; on Cambodian media, 57–58; skin-color discrimination in Cambodia and, 59; on white babies, 56–57

media, 24, 107, 188

mental illness, 214

mestiza/mestizo (mixed ancestry), 62, 232n1; Roa and, 116

Mexican Americans, 151, 153, 166

micro-aggressions, 27; Nicdao and, 64; Thakore and, 75

Miho Iwata: audience and, 50, 51; childhood of, 48–49; cultural expectations and, 49–50, 51; foreigner treatment of, 50, 51; freckles of, 50, 51; in Japan, 38–39, 48–49, 50–51; self-image of, 51; tanning for, 48–49

Miller, Laura, 104

Minaj, Nicki, 7

Mishra, Neha, 16–17

Miss Universe Japan (2015), 125

mixed ancestry (mestiza/mestizo), 62, 116, 232n1

Miyamoto, Ariana, 125

Mizutani, Julia: on fetish, 89; *hafu* and, 78, 89; on identity, 90; as multiracial, 88, 89, 90–91; on racial imposters, 88–89; on racism, 91; on whiteness, 88

model minority stereotype: anti-blackness and, 130–31; Chanbonpin and, 163; Falcis and, 121–22

Moore, A., 127

Morrison, Toni, 138; *The Bluest Eye* by, 165

Mostiller, Marimas Hosan, 132; on Cham Muslim community, 143–44; daughter of, 143, 147; early life of, 143–44; *hapa* and, 143; *joo* and, 144; N-word and, 145–46; on privilege, 146–47; on stereotypes, 145–46

mother and grandmother pressures, 28,
196; Falcis and, 119–22; Goveas and,
39, 44–47; Miho and, 38–39; Roa and,
116–17, 118
Muhammad, Zaharaddeen, 126
multiracial and biracial: contributors, 32–
33, 35; identity, belonging and, 150, 151;
stereotypes and, 30–31. *See also specific
topics*
multiracial Japanese (*hafu*), 78, 89, 125

Nadal, Kevin, 16
Nalkur, Sonal, 80–81; border patrol and,
96; cell mates of, 93–94; criminal justice system and, 92–95; expired license
of, 92–93; friend reactions to, 95; on
India and Canada, 95–96; in Saudi
Arabia, 94
nanny question, 160
Native Americans, 146, 157
New York Times, 79, 86, 103, 125
Nicdao, Ethel, 40–41, 66; class and, 63;
on cosmetic surgery, 65; on cultural
capital, 65; derogatory slurs and, 62–
63; LGBTQ community and, 65–66;
micro-aggressions and, 64; in Philippines, 61; on physical characteristics,
64–65; in San Francisco, 62; skin
whitening and, 64; in Taiwan, 63
nose, 37, 38, 62, 64, 82, 180, 188, 189, 190,
191, 194, 197, 198, 209–10, 212, 213, 214,
216, 217; cosmetic surgery and, 20–21,
26, 27, 65

Obama, Barack, 5–6; racist stereotypes
and, 130
Obama, Michelle, 130
O'Brien, Soledad, 150
O'Connor, Maureen, 21
Okyere, Sam, 128–29
one-drop rule, 90, 223n25
1.5 generation immigrants, 197, 232n3
Ota-Malloy, Brittany, 81; as biracial, 97;
blackness challenged for, 99; in China,
98–99; family of, 98; hair of, 98, 99–

100; invisibility of, 99; racial identities
of, 101; racialized experiences of, 98;
Shea Moisture and, 100
otherness, 41, 80; cosmetic surgery and, 27;
Jansen and, 160
Ozawa, Takeo, 90, 91, 108–9
Ozawa v. the United States, 90, 91, 108–9

Pakistan, 132; "Dark Is Divine" campaign
in, 183–84; marriage in, 19–20
papaya soap, 64, 119, 196, 232n2
partial Asian ancestry (*hapa*), 143, 231n1
Patel, Sureshbhai, 86
Philippines, 231n1; Catholicism in, 108;
Chan in, 84; class and, 187, 188, 189–
90; colonialism in, 14–15, 16, 62, 63,
107–8, 120–21, 192; colorism in, 14–15,
16; Filipina domestics, 191–92; job
ads in, 205; Mangohig and, 203, 205;
marriage in, 16; mestiza/mestizo in,
62, 116, 232n1; Nicdao in, 61; papaya
soap and, 64, 119, 196, 232n2; Pila in,
194–96; Roa and, 115–16; Rondilla
and, 187–88, 189–91; status in, 107;
teleseryas in, 195–96
physical characteristics, and colorism, 37;
blonde hair and, 103–4; Nicdao on, 64–
65; nose, 20–21. *See also* eyes
Pickford, Mary, 85
Pila, Daniela, 185; body hate of, 195, 196;
in California, 196–97; performing arts
and, 196; in Philippines, 194–96; physical appearance of, 194; relationships of,
197–98; reprogramming for, 197–98
Pond's White Beauty, 2–3, *3*
presidential election (2016), 66
privilege, 28–29, 35; African Americans
and, 5; albinism and, 152–53; audience
and, 80, 81; Chan and, 78, 84–87; of
Chen, R., 77; context and, 80; *Crazy
Rich Asians* and, 79–80; Goveas and,
78; Manglani and, 77–78, 82–83; Mc-
Intosh and, 78; Mizutani on, 78, 88–91;
Mostiller on, 146–47; Nalkur and, 80–
81, 92–96; Ota-Malloy on, 81, 97–101;

Shashri and, 172; South Asians and, 79; Taiwo and, 140; Tran-Peters and, 212

The Proud Family, 6

racial profiling, 27, 78; Patel and, 86; South Asians and, 80

racial slurs, 41

racism, 34; advertising and, 1–2, 3–4; in Cambodia, 144–45; colorism and, 4, 35, 189; in India, 126; Jansen and, 157, 159, 160; Ma on, 53–54; Mizutani on, 91. *See also* anti-blackness

Raghunathan, Suman, 130–31

Ramon, Cheyanne, vii

"Real Beauty" campaign, 65, 228n2

redefining skin color: DeCook and, 185, 208–11; East Asia and, 185; India "Dark Is Beautiful" campaign and, 183; Liu and, 186, 216–20; Lu, on, 185, 199–202; #MagandangMorenx and, 184; Mangohig and, 185, 203–7; Pakistan "Dark Is Divine" campaign and, 183–84; Pila and, 185, 194–98; reprogramming and, 31, 197–98; Rondilla and, 187–93; social media and, 184; Tran-Peters and, 186, 212–15; #UnfairAndLovely and, 184

Reichard, Raquel, 8

Reid, Harry, 5–6

rhinoplasty, 20–21, 65

Roa, Agatha, 107; on eyes, 114; mestiza grandmother of, 116; mother-daughter relationship and, 116–17, 118; Philippines and, 115–16; rebellion of, 116–17; Santos and, 114–15, 117; YouTube skin-whitening and, 114–15, 117–18

Roberts, Doris, 193

Rock, Chris, 26

Romero, Eliza, 105–6

Rondilla, Joanne, 11, 12, 14, 15, 185; on Asian beauty standards, 22, 110; on Asian immigrants, 23; *Bakekang* and, 188; class and, 104, 187, 189–90; Filipina domestics and, 191–92; on happiness, 191; healing for, 193; intelligence and, 191, 192; on marrying up, 16; parents of,

187–88; Philippines and, 187–88, 189–91; redefining skin color and, 187–93; Roberts and, 193; tanning and, 190; teaching for, 191–92, 193

Roseanne, 130

SAALT. *See* South Asian Americans Leading Together

Same Family, Different Colors (Tharps), 183

sang duc ho (born good looking), 52

Sartaj, Maria, 19–20

School Daze, 188–89

Seasonal Affective Disorder, 206–7

self-acceptance. *See* redefining skin color

self-hate: cosmetic surgery and, 54; Husain on, 132, 134; Jindal and, 132; Lee, Erika, and, 176; Ma on, 54

self-love, 54. *See also* redefining skin color

September 11th terrorist attacks (2001): Tran-Peters and, 213; violence and, 80, 213

shai hei (to dry until one turns black), 84, 87

Shashri, Kamna: albinism and, 152, 169–71; Bollywood and, 170, 172–73; cultural capital and, 170; distance for, 173–74; early life of, 169–71, 174; in India, 170–71; Indian American identity and, 169–70; invisibility of, 171–72; on matrimonial ads, 173; privilege and, 172

Shea Moisture, 100

shimi (freckles), 50, 51

Shrestha, Sriya, 25–26

Sidibe, Gabby, 7

The Simpsons, 73

skin-color discrimination, 27–28; mental, physical health and, 64; origins of, 103; privilege and, 34. *See also specific topics*

skin-whitening, 9, 89; advertising and, 1–2, 3, 3–4, 10, 14, 15, *15*, 25, 37, 89, 98–99, 103, 114–15, 118, 205; aspirational whiteness and, 110; Bird's Nest and, 2; Cambodian and, 58, 59, 60; Chan and, 84–85; in China, 12, 13–14; Dr. Fred Palmer's Skin Whitener, 5; Elisha Coy and, 103;

skin-whitening (*cont.*)
 Estee Lauder, 25; Fair & Lovely and, 2,
 27, 83, 184; Glutamax, 2; in India, 17–18,
 24–25; Jim Crow era and, 5; Lancôme,
 15, *15*; L'Oreal, 2, 7, 25; in Malaysia, 11;
 Manglani and, 82–83; Mangohig and,
 204, 205–6; Nadinola, 5; Nicdao and,
 64; papaya soap as, 64, 119, 196, 232n2;
 Pond's White Beauty and, 2–3, *3*; product tag lines for, 2–3, *3*; Snowz and, 1–2;
 in Taiwan, 11–12; tanning and, 25–26;
 Thakore and, 72; Watson and, 15, *15*;
 YouTube and, 114–15, 117–18
slavery, 5, 97, 130, 163; Taiwo and, 140–41
Snowz commercial, 1–2
social media: racial identities and, 111; redefining skin color and, 184; Tran-Peters
 and, 213–14
socioeconomic status, 109–10; Santos and,
 118. *See also* class
Sodi, Balbir Singh, 80
Sosa, Sammy, 8
South Asia, 3, 19–20, 25, 32, 78, 79, 82, 92,
 105, 107, 153, 172, 174, 183–84; emojis
 and, 112–13; hate crimes and, 80; marriage in, 18–19, 173
South Asian Americans Leading Together
 (SAALT), 130–31
Spickard, Paul, 11, 12, 16; on Asian beauty
 standards, 22; on Asian immigrants, 23;
 class and, 104
Star Trek into Darkness, 85
Steele, Catherine Knight, 6
stereotypes, 26–27; American, 40;
 anti-blackness and, 30, 40, 125–26,
 128, 130, 132, 145, 146; ape, 130; of
 Asian Americans, 86; black women,
 139; Cantonese, 200–201; Lee, Erika,
 on country and beauty, 175–76; of
 light skin, 8, 17, 24, 26, 37, 77; model
 minority, 121–22, 130–31, 163; Mostiller on, 145–46; multiracial, 30–31;
 Native American, 146; Obama, B.,
 and, 130
Stone, Emma, 85–86

Super Brian, 127
Supreme Court cases, 229n16; *Brown v.
 Board of Education*, 90; *Ozawa v. the
 United States*, 90, 91, 108–9; *Thind v. the
 United States*, 90, 91, 108–9
Sutherland, George, 90, 109

Tahmahkera, Dustin, 146
Taiwan: anti-blackness in, 127–28; English
 teacher advertisement in, 127–28;
 Nicdao and, 63; skin-whitening industry in, 11–12
Taiwo, Wendy Thompson, 132; children
 of, 142; colonialism and, 139; generational trauma and, 141; interracial sex
 and, 137–39; melanin and, 142; mother
 appearance and, 137–39, 141; privilege
 and, 140; sexual desirability and, 139;
 slavery and, 140–41; tanning and, 141;
 white groups and, 140
Tan, Amy, 155–56, 161
tanning, 39; Cambodia and, 55, 59; Chan
 and, 84; DeCook and, 209, 210–11;
 Goveas and, 45–46; Husain and, 134;
 Indian Americans and, 23; Lu and,
 199–200, 201–2; Mangohig and, 203,
 206, 207; Miho and, 48–49; Rondilla
 and, 190; skin-whitening and, 25–26;
 Taiwo and, 141
teleseryas, 195–96
television and film: *Aloha*, 85–86;
 Bakekang, 188; Bollywood and, 16, 170,
 172–73, 183; *Crazy Rich Asians*, 79–80;
 Ghost in the Shell, 86; *Madame Butterfly*,
 85; *School Daze*, 188–89; *Star Trek into
 Darkness*, 85; *teleseryas*, 195–96; whitewashing in, 85–86
Thailand, 1–2, 9–10, 32, 58, 89, 105
Thakore, Bhoomi K., 41–42; extended
 family of, 72; Indian identity and,
 72–73, 75; job market and, 75; micro-
 aggressions and, 75; physical appearance of daughter and, 72; school
 for, 73–74; skin-lightening products
 and, 72

Tharps, Lori, 17, 151; *Same Family, Different Colors* by, 183
Thind, Bhagat Singh, 90, 91, 108–9
Thind v. the United States, 90, 91, 108–9
Tiantian, Ye, 13–14
Townsend, Tyrus, 131
Tran-Peters, Kathy, 186, 215; generational trauma and, 213; harassment and, 212; mental illness and, 214; multiracial child of, 212–13; privilege and, 212; September 11th terrorist attacks and, 213; social media and, 213–14; white men and, 214
Trump, Donald, 214
Tuan, Mia, 26–27, 40

#UnfairAndLovely, 184
UNIQLO, 199
"Unpacking the Invisible Knapsack" (McIntosh), 78
US-Mexican border wall, 66

Vaid, Jyotsna, 16, 17
Verghese, Sabina, 26
Vietnam, 213; Cham people and, 231n2

violence: Africans in India and, 126; September 11th terrorist attacks and, 80, 213
Vogue India, 105–6
Vogue Japan, 105–6

Walker, Alice, 4
Washington, Kerry, 7
Watson, Emma, 15, *15*
wheatish, 19, 43, 68, 173, 227n1
white colorism, 8
whiteness, 29; defining, 88. *See also* aspirational whiteness
whitening. *See* skin-whitening
white supremacy, 91, 163, 214
white worship, 103
Wilder, JeffriAnne, 40

Xu, Gary, 12–13

Yamashita, Seimi, 10
Yeung, Evelyn, 14
YouTube: Santos on, 114–15, 117–18; social class and, 117–18

Zendaya, 6